Celtic Mythology

This edition published in 2023 by Arcturus Publishing Limited
26/27 Bickels Yard, 151–153 Bermondsey Street,
London SE1 3HA

Copyright © Arcturus Holdings Limited

All rights reserved. No part of this publication may be reproduced, stored in a retrieval system, or transmitted, in any form or by any means, electronic, mechanical, photocopying, recording or otherwise, without written permission in accordance with the provisions of the Copyright Act 1956 (as amended). Any person or persons who do any unauthorised act in relation to this publication may be liable to criminal prosecution and civil claims for damages.

Typesetting by Sooky Choi

Cover design: Peter Ridley

AD011674UK

Printed in the UK

CELTIC
MYTHOLOGY

CONTENTS

Introduction 7

THE GAELIC GODS AND THEIR STORIES.................... 9

    I. The Gods of the Gaels 10

    II. The Gods Arrive 23

    III. The Rise of the Sun-god.....................................33

    IV. The Gaelic Argonauts..42

    V. The War with the Giants 56

    VI. The Conquest of the Gods by Mortals 66

    VII. The Gods in Exile..76

    VIII. The Irish Iliad...94

    IX. Some Gaelic Love-stories.................................119

    X. Finn and the Fenians..133

    XI. The Decline and Fall of the Gods.....................154

THE BRITISH GODS AND THEIR STORIES............... 171

    XII. The Gods of the Britons..................................172

    XIII. The Adventures of the Gods of Hades...........193

XIV. The Wooing of Branwen and the Beheading
 of Brân...202

XV. The War of Enchantments 209

XVI. The Victories of Light over Darkness............215

XVII. The Mythological 'Coming of Arthur'..........221

XVIII. The Treasures of Britain 240

XIX. The Gods as King Arthur's Knights................255

XX. The Decline and Fall of the Gods 268

INTRODUCTION

This book is what its author believes to be the only attempt yet made to put the English reader into possession, in clear, compact, and what it is hoped may prove agreeable, form, of the mythical, legendary, and poetic traditions of the earliest inhabitants of our islands who have left us written records – the Gaelic and the British Celts. Many admirable translations and paraphrases of much of Gaelic mythical saga have been published, but often these books only cover a portion of the whole ground, and contain little elucidatory matter. Their characters stand isolated and unexplained; and the details that would explain them must be sought for with considerable trouble in the lectures and essays of scholars to learned societies.

In this book, readers will at last make the formal acquaintance of all the chief characters of Celtic myth: of the Gaelic gods and the giants against whom they struggled; of the 'Champions of the Red Branch' of Ulster, heroes of a martial epopee almost worthy to be placed beside 'the tale of Troy divine'; and of Finn and his Fenians. They will meet also the heroic personages of the ancient Britons: with their earliest gods, kin to the members of the Gaelic Pantheon; as well as with Arthur and his Knights. Of all these mighty figures the histories will be briefly recorded, from the time of their unquestioned godhood, through their various transformations, to the last doubtful, dying recognition of them in the present day, as 'fairies'.

This book aims to interest the reader familiar with the mythologies of Greece, Rome, and Scandinavia in another, and a nearer, source of poetry. Its author's wish is to offer those who have fallen, or will fall, under the attraction of Celtic legend and romance, just such a volume as he himself would once have welcomed, and for which he sought in vain.

To acknowledge, as far as possible, such debts is now the author's pleasing duty. First and foremost, he has relied upon the volumes of M. H. d'Arbois de Jubainville's *Cours de Littérature celtique*, and the *Hibbert Lectures* for 1886 of John Rhys, Professor of Celtic in the University of Oxford, with their sequel entitled *Studies in the Arthurian Legend*. From the writings of Mr. Alfred Nutt he has also obtained much help. With regard to direct translations, it seems almost superfluous to refer to Lady Charlotte Guest's *Mabinogion* and Mr. W. F. Skene's *Four Ancient Books of Wales*, or to the work of such well-known Gaelic scholars as Mr. Eugene O'Curry, Dr. Kuno Meyer, Dr. Whitley Stokes, Dr. Ernest Windisch, Mr. Standish Hayes O'Grady (to mention no others), as contained in such publications as the *Revue Celtique*, the *Atlantis*, and the *Transactions of the Ossianic* Society, in Mr. O'Grady's *Silva Gadelica*, Mr. Nutt's *Voyage of Bran, Son of Febal*, and Miss Hull's *Cuchullin Saga*. But space is lacking to do justice to all.

Finally, perhaps, a word should be said upon that vexed question, the transliteration of Gaelic. As yet there is no universal or consistent method of spelling. The author has therefore chosen the forms which seemed most familiar to himself, hoping in that way to best serve the uses of others.

THE GAELIC GODS AND THEIR STORIES

I
THE GODS OF THE GAELS

Of the two Celtic races that settled in our islands, it is the earlier, the Gaels, that has best preserved its old mythology. It is true that we have in few cases such detailed account of the Gaelic gods as we gain of the Hellenic deities from the Greek poets, of the Indian Devas from the Rig Veda, or of the Norse Æsir from the Eddas. Yet none the less may we draw from the ancient Irish manuscripts quite enough information to enable us to set forth their figures with some clearness. We find them, as might have been anticipated, very much like the divine hierarchies of other Aryan peoples.

We also find them separated into two opposing camps, a division common to all the Aryan religions. Just as the Olympians struggled with the Giants, the Æsir fought the Jötuns, and the Devas the Asuras, so there is warfare in the Gaelic spiritual world between two superhuman hosts. On one side are ranged the gods of day, light, life, fertility, wisdom, and good; on the other, the demons of night, darkness, death, barrenness, and evil. The first were the great spirits symbolizing the beneficial aspects of nature and the arts and intelligence of man; the second were the hostile powers thought to be behind such baneful manifestations as storm and fog, drought and disease. The first are ranged as a divine family round a goddess called Danu, from whom they took their well-known name of *Tuatha Dé Danann*, 'Tribe' or 'Folk of the Goddess

Danu'. The second owned allegiance to a female divinity called Domnu; their king, Indech, is described as her son, and they are all called 'Domnu's gods'. The word 'Domnu' appears to have signified the abyss or the deep sea, and the same idea is also expressed in their better-known name of 'Fomors', derived from two Gaelic words meaning 'under sea'. The waste of water seems to have always impressed the Celts with the sense of primeval ancientness; it was connected in their minds with vastness, darkness, and monstrous births – the very antithesis of all that was symbolized by the earth, the sky, and the sun.

Therefore the Fomors were held to be more ancient than the gods, before whom they were, however, destined to fall in the end. Offspring of 'Chaos and Old Night', they were, for the most part, huge and deformed. Some had but one arm and one leg apiece, while others had the heads of goats, horses, or bulls. The most famous, and perhaps the most terrible of them all was Balor, whose father is said to have been one Buarainech, that is, the 'cow-faced', and who combined in himself the two classical rôles of the Cyclops and the Medusa. Though he had two eyes, one was always kept shut, for it was so venomous that it slew anyone on whom its look fell. This malignant quality of Balor's eye was not natural to him, but was the result of an accident. Urged by curiosity, he once looked in at the window of a house where his father's sorcerers were preparing a magic potion, and the poisonous smoke from the cauldron reached his eye, infecting it with so much of its own deadly nature as to make it disastrous to others. Neither god nor giant seems to have been exempt from its dangers; so that Balor was only allowed to live on condition that he kept his terrible eye shut. On days of battle he was placed opposite to the enemy, the lid of the destroying eye was lifted up with a hook, and its gaze withered all who stood before it. The memory of Balor and his eye still lingers in Ireland: the 'eye of Balor' is the name for what the peasantry of other countries call the 'evil eye'; stories are still told of *Balar Beimann*, or 'Balor of the Mighty Blows'; and 'Balor's Castle' is the name of a curious cliff on Tory Island. This island, off the coast of Donegal, was the Fomorian outpost upon earth, their real abode being in the cold depths of the sea.

This rule, however, as to the hideousness of the Fomors had its exceptions. Elathan, one of their chiefs, is described in an old manuscript as of magnificent presence – a Miltonic prince of darkness. 'A man of fairest form,' it says, 'with golden hair down to his shoulders. He wore a mantle of gold braid over a shirt interwoven with threads of gold. Five golden necklaces were round his neck, and a brooch of gold with a shining precious stone thereon was on his breast. He carried two silver spears with rivets of bronze, and his sword was golden-hilted and golden-studded.' Nor was his son less handsome. His name was Bress, which means 'beautiful', and we are told that every beautiful thing in Ireland, 'whether plain, or fortress, or ale, or torch, or woman, or man', was compared with him, so that men said of them, 'that is a Bress'.

Balor, Bress, and Elathan are the three Fomorian personages whose figures, seen through the mists of antiquity, show clearest to us. But they are only a few out of many, nor are they the oldest. We can learn, however, nothing but a few names of any ancestors of the Gaelic giants. This is equally true of the Gaelic gods. Those we know are evidently not without parentage, but the names of their fathers are no more than shadows following into oblivion the figures they designated. The most ancient divinity of whom we have any knowledge is Danu herself, the goddess from whom the whole hierarchy of gods received its name of Tuatha Dé Danann.

She was also called Anu or Ana, and her name still clings to two well-known mountains near Killarney, which, though now called simply 'The Paps', were known formerly as the 'Paps of Ana'. She was the universal mother; 'well she used to cherish the gods', says the commentator of a ninth-century Irish glossary. Her husband is never mentioned by name, but one may assume him, from British analogies, to have been Bilé, known to Gaelic tradition as a god of Hades, a kind of Celtic Dis Pater from whom sprang the first men. Danu herself probably represented the earth and its fruitfulness, and one might compare her with the Greek Demeter. All the other gods are, at least by title, her children. The greatest of these would seem to have been Nuada, called *Argetlám*, or 'He of the Silver Hand'. He was at once the Gaelic Zeus, or Jupiter, and their war-god; for among primitive nations, to whom success in war is all-important, the god of battles is the supreme god. Among the Gauls, Camulus, whose name meant 'Heaven', was identified by the Romans with Mars; and other such instances come readily to the mind. He was possessed of an invincible sword, one of the four chief treasures of the Tuatha Dé Danann, over whom he was twice king; and there is little doubt that he was one of the most important gods of both the Gaels and the Britons, for his name is spread over the whole of the British Isles, which we may surmise the Celts conquered under his auspices. We may picture him as a more savage Mars, delighting in battle and slaughter, and worshipped, like his Gaulish affinities, Teutates and Hesus, of whom the Latin poet Lucan tells us, with human sacrifices, shared in by his female consorts, who, we may imagine, were not more merciful than himself, or than that Gaulish Taranis whose cult was 'no gentler than that of the Scythian Diana', and who completes Lucan's triad as a fit companion to the 'pitiless

Teutates' and the 'horrible Hesus'. Of these warlike goddesses there were five – Fea, the 'Hateful', Nemon, the 'Venomous', Badb, the 'Fury', Macha, a personification of 'battle', and, over all of them, the Morrígú, or 'Great Queen'. This supreme war-goddess of the Gaels, who resembles a fiercer Herê, perhaps symbolized the moon, deemed by early races to have preceded the sun, and worshipped with magical and cruel rites. She is represented as going fully armed, and carrying two spears in her hand. As with Arês and Poseidon in the 'Iliad', her battle-cry was as loud as that of ten thousand men. Wherever there was war, either among gods or men, she, the great queen, was present, either in her own shape or in her favourite disguise, that of a 'hoodie' or carrion crow. An old poem shows her inciting a warrior:

'Over his head is shrieking A lean hag, quickly
hopping Over the points of the weapons and shields;
She is the gray-haired Morrígú'.

With her, Fea and Nemon, Badb and Macha also hovered over the fighters, inspiring them with the madness of battle. All of these were sometimes called by the name of 'Badb'. An account of the Battle of Clontarf, fought by Brian Boru, in 1014, against the Norsemen, gives a gruesome picture of what the Gaels believed to happen in the spiritual world when battle lowered and men's blood was aflame. 'There arose a wild, impetuous, precipitate, mad, inexorable, furious, dark, lacerating, merciless, combative, contentious *badb*, which was shrieking and fluttering over their heads. And there arose also the satyrs, and sprites, and the maniacs of the valleys, and the witches and goblins and owls, and destroying demons of the air and firmament, and the demoniac phantom host;

and they were inciting and sustaining valour and battle with them.' When the fight was over, they revelled among the bodies of the slain; the heads cut off as barbaric trophies were called 'Macha's acorn crop'. These grim creations of the savage mind had immense vitality. While Nuada, the supreme war-god, vanished early out of the Pantheon – killed by the Fomors in the great battle fought between them and the gods – Badb and the Morrígú lived on as late as any of the Gaelic deities. Indeed, they may be said to still survive in the superstitious dislike and suspicion shown in all Celtic-speaking countries for their *avatar*, the hoodie-crow.

After Nuada, the greatest of the gods was the Dagda, whose name seems to have meant the 'Good God'. The old Irish tract called 'The Choice of Names' tells us that he was a god of the earth; he had a cauldron called 'The Undry', in which everyone found food in proportion to his merits, and from which none went away unsatisfied. He also had a living harp; as he played upon it, the seasons came in their order – spring following winter, and summer succeeding spring, autumn coming after summer, and, in its turn, giving place to winter. He is represented as of venerable aspect and of simple mind and tastes, very fond of porridge, and a valiant consumer of it. In an ancient tale we have a description of his dress. He wore a brown, low-necked tunic which only reached down to his hips, and, over this, a hooded cape which barely covered his shoulders. On his feet and legs were horse-hide boots, the hairy side outwards. He carried, or, rather, drew after him on a wheel, an eight-pronged war-club, so huge that eight men would have been needed to carry it; and the wheel, as he towed the whole weapon along, made a track like a territorial boundary. Ancient and gray-headed as he was, and sturdy porridge-eater, it will be seen from this that he was a formidable fighter.

He did great deeds in the battle between the gods and the Fomors, and, on one occasion, is even said to have captured single-handed a hundred-legged and four-headed monster called Mata, dragged him to the 'Stone of Benn', near the Boyne, and killed him there.

The Dagda's wife was called Boann. She was connected in legend with the River Boyne, to which she gave its name, and, indeed, its very existence. Formerly there was only a well, shaded by nine magic hazel-trees. These trees bore crimson nuts, and it was the property of the nuts that whoever ate of them immediately became possessed of the knowledge of everything that was in the world. The story is, in fact, a Gaelic version of the Hebrew myth of 'the Tree of the Knowledge of Good and Evil'. One class of creatures alone had this privilege – divine salmon who lived in the well, and swallowed the nuts as they dropped from the trees into the water, and thus knew all things, and appear in legend as the 'Salmons of Knowledge'. All others, even the highest gods, were forbidden to approach the place. Only Boann, with the proverbial woman's curiosity, dared to disobey this fixed law. She came towards the sacred well, but, as she did so, its waters rose up at her, and drove her away before them in a mighty, rushing flood. She escaped; but the waters never returned. They made the Boyne; and as for the all-knowing inhabitants of the well, they wandered disconsolately through the depths of the river, looking in vain for their lost nuts. One of these salmon was afterwards eaten by the famous Finn mac Coul, upon whom all its omniscience descended. This way of accounting for the existence of a river is a favourite one in Irish legend. It is told also of the Shannon, which burst, like the Boyne, from an inviolable well, to pursue another presumptuous nymph called Sinann, a granddaughter of the sea-god Lêr.

The Dagda had several children, the most important of whom are Brigit, Angus, Mider, Ogma, and Bodb the Red. Of these, Brigit will be already familiar to English readers who know nothing of Celtic myth. Originally she was a goddess of fire and the hearth, as well as of poetry, which the Gaels deemed an immaterial, supersensual form of flame. But the early Christianizers of Ireland adopted the pagan goddess into their roll of saintship, and, thus canonized, she obtained immense popularity as Saint Bridget, or Bride.

Angus was called *Mac Oc*, which means the 'Son of the Young', or, perhaps, the 'Young God'. This most charming of the creations of the Celtic mythology is represented as a Gaelic Eros, an eternally youthful exponent of love and beauty. Like his father, he had a harp, but it was of gold, not oak, as the Dagda's was, and so sweet was its music that no one could hear and not follow it. His kisses became birds which hovered invisibly over the young men and maidens of Erin, whispering thoughts of love into their ears. He is chiefly connected with the banks of the Boyne, where he had a 'brugh', or fairy palace; and many stories are told of his exploits and adventures.

Mider, also the hero of legends, would seem to have been a god of the underworld, a Gaelic Pluto. As such, he was connected with the Isle of Falga – a name for what was otherwise, and still is, called the Isle of Man – where he had a stronghold in which he kept three wonderful cows and a magic cauldron. He was also the owner of the 'Three Cranes of Denial and Churlishness', which might be described flippantly as personified 'gentle hints'. They stood beside his door, and when anyone approached to ask for hospitality, the first one said: 'Do not come! do not come!' and the second added: 'Get away! get away!' while the third chimed in with: 'Go past the house! go past the house!' These three birds were, however, stolen from Mider by Aitherne, an avaricious poet, to whom they would seem to have been more appropriate than to their owner, who does not otherwise appear as a churlish and illiberal deity. On the contrary, he is represented as the victim of others, who plundered him freely. The god Angus took away his wife Etain, while his cows, his cauldron, and his beautiful daughter Blathnat were carried off as spoil by the heroes or demi-gods who surrounded King Conchobar in the golden age of Ulster.

Ogma, who appears to have been also called Cermait, that is, the 'honey-mouthed', was the god of literature and eloquence. He married Etan, the daughter of Diancecht, the god of medicine, and had several children, who play parts more or less prominent in the mythology of the Gaelic Celts. One of them was called Tuirenn, whose three sons murdered the father of the sun-god, and were compelled, as expiation, to pay the greatest fine ever heard of – nothing less than the chief treasures of the world. Another son, Cairpré, became the professional bard of the Tuatha Dé Danann, while three others reigned for a short time over the divine race. As patron of literature, Ogma was naturally credited with having been the inventor of the famous *Ogam* alphabet. This was an indigenous script of Ireland, which spread afterwards to Great Britain, inscriptions in ogmic characters having been found in Scotland, the Isle of Man, South Wales, Devonshire, and at Silchester in Hampshire, the Roman city of Calleva Attrebatum. It was originally intended for inscriptions upon upright pillar-stones or upon wands, the equivalents for letters being notches cut across, or strokes made upon one of the faces of the angle:

When afterwards written in manuscript, the strokes were placed over, under, or through a horizontal line; and the vowels were represented by short lines instead of notches.

A good example of an ogmic inscription is given in Professor Rhys's *Hibbert Lectures*. It comes from a pillar on a small promontory near Dunmore Head, in the west of Kerry, and, read horizontally, reads:

ERC, THE SON OF THE SON OF ERCA (DESCENDANT OF) MODOVINIA.

The origin of this alphabet is obscure. Some authorities consider it of great antiquity, while others believe it entirely post-Christian. It seems, at any rate, to have been based upon, and consequently to presuppose a knowledge of, the Roman alphabet.

Ogma, besides being the patron of literature, was the champion, or professional strong man of the Tuatha Dé Danann. His epithet is *Grianainech*, that is, the 'Sunny-faced', from his radiant and shining countenance.

The last of the Dagda's more important children is Bodb the Red, who plays a greater part in later than in earlier legend. He succeeded his father as king of the gods. He is chiefly connected with the south of Ireland, especially with the Galtee Mountains, and with Lough Dearg, where he had a famous *sídh*, or underground palace.

The Poseidon of the Tuatha Dé Danann Pantheon was called Lêr, but we hear little of him in comparison with his famous son, Manannán, the greatest and most popular of his many children. Manannán mac Lir was the special patron of sailors, who invoked him as 'God of Headlands', and of merchants, who claimed him as the first of their guild. His favourite haunts were the Isle of Man, to which he gave his name, and the Isle of Arran, in the Firth of Clyde, where he had a palace called 'Emhain of the Apple-Trees'. He had many famous weapons – two spears called 'Yellow Shaft' and 'Red Javelin', a sword called 'The Retaliator', which never failed to slay, as well as two others known as the 'Great Fury' and the 'Little Fury'. He had a boat called 'Wave-sweeper', which propelled and guided itself wherever its owner wished, and a horse called 'Splendid Mane', which was swifter than the spring wind, and travelled equally fast on land or over the waves of the sea. No weapon could hurt him through his magic mail and breast-plate, and on his helmet there shone two magic jewels bright as the sun. He endowed the gods with the mantle which made them invisible at will, and he fed them from his pigs, which, like the boar Sæhrimnir, in the Norse Valhalla, renewed themselves as soon as they had been eaten. Of these, no doubt, he made his 'Feast of Age', the banquet at which those who ate never grew old. Thus the people of the goddess Danu preserved their immortal youth, while the ale of Goibniu the Smith-God bestowed invulnerability upon them. It is fitting that Manannán himself should have been blessed beyond all the other gods with inexhaustible life; up to the latest days of Irish heroic literature his luminous figure shines prominent, nor is it even yet wholly forgotten.

Goibniu, the Gaelic Hephaestus, who made the people of the goddess Danu invulnerable with his magic drink, was also the forger of their weapons. It was he who, helped by Luchtainé, the divine carpenter, and Credné, the divine bronze-worker, made the armoury with which the Tuatha Dé Danann conquered the Fomors. Equally useful to them was Diancecht, the god of medicine. It was he who once saved Ireland, and was indirectly the cause of the name of the River Barrow. The Morrígú, the heaven-god's fierce wife, had borne a son of such terrible aspect that the physician of the gods, foreseeing danger, counselled that he should be destroyed in his infancy. This was done; and Diancecht opened the infant's heart, and found within it three serpents, capable, when they grew to full size, of depopulating Ireland. He lost no time in destroying these serpents also, and burning them into ashes, to avoid the evil which even their dead bodies might do. More than this, he flung the ashes into the nearest river, for he feared that there might be danger even in them; and, indeed, so venomous were they that the river boiled up and slew every living creature in it, and therefore has been called 'Barrow' (boiling) ever since.

Diancecht had several children, of whom two followed their father's profession. These were Miach and his sister Airmid. There were also another daughter, Etan, who married Cermait (or Ogma), and three other sons called Cian, Cethé, and Cu. Cian married Ethniu, the daughter of Balor the Fomor, and they had a son who was the crowning glory of the Gaelic Pantheon – its Apollo, the Sun-God, – Lugh, called *Lamhfada*, which means the 'Long-handed', or the 'Far-shooter'. It was not, however, with the bow, like the Apollo of the Greeks, but with the rod-sling that Lugh performed his feats; his worshippers sometimes saw the terrible weapon in the sky as a rainbow, and the Milky Way was called 'Lugh's Chain'. He also had a magic spear, which, unlike the rod-sling, he had no need to wield, himself; for it was alive, and thirsted so for blood that only by steeping its head in a sleeping-draught of pounded poppy leaves could it be kept at rest. When battle was near, it was drawn out; then it roared and struggled against its thongs; fire flashed from it; and, once slipped from the leash, it tore through and through the ranks of the enemy, never tired of slaying. Another of his possessions was a magic hound which an ancient poem, attributed to the Fenian hero, Caoilte, calls –

'That hound of mightiest deeds, Which was irresistible in hardness of combat, Was better than wealth ever known, A ball of fire every night.

'Other virtues had that beautiful hound (Better this property than any other property), Mead or wine would grow of it, Should it bathe in spring water.'

This marvellous hound, as well as the marvellous spear, and the indestructible pigs of Manannán were obtained for Lugh by the sons of Tuirenn as part of the blood-fine he exacted from them for the murder of his father Cian. A hardly less curious story is that which tells how Lugh got his name of the *Ioldanach*, or the 'Master of All Arts'.

These are, of course, only the greater deities of the Gaelic Pantheon, their divinities which answered to such Hellenic figures as Demeter, Zeus, Herê, Cronos, Athena, Eros, Hades, Hermes, Hephaestus, Aesculapius, and Apollo. All of them had many descendants, some of whom play prominent parts in the heroic cycles of the 'Red Branch of Ulster' and of the 'Fenians'. In addition to these, there must have been a multitude of lesser gods who stood in much the same relation to the great gods as the rank and file of tribesmen did to their chiefs. Most of these were probably local deities of the various clans – the gods their heroes swore by. But it is also possible that some may have been divinities of the aboriginal race. Professor Rhys thinks that he can still trace a few of such Iberian gods by name, as Nêt, Ri or Roi, Corb, and Beth. But they play no recognizable part in the stories of the Gaelic gods.

II

THE GODS ARRIVE

The people of the goddess Danu were not the first divine inhabitants of Ireland. Others had been before them, dwellers in 'the dark backward and abysm of time'. In this the Celtic mythology resembles those of other nations, in almost all of which we find an old, dim realm of gods standing behind the reigning Pantheon. Such were Cronos and the Titans, dispossessed by the Zeus who seemed, even to Hesiod, something of a *parvenu* deity. Gaelic tradition recognizes two divine dynasties anterior to the Tuatha Dé Danann. The first of these was called 'The Race of Partholon'. Its head and leader came – as all gods and men came, according to Celtic ideas – from the Other World, and landed in Ireland with a retinue of twenty-four males and twenty-four females upon the first of May, the day called 'Beltaine', sacred to Bilé, the god of death. At this remote time, Ireland consisted of only one treeless, grassless plain, watered by three lakes and nine rivers. But, as the race of Partholon increased, the land stretched, or widened, under them – some said miraculously, and others, by the labours of Partholon's people. At any rate, during the three hundred years they dwelt there, it grew from one plain to four, and acquired seven new lakes; which was fortunate, for the race of Partholon increased from forty-eight members to five thousand, in spite of battles with the Fomors.

These would seem to have been inevitable. Whatever gods ruled, they found themselves in eternal opposition to the not-gods – the powers of darkness, winter, evil, and death. The race of Partholon warred against them with success. At the Plain of Ith, Partholon defeated their leader, a gigantic demon called Cichol the Footless, and dispersed his deformed and monstrous host. After this there was quiet for three hundred years. Then – upon the same fatal first of May – there began a mysterious epidemic, which lasted a week, and destroyed them all. In premonition of their end, they foregathered upon the original, first-created plain – then called Sen Mag, or the 'Old Plain', – so that those who survived might the more easily bury those that died. Their funeral-place is still marked by a mound near Dublin, called 'Tallaght' in the maps, but formerly known as *Tamlecht Muintre Partholain*, the 'Plague-grave of Partholon's People'. This would seem to have been a development of the very oldest form of the legend – which knew nothing of a plague, but merely represented the people of Partholon as having returned, after their sojourn in Ireland, to the other world, whence they came – and is probably due to the gradual euhemerization of the ancient gods into ancient men.

Following the race of Partholon, came the race of Nemed, which carried on the work and traditions of its forerunner. During its time, Ireland again enlarged herself, to the extent of twelve new plains and four more lakes. Like the people of Partholon, the race of Nemed struggled with the Fomors, and defeated them in four consecutive battles. Then Nemed died, with two thousand of his people, from an epidemic, and the remnant, left without their leader, were terribly oppressed by the Fomors. Two Fomorian kings – Morc, son of Dela, and Conann, son of Febar – had built a tower of glass upon Tory Island, always their chief stronghold, and where stories of them still linger, and from this vantage-point they dictated a tax which recalls that paid, in Greek story, to the Cretan Minotaur. Two-thirds of the children born to the race of Nemed during the year were to be delivered up on each day of Samhain. Goaded by this to a last desperate effort, the survivors of Nemed's people attacked the tower, and took it, Conann perishing in the struggle. But their triumph was short. Morc, the other king, collected his forces, and inflicted such a slaughter upon the people of Nemed that, out of the sixteen thousand who had assembled for the storming of the tower, only thirty survived. And these returned whence they came, or died – the two acts being, mythologically speaking, the same.

One cannot help seeing a good deal of similarity between the stories of these two mythical invasions of Ireland. Especially noticeable is the account of the epidemic which destroyed all Partholon's people and nearly all of Nemed's. Hence it has been held that the two legends are duplicates, and that there was at first only one, which has been adapted somewhat differently by two races, the Iberians and the Gaels. Professor Rhys considers the account of Nemed to have been the original Celtic one, and the Partholon story, the version of it which the native races made to please themselves. The name 'Partholon', with its initial p, is entirely foreign to the genius of Gaelic speech. Moreover, Partholon himself is given, by the early chroniclers, ancestors whose decidedly non-Aryan names reappear afterwards as the names of Fir Bolg chiefs. Nemed was later than Partholon in Ireland, as the Gaels, or 'Milesians', were later than the Iberians, or 'Fir Bolgs'.

These 'Fir Bolgs' are found in myth as the next colonizers of Ireland. Varying traditions say that they came from Greece, or from 'Spain' – which was a post-Christian euphemism for the

Celtic Hades. They consisted of three tribes, called the 'Fir Domnann' or 'Men of Domnu', the 'Fir Gaillion' or 'Men of Gaillion', and the 'Fir Bolg' or 'Men of Bolg'; but, in spite of the fact that the first-named tribe was the most important, they are usually called collectively after the last. Curious stories are told of their life in Greece, and how they came to Ireland; but these are somewhat factitious, and obviously do not belong to the earliest tradition.

In the time of their domination they had, we are told, partitioned Ireland among them: the Fir Bolg held Ulster; the Fir Domnann, divided into three kingdoms, occupied North Munster, South Munster, and Connaught; while the Fir Gaillion owned Leinster. These five provinces met at a hill then called 'Balor's Hill', but afterwards the 'Hill of Uisnech'. It is near Rathconrath, in the county of West Meath, and was believed, in early times, to mark the exact centre of Ireland. They held the country from the departure of the people of Nemed to the coming of the people of the goddess Danu, and during this period they had nine supreme kings. At the time of the arrival of the gods, their king's name was Eochaid son of Erc, surnamed 'The Proud'.

We have practically no other details regarding their life in Ireland. It is obvious, however, that they were not really gods, but the pre-Aryan race which the Gaels, when they landed in Ireland, found already in occupation. There are many instances of peoples at a certain stage of culture regarding tribes in a somewhat lower one as semi-divine, or, rather, half-diabolical. The suspicion and fear with which the early Celts must have regarded the savage aborigines made them seem 'larger than human'. They feared them for the weird magical rites which they practised in their inaccessible forts among the hills, amid storms and mountain mists. The Gaels, who held themselves to be the children of light, deemed these 'dark Iberians' children of the dark. Their tribal names seem to have been, in several instances, founded upon this idea. There were the *Corca-Oidce* ('People of Darkness') and the *Corca-Duibhne* ('People of the Night'). The territory of the western tribe of the *Hi Dorchaide* ('Sons of Dark') was called the 'Night Country'. The Celts, who held their own gods to have preceded them into Ireland, would not believe that even the Tuatha Dé Danann could have wrested the land from these magic-skilled Iberians without battle.

They seem also to have been considered as in some way connected with the Fomors. Just as the largest Iberian tribe was called the 'Men of Domnu', so the Fomors were called the 'Gods of Domnu', and Indech, one of their kings, is a 'son of Domnu'. Thus eternal battle between the gods, children of Danu, and the giants, children of Domnu, would reflect, in the supernatural world, the perpetual warfare between invading Celt and resisting Iberian. It is shadowed, too, in the later heroic cycle. The champions of Ulster, Aryans and Gaels par excellence, have no such bitter enemies as the Fir Domnann of Munster and the Fir Gaillion of Leinster. A few scholars would even see in the later death-struggle between the High King of Ireland and his rebellious Fenians the last historic or mythological adumbration of racial war.

The enemies alike of Fir Bolg and Fomor, the Tuatha Dé Danann, gods of the Gaels, were the next to arrive. What is probably the earliest account tells us that they came from the sky. Later versions, however, give them a habitation upon earth – some say in the north, others in the 'southern isles of the world'. They had dwelt in four mythical cities called Findias, Gorias, Murias, and Falias, where they had learned poetry and magic – to the primitive mind two not very dissimilar things – and whence they had brought to Ireland their four chief treasures. From Findias came Nuada's sword, from whose stroke no one ever escaped or recovered; from Gorias, Lugh's terrible lance; from Murias, the Dagda's cauldron; and from Falias, the Stone of Fál, better known as the 'Stone of Destiny', which afterwards fell into the hands of the early kings of Ireland. According to legend, it had the magic property of uttering a human cry when touched by the rightful King of Erin. Some have recognized in this marvellous stone the same rude block which Edward I brought from Scone in the year 1300, and placed in Westminster Abbey, where it now forms part of the Coronation Chair.

It is a curious fact that, while Scottish legend asserts this stone to have come to Scotland from Ireland, Irish legend should also declare that it was taken from Ireland to Scotland. This would sound like conclusive evidence, but it is none the less held by leading modern archæologists – including Dr. W. F. Skene, who has published a monograph on the subject – that the Stone of Scone and the Stone of Tara were never the same. Dr. Petrie identifies the real *Lia Fáil* with a stone which has always remained in Ireland, and which was removed from its original position on Tara Hill, in 1798, to mark the tomb of the rebels buried close by under a mound now known as 'the Croppies' grave'.

Whether the Tuatha Dé Danann came from earth or heaven, they landed in a dense cloud upon the coast of Ireland on the mystic first of May without having been opposed, or even noticed by the people whom it will be convenient to follow the manuscript authorities in calling the 'Fir Bolgs'. That those might still be ignorant of their coming, the Morrígú, helped by Badb and Macha, made use of the magic they had learned in Findias, Gorias, Murias, and Falias. They spread 'druidically-formed showers and fog-sustaining shower-clouds' over the country, and caused the air to pour down fire and blood upon the Fir Bolgs, so that they were obliged to shelter themselves for three days and three nights. But the Fir Bolgs had druids of their own, and, in the end, they put a stop to these enchantments by counter-spells, and the air grew clear again.

The Tuatha Dé Danann, advancing westward, had reached a place called the 'Plain of the Sea', in Leinster, when the two armies met. Each sent out a warrior to parley. The two adversaries approached each other cautiously, their eyes peeping over the tops of their shields. Then, coming gradually nearer, they spoke to one another, and the desire to examine each other's weapons made them almost friends.

The envoy of the Fir Bolgs looked with wonder at the 'beautifully-shaped, thin, slender, long, sharp-pointed spears' of the warrior of the Tuatha Dé Danann, while the ambassador of the tribe of the goddess Danu was not less impressed by the lances of the Fir Bolgs, which were 'heavy, thick, pointless, but sharply-rounded'. They agreed to exchange weapons, so that each side might, by an examination of them, be able to come to some opinion as to its opponent's strength. Before parting, the envoy of the Tuatha Dé Danann offered the Fir Bolgs, through their representative, peace, with a division of the country into two equal halves.

The Fir Bolg envoy advised his people to accept this offer. But their king, Eochaid, son of Erc, would not. 'If we once give these people half,' he said, 'they will soon have the whole.'

The people of the goddess Danu were, on the other hand, very much impressed by the sight of the Fir Bolgs' weapons. They decided to secure a more advantageous position, and, retreating farther west into Connaught, to a plain then called Nia, but now Moytura, near the present village of Cong, they drew up their line at its extreme end, in front of the pass of Balgatan, which offered a retreat in case of defeat.

The Fir Bolgs followed them, and encamped on the nearer side of the plain. Then Nuada, King of the Tuatha Dé Danann, sent an ambassador offering the same terms as before. Again the Fir Bolgs declined them.

'Then when', asked the envoy, 'do you intend to give battle?'

'We must have a truce,' they said, 'for we want time to repair our armour, burnish our helmets, and sharpen our swords. Besides, we must have spears like yours made for us, and you must have spears like ours made for you.'

The result of this chivalrous, but, to modern ideas, amazing, parley was that a truce of one hundred and five days was agreed upon.

It was on Midsummer Day that the opposing armies at last met. The people of the goddess Danu appeared in 'a flaming line', wielding their 'red-bordered, speckled, and firm shields'. Opposite to them were ranged the Fir Bolgs, 'sparkling, brilliant, and flaming, with their swords, spears, blades, and trowel-spears'. The proceedings began with a kind of deadly hurley-match, in which thrice nine of the Tuatha Dé Danann played the same number of the Fir Bolgs, and were defeated and killed. Then followed another parley, to decide how the battle should be carried on, whether there should be fighting every day or only on every second day. Moreover, Nuada obtained from Eochaid an assurance that the battles should always be fought with equal numbers, although this was, we are told, 'very disagreeable to the Fir Bolg king, because he had largely the advantage in the numbers of his army'. Then warfare recommenced with a series of single combats, like those of the Greeks and Trojans in the 'Iliad'. At the end of each day the conquerors on both sides went back to their camps, and were refreshed by being bathed in healing baths of medicinal herbs.

So the fight went on for four days, with terrible slaughter upon each side. A Fir Bolg champion called Sreng fought in single combat with Nuada, the King of the Gods, and shore off his hand and half his shield with one terrific blow. Eochaid, the King of the Fir Bolgs, was even less fortunate than Nuada; for he lost his life. Suffering terribly from thirst, he went, with a hundred of his men, to look for water, and was followed, and pursued as far as the strand of Ballysadare, in Sligo. Here he turned to bay, but was killed, his grave being still marked by a tumulus. The Fir Bolgs, reduced at last to three hundred men, demanded single combat until all upon one side were slain. But, sooner than consent to this, the Tuatha Dé Danann offered them a fifth part of Ireland, whichever province they might choose. They agreed, and chose Connaught, ever afterwards their especial home, and where, until the middle of the seventeenth century, men were still found tracing their descent from Sreng.

The whole story has a singularly historical, curiously unmythological air about it, which contrasts strangely with the account of the other battle of the same name which the Tuatha Dé Danann waged afterwards with the Fomors. The neighbourhood of Cong still preserves both relics and traditions of the fight. Upon the plain of 'Southern Moytura' (as it is called, to distinguish it from the 'Northern Moytura' of the second battle) are many circles and tumuli. These circles are especially numerous near the village itself; and it is said that there were formerly others, which have been used for making walls and dykes. Large cairns of stones, too, are scattered over what was certainly once the scene of a great battle. These various prehistoric monuments each have their still-told story; and Sir William Wilde, as he relates in his Lough Corrib, was so impressed by the unexpected agreement between the details of the legendary battle, as he read them in the ancient manuscript, and the traditions still attaching to the mounds, circles, and cairns, that he tells us he could not help coming to the conclusion that the account was absolutely historical. Certainly the coincidences are curious. His opinion was that the 'Fir Bolgs' were a colony of Belgæ, and that the 'Tuatha Dé Danann' were Danes. But the people of the goddess Danu are too obviously mythical to make it worth while to seek any standing-ground for them in the world of reality. In their superhuman attributes, they are quite different from the Fir Bolgs. In the epical cycle it is made as clear that the Tuatha Dé Danann are divine beings as it is that the Fir Bolg, the Fir Domnann, and the Fir Gaillion stand on exactly the same footing as the men of Ulster. Later history records by what Milesian kings and on what terms of rack-rent the three tribes were allowed settlements in other parts of Ireland than their native Connaught. They appear in ancient, mediæval, and almost modern chronicles as the old race of the land. The truth seems to be that the whole story of the war between the gods and the Fir Bolgs is an invention of comparatively late times. In the earliest documents there is only one battle of Moytura, fought between the people of the goddess Danu and the Fomors. The idea of doubling it seems to date from after the eleventh century; and its inventor may very well have used the legends concerning this battle-field, where two unknown armies had fought in days gone by, in compiling his story. It never belonged to the same genuine mythological stratum as the legend of the original battle fought by the Tuatha Dé Danann, the gods of the Gaels, against the Fomors, the gods of the Iberians.

III

THE RISE OF THE SUN-GOD

It was as a result of the loss of his hand in this battle with the Fir Bolgs that Nuada got his name of *Argetlám*, that is, the 'Silver Handed'. For Diancecht, the physician of the Tuatha Dé Danann, made him an artificial hand of silver, so skilfully that it moved in all its joints, and was as strong and supple as a real one. But, good as it was of its sort, it was a blemish; and, according to Celtic custom, no maimed person could sit upon the throne. Nuada was deposed; and the Tuatha Dé Danann went into council to appoint a new king.

They agreed that it would be a politic thing for them to conciliate the Fomors, the giants of the sea, and make an alliance with them. So they sent a message to Bress, the son of the Fomorian king, Elathan, asking him to come and rule over them. Bress accepted this offer; and they made a marriage between him and Brigit, the daughter of the Dagda. At the same time, Cian, the son of Diancecht, the physician of the Tuatha Dé Danann, married Ethniu, the daughter of the Fomor, Balor. Then Bress was made king, and endowed with lands and a palace; and he, on his part, gave hostages that he would abdicate if his rule ever became unpleasing to those who had elected him.

But, in spite of all his fair promises, Bress, who belonged in heart to his own fierce people, began to oppress his subjects with excessive taxes. He put a tax upon every hearth, upon every kneading-trough, and upon every quern, as well as a poll-tax of an ounce of gold upon every member of the Tuatha Dé Danann. By a crafty trick, too, he obtained the milk of all their cattle. He asked at first only for the produce of any cows which happened to be brown and hairless, and the people of the goddess Danu granted him this cheerfully. But Bress passed all the cattle in Ireland between two fires, so that their hair was singed off, and thus obtained the monopoly of the main source of food. To earn a livelihood, all the gods, even the greatest, were now forced to labour for him. Ogma, their champion, was sent out to collect firewood, while the Dagda was put to work building forts and castles.

One day, when the Dagda was at his task, his son, Angus, came to him. 'You have nearly finished that castle,' he said. 'What reward do you intend to ask from Bress when it is done?' The Dagda replied that he had not yet thought of it. 'Let me give you some advice,' said Angus. 'Ask Bress to have all the cattle in Ireland gathered together upon a plain, so that you can pick out one for yourself. He will consent to that. Then choose the black-maned heifer called 'Ocean'.'

The Dagda finished building the fort, and then went to Bress for his reward. 'What will you have?' asked Bress. 'I want all the cattle in Ireland gathered together upon a plain, so that I may choose one of them for myself.' Bress did this; and the Dagda took the black-maned heifer Angus had told him of. The king, who had expected to be asked very much more, laughed at what he thought was the Dagda's simplicity. But Angus had been wise; as will be seen hereafter.

Meanwhile Bress was infuriating the people of the goddess Danu by adding avarice to tyranny. It was for kings to be liberal to all-comers, but at the court of Bress no one ever greased his knife with fat, or made his breath smell of ale. Nor were there ever any poets or musicians or jugglers or jesters there to give pleasure to the people; for Bress would distribute no largess. Next, he cut down the very subsistence of the gods. So scanty was his allowance of food that they began to grow weak with famine. Ogma, through feebleness, could only carry one-third of the wood needed for fuel; so that they suffered from cold as well as from hunger.

It was at this crisis that two physicians, Miach, the son, and Airmid, the daughter, of Diancecht, the god of medicine, came to the castle where the dispossessed King Nuada lived. Nuada's porter, blemished, like himself (for he had lost an eye), was sitting at the gate, and on his lap was a cat curled up asleep. The porter asked the strangers who they were. 'We are good doctors,' they said. 'If that is so,' he replied, 'perhaps you can give me a new eye.' 'Certainly,' they said, 'we could take one of the eyes of that cat, and put it in the place where your lost eye used to be.' 'I should be very pleased if you would do that,' answered the porter, So Miach and Airmid removed one of the cat's eyes, and put it in the hollow where the man's eye had been.

The story goes on to say that this was not wholly a benefit to him; for the eye retained its cat's nature, and, when the man wished to sleep at nights, the cat's eye was always looking out for mice, while it could hardly be kept awake during the day. Nevertheless, he was pleased at the time, and went and told Nuada, who commanded that the doctors who had performed this marvellous cure should be brought to him.

As they came in, they heard the king groaning, for Nuada's wrist had festered where the silver hand joined the arm of flesh.

Miach asked where Nuada's own hand was, and they told him that it had been buried long ago. But he dug it up, and placed it to Nuada's stump; he uttered an incantation over it, saying: 'Sinew to sinew, and nerve to nerve be joined!' and in three days and nights the hand had renewed itself and fixed itself to the arm, so that Nuada was whole again.

When Diancecht, Miach's father, heard of this he was very angry to think that his son should have excelled him in the art of medicine. He sent for him, and struck him upon the head with a sword, cutting the skin, but not wounding the flesh. Miach easily healed this. So Diancecht hit him again, this time to the bone. Again Miach cured himself. The third time his father smote him, the sword went right through the skull to the membrane of the brain, but even this wound Miach was able to leech. At the fourth stroke, however, Diancecht cut the brain in two, and Miach could do nothing for that. He died, and Diancecht buried him. And upon his grave there grew up three hundred and sixty-five stalks of grass, each one a cure for any illness of each of the three hundred and sixty-five nerves in a man's body. Airmid, Miach's sister, plucked all these very carefully, and arranged them on her mantle according to their properties. But her angry and jealous father overturned the cloak, and hopelessly confused them. If it had not been for that act, says the early writer, men would know how to cure every illness, and would so be immortal.

The healing of Nuada's blemish happened just at the time when all the people of the goddess Danu had at last agreed that the exactions and tyranny of Bress could no longer be borne. It was the insult he put upon Cairpré, son of Ogma the god of literature, that caused things to come to this head. Poets were always held by the Celts in great honour; and when Cairpré, the bard of the Tuatha Dé Danann, went to visit Bress, he expected to be treated with much consideration, and fed at the king's own table. But, instead of doing so, Bress lodged him in a small, dark room where there was no fire, no bed, and no furniture except a mean table on which small cakes of dry bread were put on a little dish for his food. The next morning, Cairpré rose early and left the palace without having spoken to Bress. It was the custom of poets when they left a king's court to utter a panegyric on their host, but Cairpré treated Bress instead to a magical satire. It was the first satire ever made in Ireland, and seems to us to bear upon it all the marks of an early effort. Roughly rendered, it said:

> 'No meat on the plates, No milk of the cows; No shelter for the belated; No money for the minstrels: May Bress's cheer be what he gives to others!'

This satire of Cairpré's was, we are assured, so virulent that it caused great red blotches to break out all over Bress's face. This in itself constituted a blemish such as should not be upon a king, and the Tuatha Dé Danann called upon Bress to abdicate and let Nuada take the throne again.

Bress was obliged to do so. He went back to the country of the Fomors, underneath the sea, and complained to his father Elathan, its king, asking him to gather an army to reconquer his throne. The Fomors assembled in council – Elathan, Tethra, Balor, Indech, and all the other warriors and chiefs – and they decided to come with a great host, and take Ireland away, and put it under the sea where the people of the goddess Danu would never be able to find it again.

At the same time, another assembly was also being held at

Tara, the capital of the Tuatha Dé Danann. Nuada was celebrating his return to the throne by a feast to his people. While it was at its height, a stranger clothed like a king came to the palace gate. The porter asked him his name and errand.

'I am called Lugh,' he said. 'I am the grandson of Diancecht by Cian, my father, and the grandson of Balor by Ethniu, my mother.'

'But what is your profession?' asked the porter; 'for no one is admitted here unless he is a master of some craft.'

'I am a carpenter,' said Lugh.

'We have no need of a carpenter. We already have a very good one; his name is Luchtainé.'

'I am an excellent smith,' said Lugh.

'We do not want a smith. We have a very good one; his name is Goibniu.'

'I am a professional warrior,' said Lugh.

'We have no need of one. Ogma is our champion.'

'I am a harpist,' said Lugh.

'We have an excellent harpist already.'

'I am a warrior renowned for skilfulness rather than for mere strength.'

'We already have a man like that.'

'I am a poet and tale-teller,' said Lugh.

'We have no need of such. We have a most accomplished poet and tale-teller.'

'I am a sorcerer,' said Lugh.

'We do not want one. We have numberless sorcerers and druids.'

'I am a physician,' said Lugh.

'Diancecht is our physician.'

'I am a cup-bearer,' said Lugh.

'We already have nine of them.'

'I am a worker in bronze.'

'We have no need of you. We already have a worker in bronze. His name is Credné.'

'Then ask the king,' said Lugh, 'if he has with him a man who is master of all these crafts at once, for, if he has, there is no need for me to come to Tara.'

So the door-keeper went inside, and told the king that a man had come who called himself Lugh the *Ioldanach*, or the 'Master of all Arts', and that he claimed to know everything.

The king sent out his best chess-player to play against the stranger. Lugh won, inventing a new move called 'Lugh's enclosure'.

Then Nuada invited him in. Lugh entered, and sat down upon the chair called the 'sage's seat', kept for the wisest man.

Ogma, the champion, was showing off his strength. Upon the floor was a flagstone so large that four-score yokes of oxen would have been needed to move it. Ogma pushed it before him along the hall, and out at the door. Then Lugh rose from his chair, and pushed it back again. But this stone, huge as it was, was only a portion broken from a still greater rock outside the palace. Lugh picked it up, and put it back into its place.

The Tuatha Dé Danann asked him to play the harp to them. So he played the 'sleep-tune', and the king and all his court fell asleep, and did not wake until the same hour of the following day. Next he played a plaintive air, and they all wept. Lastly, he played a measure which sent them into transports of joy.

When Nuada had seen all these numerous talents of Lugh, he began to wonder whether one so gifted would not be of great help against the Fomors. He took counsel with the others, and, by their advice, lent his throne to Lugh for thirteen days, taking the 'sage's seat' at his side.

Lugh summoned all the Tuatha Dé Danann to a council.

'The Fomors are certainly going to make war on us,' he said. 'What can each of you do to help?'

Diancecht the Physician said: 'I will completely cure everyone who is wounded, provided his head is not cut off, or his brain or spinal marrow hurt.'

'I,' said Goibniu the Smith, 'will replace every broken lance and sword with a new one, even though the war last seven years. And I will make the lances so well that they shall never miss their mark, or fail to kill. Dulb, the smith of the Fomors, cannot do as much as that. The fate of the fighting will be decided by my lances.'

'And I,' said Credné the Bronze-worker, 'will furnish all the rivets for the lances, the hilts for the swords, and the rims and bosses for the shields.'

'And I,' said Luchtainé the Carpenter, 'will provide all the shields and lance-shafts.'

Ogma the Champion promised to kill the King of the Fomors, with thrice nine of his followers, and to capture one-third of his army.

'And you, O Dagda,' said Lugh, 'what will you do?'

'I will fight,' said the Dagda, 'both with force and craft. Wherever the two armies meet, I will crush the bones of the Fomors with my club, till they are like hailstones under a horse's feet.'

'And you, O Morrígú?' said Lugh.

'I will pursue them when they flee,' she replied. 'And I always catch what I chase.'

'And you, O Cairpré, son of Etan?' said Lugh to the poet, 'what can you do?'

'I will pronounce an immediately-effective curse upon them; by one of my satires I will take away all their honour, and, enchanted by me, they shall not be able to stand against our warriors.'

'And ye, O sorcerers, what will ye do?'

'We will hurl by our magic arts,' replied Mathgan, the head sorcerer, 'the twelve mountains of Ireland at the Fomors. These mountains will be Slieve League, Denna Ulad, the Mourne Mountains, Bri Ruri, Slieve Bloom, Slieve Snechta, Slemish, Blai-Sliab, Nephin, Sliab Maccu Belgodon, Segais, and Cruachan Aigle'.

Then Lugh asked the cup-bearers what they would do.

'We will hide away by magic,' they said, 'the twelve chief lakes and the twelve chief rivers of Ireland from the Fomors, so that they shall not be able to find any water, however thirsty they may be; those waters will conceal themselves from the Fomors so that they shall not get a drop, while they will give drink to the people of the goddess Danu as long as the war lasts, even if it last seven years.' And they told Lugh that the twelve chief lakes were Lough Derg, Lough Luimnigh,

Lough Corrib, Lough Ree, Lough Mask, Strangford Lough, Lough Læig, Lough Neagh, Lough Foyle, Lough Gara, Lough Reagh, and Márloch, and that the twelve chief rivers were the Bush, the Boyne, the Bann, the Nem, the Lee, the Shannon, the Moy, the Sligo, the Erne, the Finn, the Liffey, and the Suir.

Finally, the Druid, Figol, son of Mamos, said: 'I will send three streams of fire into the faces of the Fomors, and I will take away two-thirds of their valour and strength, but every breath drawn by the people of the goddess Danu will only make them more valorous and strong, so that even if the fighting lasts seven years, they will not be weary of it.

All decided to make ready for a war, and to give the direction of it to Lugh.

IV

THE GAELIC ARGONAUTS

The preparations for this war are said to have lasted seven years. It was during the interval that there befel an episode which might almost be called the 'Argonautica' of the Gaelic mythology.

In spite of the dethronement of Bress, the Fomors still claimed their annual tribute from the tribe of the goddess Danu, and sent their tax-gatherers, nine times nine in number, to 'Balor's Hill' to collect it. But, while they waited for the gods to come to tender their submission and their subsidy, they saw a young man approaching them. He was riding upon 'Splendid Mane', the horse of Manannán son of Lêr, and was dressed in Manannán's breast-plate and helmet, through which no weapon could wound their wearer, and he was armed with sword and shield and poisoned darts. 'Like to the setting sun', says the story, 'was the splendour of his countenance and his forehead, and they were not able to look in his face for the greatness of his splendour.' And no wonder! for he was Lugh the Far-shooter, the new-come sun-god of the Gaels. He fell upon the Fomorian tax-gatherers, killing all but nine of them, and these he only spared that they might go back to their kinsmen and tell how the gods had received them.

There was consternation in the under-sea country. 'Who can this terrible warrior be?' asked Balor. 'I know,' said Balor's wife; 'he must be the son of our daughter Ethniu; and I foretell that, since he has cast in his lot with his father's people, we shall never bear rule in Erin again.'

The chiefs of the Fomors saw that this slaughter of their tax-gatherers signified that the Tuatha Dé Danann meant fighting. They held a council to debate on it. There came to it Elathan and Tethra and Indech, kings of the Fomors; Bress himself, and Balor of the stout blows; Cethlenn the crooked tooth, Balor's wife; Balor's twelve white-mouthed sons; and all the chief Fomorian warriors and druids.

Meanwhile, upon earth, Lugh was sending messengers all over Erin to assemble the Tuatha Dé Danann. Upon this errand went Lugh's father Cian, who seems to have been a kind of lesser solar deity, son of Diancecht, the god of medicine. As Cian was going over the plain of Muirthemne, he saw three armed warriors approaching him, and, when they got nearer, he recognized them as the three sons of Tuirenn, son of Ogma, whose names were Brian, Iuchar, and Iucharba. Between these three and Cian, with his brothers Cethé and Cu, there was, for some reason, a private enmity. Cian saw that he was now at a disadvantage. 'If my brothers were with me,' he said to himself, 'what a fight we would make; but, as I am alone, it will be best for me to conceal myself.' Looking round, he saw a herd of pigs feeding on the plain. Like all the gods, he had the faculty of shape-shifting; so, striking himself with a magic wand, he changed himself into a pig, joined the herd, and began feeding with them.

But he had been seen by the sons of Tuirenn. 'What has become of the warrior who was walking on the plain a moment ago?' said Brian to his brothers. 'We saw him then,' they replied, 'but we do not know where he is now.' 'Then you have not used the proper vigilance which is needed in time of war,' said the elder brother.

'However, I know what has become of him. He has struck himself with a druidical wand, and changed himself into a pig, and there he is, in that herd, rooting up the ground, just like all the other pigs. I can also tell you who he is. His name is Cian, and you know that he is no friend of ours.'

'It is a pity that he has taken refuge among the pigs,' they replied, 'for they belong to some one of the Tuatha Dé Danann, and, even if we were to kill them all, Cian might still escape us.'

Again Brian reproached his brothers. 'You are very ignorant,' he said, 'if you cannot distinguish a magical beast from a natural beast. However, I will show you.' And thereupon he struck his two brothers with his own wand of shape-changing, and turned them into two swift, slender hounds, and set them upon the pigs.

The magic hounds soon found the magic pig, and drove it out of the herd on to the open plain. Then Brian threw his spear, and hit it. The wounded pig came to a stop. 'It was an evil deed of yours, casting that spear,' it cried, in a human voice, 'for I am not a pig, but Cian, son of Diancecht. So give me quarter.'

Iuchar and Iucharba would have granted it, and let him go; but their fiercer brother swore that Cian should be put an end to, even if he came back to life seven times. So Cian tried a fresh ruse. 'Give me leave', he asked, 'only to return to my own shape before you slay me.' 'Gladly,' replied Brian, 'for I would much rather kill a man than a pig.'

So Cian spoke the befitting spell, cast off his pig's disguise, and stood before them in his own shape. 'You will be obliged to spare my life now,' he said. 'We will not,' replied Brian. 'Then it will be the worst day's work for all of you that you ever did in your lives,' he answered; 'for, if you had killed me in the shape of a pig, you would only have had to pay the value of a pig, but if you kill me now, I tell you that there never has been, and there never will be, anyone killed in this world for whose death a greater blood-fine will be exacted than for mine.'

But the sons of Tuirenn would not listen to him. They slew him, and pounded his body with stones until it was a crushed mass. Six times they tried to bury him, and the earth cast him back in horror; but, the seventh time, the mould held him, and they put stones upon him to keep him down. They left him buried there, and went to Tara.

Meanwhile Lugh had been expecting his father's return. As he did not come, he determined to go and look for him. He traced him to the Plain of Muirthemne, and there he was at fault. But the indignant earth itself, which had witnessed the murder, spoke to Lugh, and told him everything. So Lugh dug up his father's corpse, and made certain how he had come to his death; then he mourned over him, and laid him back in the earth, and heaped a barrow over him, and set up a pillar with his name on it in 'ogam'.

He went back to Tara, and entered the great hall. It was filled with the people of the goddess Danu, and among them Lugh saw the three sons of Tuirenn. So he shook the 'chiefs' chain', with which the Gaels used to ask for a hearing in an assembly, and when all were silent, he said:

'People of the goddess Danu, I ask you a question. What would be the vengeance that any of you would take upon one who had murdered his father?'

A great astonishment fell upon them, and Nuada, their king, said: 'Surely it is not your father that has been murdered?'

'It is,' replied Lugh. 'And I am looking at those who murdered him; and they know how they did it better than I do.'

'Then Nuada declared that nothing short of hewing the murderer of his father limb from limb would satisfy him, and all the others said the same, including the sons of Tuirenn.

'The very ones who did the deed say that,' cried Lugh. 'Then let them not leave the hall till they have settled with me about the blood-fine to be paid for it.'

'If it was I who had killed your father,' said the king, 'I should think myself lucky if you were willing to accept a fine instead of vengeance.'

The sons of Tuirenn took counsel together in whispers. Iuchar and Iucharba were in favour of admitting their guilt, but Brian was afraid that, if they confessed, Lugh would withdraw his offer to accept a fine, and would demand their deaths. So he stood out, and said that, though it was not they who had killed Cian, yet, sooner than remain under Lugh's anger, as he suspected them, they would pay the same fine as if they had.

'Certainly you shall pay the fine,' said Lugh, 'and I will tell you what it shall be. It is this: three apples; and a pig's-skin; and a spear; and two horses and a chariot; and seven pigs; and a hound-whelp; and a cooking-spit; and three shouts on a hill: that is the fine, and, if you think it is too much, I will remit some of it, but, if you do not think it is too much, then pay it.'

'If it were a hundred times that,' replied Brian, 'we should not think it too much. Indeed, it seems so little that I fear there must be some treachery concealed in it.'

'I do not think it too little,' replied Lugh. 'Give me your pledge before the people of the goddess Danu that you will pay it faithfully, and I will give you mine that I will ask no more.'

So the sons of Tuirenn bound themselves before the Tuatha Dé Danann to pay the fine to Lugh.

When they had sworn, and given sureties, Lugh turned to them again. 'I will now', he said, 'explain to you the nature of the fine you have pledged yourselves to pay me, so that you may know whether it is too little or not.' And, with foreboding hearts, the sons of Tuirenn set themselves to listen.

'The three apples that I have demanded,' he began, 'are three apples from the Garden of the Hesperides, in the east of the world. You will know them by three signs. They are the size of the head of a month-old child, they are of the colour of burnished gold, and they taste of honey. Wounds are healed and diseases cured by eating them, and they do not diminish in any way by being eaten. Whoever casts one of them hits anything he wishes, and then it comes back into his hand. I will accept no other apples instead of these. Their owners keep them perpetually guarded because of a prophecy that three young warriors from the west of the world will come to take them by force, and, brave as you may be, I do not think that you will ever get them.

'The pig's-skin that I have demanded is the pig's-skin of Tuis, King of Greece. It has two virtues: its touch perfectly cures all wounded or sick persons if only there is any life still left in them; and every stream of water through which it passes is turned into wine for nine days. I do not think that you will get it from the King of Greece, either with his consent or without it.

'And can you guess what spear it is that I have demanded?' asked Lugh. 'We cannot,' they said. 'It is the poisoned spear of Pisear, King of Persia; it is irresistible in battle; it is so fiery that its blade must always be held under water, lest it destroy the city in which it is kept. You will find it very difficult to obtain.

'And the two horses and the chariot are the two wonderful horses of Dobhar, King of Sicily, which run equally well over land and sea; there are no other horses in the world like them, and no other vehicle equal to the chariot.

'And the seven pigs are the pigs of Easal, King of the Golden

Pillars; though they may be killed every night, they are found alive again the next day, and every person that eats part of them can never be afflicted with any disease.

'And the hound-whelp I claim is the hound-whelp of the King of Ioruaidhe; her name is Failinis; every wild beast she sees she catches at once. It will not be easy for you to secure her.

'The cooking-spit which you must get for me is one of the cooking-spits of the women of the Island of Fianchuivé, which is at the bottom of the sea, between Erin and Alba.

'You have also pledged yourselves to give three shouts upon a hill. The hill upon which they must be given is the hill called Cnoc Miodhchaoin, in the north of Lochlann. Miodhchaoin and his sons do not allow shouts to be given on that hill; besides this, it was they who gave my father his military education, and, even if I were to forgive you, they would not; so that, though you achieve all the other adventures, I think that you will fail in this one.

'Now you know what sort of a fine it is that you have bargained to pay me,' said Lugh.

And fear and astonishment fell upon the sons of Tuirenn.

This tale is evidently the work of some ancient Irish story-teller who wished to compile from various sources a more or less complete account of how the Gaelic gods obtained their legendary possessions. The spear of Pisear, King of Persia, is obviously the same weapon as the lance of Lugh, which another tradition describes as having been brought by the Tuatha Dé Danann from their original home in the city of Gorias; Failinis, the whelp of the King of Ioruaidhe, is Lugh's 'hound of mightiest deeds', which was irresistible in battle, and which turned any running water it bathed in into wine, a property here transferred to the magic pig's-skin of King Tuis: the seven swine of the King of the Golden Pillars must be the same undying porkers from whose flesh Manannán mac Lir made the 'Feast of Age' which preserved the eternal youth of the gods; it was with horses and chariot that ran along the surface of the sea that Manannán used to journey to and fro between Erin and the Celtic Elysium in the West; the apples that grew in the Garden of the Hesperides were surely of the same celestial growth as those that fed the inhabitants of that immortal country; while the cooking-spit reminds us of three such implements at Tara, made by Goibniu and associated with the names of the Dagda and the Morrígú.

The burden of collecting all these treasures was placed upon the shoulders of the three sons of Tuirenn.

They consulted together, and agreed that they could never hope to succeed unless they had Manannán's magic horse, 'Splendid Mane', and Manannán's magic coracle, 'Wave-sweeper'. But both these had been lent by Manannán to Lugh himself. So the sons of Tuirenn were obliged to humble themselves to beg them from Lugh. The sun-god would not lend them the horse, for fear of making their task too easy, but he let them have the boat, because he knew how much the spear of Pisear and the horses of Dobhar would be needed in the coming war with the Fomors. They bade farewell to their father, and went down to the shore and put out to sea, taking their sister with them.

'Which portion of the fine shall we seek first?' said the others to Brian. 'We will seek them in the order in which they were demanded,' he replied. So they directed the magic boat to sail to the Garden of the Hesperides, and presently they arrived there.

They landed at a harbour, and held a council of war. It was decided that their best chance of obtaining three of the apples would be by taking the shapes of hawks. Thus they would have strength enough in their claws to carry the apples away, together with sufficient quickness upon the wing to hope to escape the arrows, darts, and sling-stones which would be shot and hurled at them by the warders of the garden.

They swooped down upon the orchard from above. It was done so swiftly that they carried off the three apples, unhit either by shaft or stone. But their difficulties were not yet over. The king of the country had three daughters who were well skilled in witchcraft. By sorcery they changed themselves into three ospreys, and pursued the three hawks. But the sons of Tuirenn reached the shore first, and, changing themselves into swans, dived into the sea. They came up close to their coracle, and got into it, and sailed swiftly away with the spoil.

Thus their first quest was finished, and they voyaged on to Greece, to seek the pig's-skin of King Tuis. No one could go without some excuse into a king's court, so they decided to disguise themselves as poets, and to tell the door-keeper that they were professional bards from Erin, seeking largess at the hands of kings. The porter let them into the great hall, where the poets of Greece were singing before the king.

When those had all finished, Brian rose, and asked permission to show his art. This was accorded; and he sang:

> 'O Tuis, we conceal not thy fame. We praise thee as the oak above the kings; The skin of a pig, bounty without hardness! This is the reward which I ask for it.
> 'A stormy host and raging sea Are a dangerous power, should one oppose it. The skin of a pig, bounty without hardness! This is the reward I ask, O Tuis.'

'That is a good poem,' said the king, 'only I do not understand it.'

'I will explain it,' said Brian. "*We praise thee as the oak above the kings*'; this means that, as the oak excels all other trees, so do you excel all other kings in nobility and generosity. '*The skin of a pig, bounty without hardness*'; that is a pig's-skin which you have, O Tuis, and which I should like to receive as the reward of my poem. '*A stormy host and raging sea are a dangerous power, should one oppose it*'; this means to say, that we are not used to going without anything on which we have set our hearts, O Tuis.'

'I should have liked your poem better,' replied the king, 'if my pig's-skin had not been mentioned in it. It was not a wise thing for you to have done, O poet. But I will measure three fills of red gold out of the skin, and you shall have those.'

'May all good be thine, O King!' answered Brian. 'I knew that I should get a noble reward.'

So the king sent for the pig's-skin to measure out the gold with. But, as soon as Brian saw it, he seized it with his left hand, and slew the man who was holding it, and Iuchar and Iucharba also hacked about them; and they cut their way down to the boat, leaving the King of Greece among the dead behind them.

'And now we will go and get King Pisear's spear,' said Brian. So, leaving Greece, they sailed in their coracle to Persia.

Their plan of disguising themselves as poets had served them so well that they decided to make use of it again. So they went into the King of Persia's hall in the same way as they had entered that of the King of Greece. Brian first listened to the poets of Persia singing; then he sang his own song:

'Small the esteem of any spear with Pisear; The battles
of foes are broken; No oppression to Pisear; Everyone
whom he wounds.

'A yew-tree, the finest of the wood, It is called King
without opposition. May that splendid shaft drive
on Yon crowd into their wounds of death.'

'That is a good poem, O man of Erin,' said the king, 'but why is my spear mentioned in it?'

'The meaning is this,' replied Brian: 'I should like to receive that spear as a reward for my poem.'

'You make a rash request,' said the king. 'If I spare your life after having heard it, it will be a sufficient reward for your poem.'

Brian had one of the magic apples in his hand, and he remembered its boomerang-like quality. He hurled it full in the King of Persia's face, dashing out his brains. The Persians flew to arms, but the three sons of Tuirenn conquered them, and made them yield up the spear.

They had now to travel to Sicily, to obtain the horses and chariot of King Dobhar. But they were afraid to go as poets this time, for fear the fame of their deeds might have got abroad. They therefore decided to pretend to be mercenary soldiers from Erin, and offer the King of Sicily their service. This, they thought, would be the easiest way of finding out where the horses and the chariot were kept. So they went and stood on the green before the royal court.

When the King of Sicily heard that there had come mercenaries from Erin, seeking wages from the kings of the world, he invited them to take service with him. They agreed; but, though they stayed with him a fortnight and a month, they never saw the horses, or even found out where they were kept. So they went to the king, and announced that they wished to leave him.

'Why?' he asked, for he did not want them to go.

'We will tell you, O King!' replied Brian. 'It is because we have not been honoured with your confidence, as we have been accustomed with other kings. You have two horses and a chariot, the best in the world, and we have not even been allowed to see them.'

'I would have shown them to you on the first day if you had asked me,' said the king; 'and you shall see them at once, for I have seldom had warriors with me so good as you are, and I do not wish you to leave me.'

So he sent for the steeds, and had them yoked to the chariot, and the sons of Tuirenn were witnesses of their marvellous speed, and how they could run equally well over land or water.

Brian made a sign to his brothers, and they watched their opportunity carefully, and, as the chariot passed close beside them, Brian leaped into it, hurling its driver over the side. Then, turning the horses, he struck King Dobhar with Pisear's spear, and killed him. He took his two brothers up into the chariot and they drove away.

By the time the sons of Tuirenn reached the country of Easal, King of the Pillars of Gold, rumour had gone before them. The king came down to the harbour to meet them, and asked them if it were really true that so many kings had fallen at their hands. They replied that it was true, but that they had no quarrel with any of them; only they must obtain at all costs the fine demanded by Lugh. Then Easal asked them why they had come to his land, and they told him that they needed his seven pigs to add to the tribute. So Easal thought it better to give them up, and to make friends with the three sons of Tuirenn, than to fight with such warriors. The sons of Tuirenn were very glad at this, for they were growing weary of battles.

It happened that the King of Ioruaidhe, who had the hound-whelp that Lugh had demanded, was the husband of King Easal's daughter. Therefore King Easal did not wish that there should be fighting between him and the three sons of Tuirenn. He proposed to Brian and his brothers that he should sail with them to Ioruaidhe, and try to persuade the king of the country to give up the hound-whelp peacefully. They consented, and all set foot safely on the 'delightful, wonderful shores of Ioruaidhe', as the manuscript calls them. But King Easal's son-in-law would not listen to reason. He assembled his warriors, and fought; but the sons of Tuirenn defeated them, and compelled their king to yield up the hound-whelp as the ransom for his life.

All these quests had been upon the earth, but the next was harder. No coracle, not even Manannán's 'Wave-sweeper', could penetrate to the Island of Fianchuivé, in the depths of the sea that severs Erin from Alba. So Brian left his brothers, and put on his 'water-dress, with his transparency of glass upon his head' – evidently an ancient Irish anticipation of the modern diver's dress. Thus equipped, he explored the bottom of the sea for fourteen days before he found the island. But when at last he reached it, and entered the hall of its queen, she and her sea-maidens were so amazed at Brian's hardihood in having penetrated to their kingdom that they presented him with the cooking-spit, and sent him back safe.

By this time, Lugh had found out by his magic arts that the sons of Tuirenn had obtained all the treasures he had demanded as the blood-fine. He desired to get them safely into his own custody before his victims went to give their three shouts upon Miodhchaoin's Hill. He therefore wove a druidical spell round them, so that they forgot the rest of their task altogether, and sailed back to Erin. They searched for Lugh, to give him the things, but he had gone away, leaving word that they were to be handed over to Nuada, the Tuatha Dé Danann king. As soon as they were in safe-keeping, Lugh came back to Tara and found the sons of

Tuirenn there. And he said to them:

'Do you not know that it is unlawful to keep back any part of a blood-fine? So have you given those three shouts upon Miodhchaoin's Hill?'

Then the magic mist of forgetfulness fell from them, and they remembered. Sorrowfully they went back to complete their task.

Miodhchaoin himself was watching for them, and, when he saw them land, he came down to the beach. Brian attacked him, and they fought with the swiftness of two bears and the ferocity of two lions until Miodhchaoin fell.

Then Miodhchaoin's three sons – Corc, Conn, and Aedh – came out to avenge their father, and they drove their spears through the bodies of the three sons of Tuirenn. But the three sons of Tuirenn also drove their spears through the bodies of the three sons of Miodhchaoin.

The three sons of Miodhchaoin were killed, and the three sons of Tuirenn were so sorely wounded that birds might have flown through their bodies from one side to the other. Nevertheless Brian was still able to stand upright, and he held his two brothers, one in each hand, and kept them on their feet, and, all together, they gave three faint, feeble shouts.

Their coracle bore them, still living, to Erin. They sent their father Tuirenn as a suppliant to Lugh, begging him to lend them the magic pig's-skin to heal their wounds.

But Lugh would not, for he had counted upon their fight with the sons of Miodhchaoin to avenge his father Cian's death. So the children of Tuirenn resigned themselves to die, and their father made a farewell song over them and over himself, and died with them.

Thus ends that famous tale – 'The Fate of the Sons of Tuirenn', known as one of the 'Three Sorrowful Stories of Erin'.

V

THE WAR WITH THE GIANTS

By this time the seven years of preparation had come to an end. A week before the Day of Samhain, the Morrígú discovered that the Fomors had landed upon Erin. She at once sent a messenger to tell the Dagda, who ordered his druids and sorcerers to go to the ford of the River Unius, in Sligo, and utter incantations against them.

The people of the goddess Danu, however, were not yet quite ready for battle. So the Dagda decided to visit the Fomorian camp as an ambassador, and, by parleying with them, to gain a little more time. The Fomors received him with apparent courtesy, and, to celebrate his coming, prepared him a feast of porridge; for it was well-known how fond he was of such food. They poured into their king's cauldron, which was as deep as five giant's fists, fourscore gallons of new milk, with meal and bacon in proportion. To this they added the whole carcasses of goats, sheep, and pigs; they boiled the mixture together, and poured it into a hole in the ground. 'Now,' said they, 'if you do eat it all, we shall put you to death, for we will not have you go back to your own people and say that the Fomors are inhospitable.' But they did not succeed in frightening the Dagda. He took his spoon, which was so large that two persons of our puny size might have reclined comfortably in the middle of it, dipped it into the porridge, and fished up halves of salted pork and quarters of bacon.

'If it tastes as good as it smells,' he said, 'it is good fare.' And so it proved; for he ate it all, and scraped up even what remained at the bottom of the hole. Then he went away to sleep it off, followed by the laughter of the Fomors; for his stomach was so swollen with food that he could hardly walk. It was larger than the biggest cauldron in a large house, and stood out like a sail before the wind.

But the Fomors' little practical joke upon the Dagda had given the Tuatha Dé Danann time to collect their forces. It was on the eve of Samhain that the two armies came face to face. Even then the Fomors could not believe that the people of the goddess Danu would offer them much resistance.

'Do you think they will really dare to give us battle?' said Bress to Indech, the son of Domnu. 'If they do not pay their tribute, we will pound their bones for them,' he replied.

The war of gods and giants naturally mirrored the warfare of the Gaels, in whose battles, as in those of most semi-barbarous people, single combat figured largely. The main armies stood still, while, every day, duels took place between ambitious combatants. But no great warriors either of the Tuatha Dé Danann or of the Fomors took part in them.

Sometimes a god, sometimes a giant would be the victor; but there was a difference in the net results that astonished the Fomors. If their own swords and lances were broken, they were of no more use, and if their own champions were killed, they never came back to life again; but it was quite otherwise with the people of the goddess Danu. Weapons shattered on one day reappeared upon the next in as good condition as though they had never been used, and warriors slain on one day came back upon the morrow unhurt, and ready, if necessary, to be killed again.

The Fomors decided to send someone to discover the secret of these prodigies. The spy they chose was Ruadan, the son of Bress and of Brigit, daughter of the Dagda, and therefore half-giant and half-god. He disguised himself as a Tuatha Dé Danann warrior, and went to look for Goibniu. He found him at his forge, together with Luchtainé, the carpenter, and Credné, the bronze-worker. He saw how Goibniu forged lance-heads with three blows of his hammer, while Luchtainé cut shafts for them with three blows of his axe, and Credné fixed the two parts together so adroitly that his bronze nails needed no hammering in. He went back and told the Fomors, who sent him again, this time to try and kill Goibniu.

He reappeared at the forge, and asked for a javelin. Without suspicion, Goibniu gave him one, and, as soon as he got it into his hand, he thrust it through the smith's body. But Goibniu plucked it out, and, hurling it back at his assailant, mortally wounded him. Ruadan went home to die, and his father Bress and his mother Brigit mourned for him, inventing for the purpose the Irish 'keening'. Goibniu, on the other hand, took no harm. He went to the physician Diancecht, who, with his daughter Airmid, was always on duty at a miraculous well called the 'spring of health'. Whenever one of the Tuatha Dé Danann was killed or wounded, he was brought to the two doctors, who plunged him into the wonder-working water, and brought him back to life and health again.

The mystic spring was not long, however, allowed to help the people of the goddess. A young Fomorian chief, Octriallach son of Indech, found it out. He and a number of his companions went to it by night, each carrying a large stone from the bed of the River Drowes. These they dropped into the spring, until they had filled it, dispersed the healing water, and formed a cairn above it. Legend has identified this place by the name of the 'Cairn of Octriallach'.

This success determined the Fomors to fight a pitched battle. They drew out their army in line. There was not a warrior in it who had not a coat of mail and a helmet, a stout spear, a strong buckler, and a heavy sword. 'Fighting the Fomors on that day', says the old author, 'could only be compared to one of three things – beating one's head against a rock, or plunging it into a fire, or putting one's hand into a serpent's nest.'

All the great fighters of the Tuatha Dé Danann were drawn out opposite to them, except Lugh. A council of the gods had decided that his varied accomplishments made his life too valuable to be risked in battle. They had, therefore, left him behind, guarded by nine warriors. But, at the last moment, Lugh escaped from his warders, and appeared in his chariot before the army. He made them a patriotic speech. 'Fight bravely,' he said, 'that your servitude may last no longer; it is better to face death than to live in vassalage and pay tribute.' With these encouraging words, he drove round the ranks, standing on tiptoe, so that all the Tuatha Dé Danann might see him.

The Fomors saw him too, and marvelled. 'It seems wonderful to me,' said Bress to his druids, 'that the sun should rise in the west to-day and in the east every other day.' 'It would be better for us if it were so,' replied the druids. 'What else can it be, then?' asked Bress. 'It is the radiance of the face of Lugh of the Long Arms,' said they.

Then the two armies charged each other with a great shout. Spears and lances smote against shields, and so great was the shouting of the fighters, the shattering of shields, the clattering of swords, the rattling of quivers, and the whistling of darts and javelins that it seemed as if thunder rolled everywhere.

They fought so closely that the heads, hands, and feet of those on one side were touching the heads, hands, and feet of those on the other side; they shed so much blood on to the ground that it became hard to stand on it without slipping; and the river of Unsenn was filled with dead bodies, so hard and swift and bloody and cruel was the battle.

Many great chiefs fell on each side. Ogma, the champion of the Tuatha Dé Danann, killed Indech, the son of the goddess Domnu. But, meanwhile, Balor of the Mighty Blows raged among the gods, slaying their king, Nuada of the Silver Hand, as well as Macha, one of his warlike wives. At last he met with Lugh. The sun-god shouted a challenge to his grandfather in the Fomorian speech. Balor heard it, and prepared to use his death-dealing eye.

'Lift up my eyelid,' he said to his henchmen, 'that I may see this chatterer who talks to me.

The attendants lifted Balor's eye with a hook, and if the glance of the eye beneath had rested upon Lugh, he would certainly have perished. But, when it was half opened, Lugh flung a magic stone which struck Balor's eye out through the back of his head. The eye fell on the ground behind Balor, and destroyed a whole rank of thrice nine Fomors who were unlucky enough to be within sight of it.

An ancient poem has handed down the secret of this magic stone. It is there called a *tathlum*, meaning a 'concrete ball' such as the ancient Irish warriors used sometimes to make out of the brains of dead enemies hardened with lime.

> 'A tathlum, heavy, fiery, firm, Which the Tuatha Dé Danann had with them, It was that broke the fierce Balor's eye, Of old, in the battle of the great armies.
>
> 'The blood of toads and furious bears, And the blood of the noble lion, The blood of vipers and of

Osmuinn's trunks; – It was of these the tathlum was composed.

'The sand of the swift Armorian sea, And the sand of the teeming Red Sea; – All these, being first purified, were used In the composition of the tathlum.

'Briun, the son of Bethar, no mean warrior, Who on the ocean's eastern border reigned; – It was he that fused, and smoothly formed, It was he that fashioned the tathlum.

'To the hero Lugh was given This concrete ball,
– no soft missile; – In Mag Tuireadh of shrieking wails, From his hand he threw the tathlum.'

This blinding of the terrible Balor turned the fortunes of the fight; for the Fomors wavered, and the Morrígú came and encouraged the people of the goddess Danu with a song, beginning 'Kings arise to the battle', so that they took fresh heart, and drove the Fomors headlong back to their country underneath the sea.

Such was the battle which is called in Irish *Mag Tuireadh na b-Fomorach*, that is to say, the 'Plain of the Towers of the Fomors', and, more popularly, the 'Battle of Moytura the Northern', to distinguish it from the other Battle of Moytura fought by the Tuatha Dé Danann against the Fir Bolgs farther to the south. More of the Fomors were killed in it, says the ancient manuscript, than there are stars in the sky, grains of sand on the sea-shore, snow-flakes in winter, drops of dew upon the meadows in spring-time, hailstones during a storm, blades of grass trodden under horses' feet, or Manannán son of Lêr's white horses, the waves of the sea, when a tempest breaks. The 'towers' or pillars said to mark the graves of the combatants still stand upon the plain of Carrowmore, near Sligo, and form, in the opinion of Dr. Petrie, the finest collection of prehistoric monuments in the world, with the sole exception of Carnac, in Brittany. Megalithic structures of almost every kind are found among them – stone cairns with dolmens in their interiors, dolmens standing open and alone, dolmens surrounded by one, two, or three circles of stones, and circles without dolmens – to the number of over a hundred. Sixty-four of such prehistoric remains stand together upon an elevated plateau not more than a mile across, and make the battle-field of Moytura, though the least known, perhaps the most impressive of all primeval ruins. What they really commemorated we may never know, but, in all probability, the place was the scene of some important and decisive early battle, the monuments marking the graves of the chieftains who were interred as the result of it. Those which have been examined were found to contain burnt wood and the half-burnt bones of men and horses, as well as implements of flint and bone. The actors, therefore, were still in the Neolithic Age. Whether the horses were domesticated ones buried with their riders, or wild ones eaten at the funeral feasts, it would be hard to decide. The history of the real event must have been long lost even at the early date when its relics were pointed out as the records of a battle between the gods and the giants of Gaelic myth.

The Tuatha Dé Danann, following the routed Fomors, overtook and captured Bress. He begged Lugh to spare his life.

'What ransom will you pay for it?' asked Lugh.

'I will guarantee that the cows of Ireland shall always be in milk,' promised Bress.

But, before accepting, Lugh took counsel with his druids.

'What good will that be,' they decided, 'if Bress does not also lengthen the lives of the cows?'

This was beyond the power of Bress to do; so he made another offer.

'Tell your people,' he said to Lugh, 'that, if they will spare my life, they shall have a good wheat harvest every year.'

But they said: 'We already have the spring to plough and sow in, the summer to ripen the crops, the autumn for reaping, and the winter in which to eat the bread; and that is all we want.'

Lugh told this to Bress. But he also said: 'You shall have your life in return for a much less service to us than that.'

'What is it?' asked Bress.

'Tell us when we ought to plough, when we ought to sow, and when we ought to harvest.'

Bress replied: 'You should plough on a Tuesday, sow on a Tuesday, and harvest on a Tuesday.'

And this lying maxim (says the story) saved Bress's life.

Lugh, the Dagda, and Ogma still pursued the Fomors, who had carried off in their flight the Dagda's harp. They followed them into the submarine palace where Bress and Elathan lived, and there they saw the harp hanging on the wall. This harp of the Dagda's would not play without its owner's leave. The Dagda sang to it:

'Come, oak of the two cries! Come, hand of fourfold music! Come, summer! Come, winter! Voice of harps, bellows, and flutes!'

For the Dagda's harp had these two names; it was called 'Oak of the two cries' and 'Hand of four-fold music'.

It leaped down from the wall, killing nine of the Fomors as it passed, and came into the Dagda's hand. The Dagda played to the Fomors the three tunes known to all clever harpists – the weeping-tune, the laughing-tune, and the sleeping-tune. While he played the weeping-tune, they were bowed with weeping; while he played the laughing-tune, they rocked with laughter; and when he played the sleeping-tune, they all fell asleep. And while they slept, Lugh, the Dagda, and Ogma got away safely.

Next, the Dagda brought the black-maned heifer which he had, by the advice of Angus son of the Young, obtained from Bress. The wisdom of Angus had been shown in this advice, for it was this very heifer that the cattle of the people of the goddess Danu were accustomed to follow, whenever it lowed. Now, when it lowed, all the cattle which the Fomors had taken away from the Tuatha Dé Danann came back again.

Yet the power of the Fomors was not wholly broken. Four of them still carried on a desultory warfare by spoiling the corn, fruit, and milk of their conquerors. But the Morrígú and Badb and Mider and Angus pursued them, and drove them out of Ireland for ever.

Last of all, the Morrígú and Badb went up on to the summits of all the high mountains of Ireland, and proclaimed the victory. All the lesser gods who had not been in the battle came round and heard the news. And Badb sang a song which began:

> Peace mounts to the heavens, The heavens descend
> to earth, Earth lies under the heavens, Everyone is strong
> . . . ',

but the rest of it has been lost and forgotten.

Then she added a prophecy in which she foretold the

approaching end of the divine age, and the beginning of a new one in which summers would be flowerless and cows milkless and women shameless and men strengthless, in which there would be trees without fruit and seas without fish, when old men would give false judgments and legislators make unjust laws, when warriors would betray one another, and men would be thieves, and there would be no more virtue left in the world.

VI

THE CONQUEST OF THE GODS BY MORTALS

Of what Badb had in mind when she uttered this prophecy we have no record. But it was true. The twilight of the Irish gods was at hand. A new race was coming across the sea to dispute the ownership of Ireland with the people of the goddess Danu. And these new-comers were not divinities like themselves, but men like ourselves, ancestors of the Gaels.

This story of the conquest of the gods by mortals – which seems such a strange one to us – is typically Celtic. The Gaelic mythology is the only one which has preserved it in any detail; but the doctrine would seem to have been common at one time to all the Celts. It was, however, of less shame to the gods than would otherwise have been; for men were of as divine descent as themselves. The dogma of the Celts was that men were descended from the god of death, and first came from the Land of the Dead to take possession of the present world. Caesar tells us, in his too short account of the Gauls, that they believed themselves to be sprung from Dis Pater, the god of the underworld. In the Gaelic mythology Dis Pater was called Bilé, a name which has for root the syllable bel, meaning 'to die'. The god Beli in British mythology was no doubt the same person, while the same idea is expressed by the same root in the name of Balor, the terrible Fomor whose glance was death.

The post-Christian Irish chroniclers, seeking to reconcile

Christian teachings with the still vital pagan mythology by changing the gods into ancient kings and incorporating them into the annals of the country, with appropriate dates, also disposed of the genuine early doctrine by substituting Spain for Hades, and giving a highly-fanciful account of the origin and wanderings of their ancestors. To use a Hibernicism, appropriate in this connection, the first Irishman was a Scythian called Fenius Farsa. Deprived of his own throne, he had settled in Egypt, where his son Niul married a daughter of the reigning Pharaoh. Her name was Scôta, and she had a son called Goidel, whose great-grandson was named Eber Scot, the whole genealogy being probably invented to explain the origin of the three names by which the Gaels called themselves – Finn, Scot, and Goidel. Fenius and his family and clan were turned out of Egypt for refusing to join in the persecution of the children of Israel, and sojourned in Africa for forty-two years. Their wanderings took them to 'the altars of the Philistines, by the Lake of Osiers'; then, passing between Rusicada and the hilly country of Syria, they travelled through Mauretania as far as the Pillars of Hercules; and thence landed in Spain, where they lived many years, greatly increasing and multiplying. The same route is given by the twelfth-century British historian, Geoffrey of Monmouth, as that taken by Brutus and the Trojans when they came to colonize Britain. Its only connection with any kind of fact is that it corresponds fairly well with what ethnologists consider must have been the westward line of migration taken, not, curiously enough, by the Aryan Celts, but by the pre-Aryan Iberians.

It is sufficient for us to find the first men in Spain, remembering that 'Spain' stood for the Celtic Hades, or Elysium. In this country Bregon, the father of two sons, Bilé and Ith, had built a watch-tower, from which, one winter's evening, Ith saw, far off over the seas, a land he had never noticed before. 'It is on winter evenings, when the air is pure, that man's eyesight reaches farthest', remarks the old tract called the 'Book of Invasions', gravely accounting for the fact that Ith saw Ireland from Spain.

Wishing to examine it nearer, he set sail with thrice thirty warriors, and landed without mishap at the mouth of the River Scêné. The country seemed to him to be uninhabited, and he marched with his men towards the north. At last he reached Aileach, near the present town of Londonderry.

Here he found the three reigning kings of the people of the goddess Danu, Mac Cuill, Mac Cecht, and Mac Greiné, the sons of Ogma, and grandsons of the Dagda. These had succeeded Nuada the Silver-handed, killed in the battle with the Fomors; and had met, after burying their predecessor in a tumulus called Grianan Aileach, which still stands on the base of the Inishowen Peninsula, between Lough Swilly and Lough Foyle, to divide his kingdom among them. Unable to arrive at any partition satisfactory to all, they appealed to the new-comer to arbitrate.

The advice of Ith was moral rather than practical. 'Act according to the laws of justice' was all that he would say to the claimants; and then he was indiscreet enough to burst into enthusiastic praises of Ireland for its temperate climate and its richness in fruit, honey, wheat, and fish. Such sentiments from a foreigner seemed to the Tuatha Dé Danann suggestive of a desire to take the country from them. They conspired together and treacherously killed Ith at a place since called 'Ith's Plain'. They, however, spared his followers, who returned to 'Spain', taking their dead leader's body with them. The indignation there was great, and Milé, Bilé's son and Ith's nephew, determined to go to Ireland and get revenge.

Milé therefore sailed with his eight sons and their wives.

THE CONQUEST OF THE GODS BY MORTALS

Thirty-six chiefs, each with his shipful of warriors, accompanied him. By the magic arts of their druid, Amergin of the Fair Knee, they discovered the exact place at which Ith had landed before them, and put in to shore there. Two alone failed to reach it alive. The wife of Amergin died during the voyage, and Aranon, a son of Milé, on approaching the land, climbed to the top of the mast to obtain a better view, and, falling off, was drowned. The rest disembarked safely upon the first of May.

Amergin was the first to land. Planting his right foot on Irish soil, he burst into a poem preserved in both the Book of Lecan and the Book of Ballymote. It is a good example of the pantheistic philosophy of the Celtic races, and a very close parallel to it is contained in an early Welsh poem, called the 'Battle of the Trees', and attributed to the famous bard Taliesin. 'I am the wind that blows upon the sea,' sang Amergin; 'I am the ocean wave; I am the murmur of the surges; I am seven battalions; I am a strong bull; I am an eagle on a rock; I am a ray of the sun; I am the most beautiful of herbs; I am a courageous wild boar; I am a salmon in the water; I am a lake upon a plain; I am a cunning artist; I am a gigantic, sword-wielding champion; I can shift my shape like a god. In what direction shall we go? Shall we hold our council in the valley or on the mountain-top? Where shall we make our home? What land is better than this island of the setting sun? Where shall we walk to and fro in peace and safety? Who can find you clear springs of water as I can? Who can tell you the age of the moon but I? Who can call the fish from the depths of the sea as I can? Who can cause them to come near the shore as I can? Who can change the shapes of the hills and headlands as I can? I am a bard who is called upon by seafarers to prophesy. Javelins shall be wielded to avenge our wrongs. I prophesy victory.

I end my song by prophesying all other good things.'

The Welsh bard Taliesin sings in the same strain as the druid Amergin his unity with, and therefore his power over, all nature, animate and inanimate. 'I have been in many shapes', he says, 'before I attained a congenial form. I have been a narrow blade of a sword; I have been a drop in the air; I have been a shining star; I have been a word in a book; I have been a book in the beginning; I have been a light in a lantern a year and a half; I have been a bridge for passing over threescore rivers; I have journeyed as an eagle; I have been a boat on the sea; I have been a director in battle; I have been a sword in the hand; I have been a shield in fight; I have been the string of a harp; I have been enchanted for a year in the foam of water. There is nothing in which I have not been.' It is strange to find Gael and Briton combining to voice almost in the same words this doctrine of the mystical Celts, who, while still in a state of semi-barbarism, saw, with some of the greatest of ancient and modern philosophers, the One in the Many, and a single Essence in all the manifold forms of life.

The Milesians (for so, following the Irish annalists, it will be convenient to call the first Gaelic settlers in Ireland) began their march on Tara, which was the capital of the Tuatha Dé Danann, as it had been in earlier days the chief fortress of the Fir Bolgs, and would in later days be the dwelling of the high kings of Ireland. On their way they met with a goddess called Banba, the wife of Mac Cuill. She greeted Amergin. 'If you have come to conquer Ireland,' she said, 'your cause is no just one.' 'Certainly it is to conquer it we have come,' replied Amergin, without condescending to argue upon the abstract morality of the matter. 'Then at least grant me one thing,' she asked. 'What is that?' replied Amergin. 'That this island shall be called by my name.'

'It shall be,' replied Amergin.

A little farther on, they met a second goddess, Fotla, the wife of Mac Cecht, who made the same request, and received the same answer from Amergin.

Last of all, at Uisnech, the centre of Ireland, they came upon the third of the queens, Eriu, the wife of Mac Greiné. 'Welcome, warriors,' she cried. 'To you who have come from afar this island shall henceforth belong, and from the setting to the rising sun there is no better land. And your race will be the most perfect the world has ever seen.' 'These are fair words and a good prophecy,' said Amergin. 'It will be no thanks to you,' broke in Donn, Milé's eldest son. 'Whatever success we have we shall owe to our own strength.' 'That which I prophesy has no concern with you,' retorted the goddess, 'and neither you nor your descendants will live to enjoy this island.' Then, turning to Amergin, she, too, asked that Ireland might be called after her. 'It shall be its principal name,' Amergin promised.

And so it has happened. Of the three ancient names of Ireland – Banba, Fotla, and Eriu – the last, in its genitive form of 'Erinn', is the one that has survived.

The invaders came to Tara, then called Drumcain, that is, the 'Beautiful Hill'. Mac Cuill, Mac Cecht, and Mac Greiné met them, with all the host of the Gaelic gods. As was usual, they held a parley. The people of the goddess Danu complained that they had been taken by surprise, and the Milesians admitted that to invade a country without having first warned its inhabitants was not strictly according to the courtesies of chivalrous warfare. The Tuatha Dé Danann proposed to the invaders that they should leave the island for three days, during which they themselves would decide whether to fight for their kingdom or to surrender it; but the Milesians did not care for this, for they knew that, as soon as they were out of the island, the Tuatha Dé Danann would oppose them with druidical enchantments, so that they would not be able to make a fresh landing. In the end, Mac Cuill, Mac Cecht, and Mac Greiné offered to submit the matter to the arbitration of Amergin, the Milesians' own lawgiver, with the express stipulation that, if he gave an obviously partial judgment, he was to suffer death at their hands. Donn asked his druid if he were prepared to accept this very delicate duty. Amergin replied that he was, and at once delivered the first judgment pronounced by the Milesians in Ireland.

> 'The men whom we found dwelling in the land, to them is possession due by right.
> It is therefore your duty to set out to sea over nine green waves;
> And if you shall be able to effect a landing again in spite of them,
> You are to engage them in battle, and I adjudge to you the land in which you found them living.
> I adjudge to you the land wherein you found them dwelling, by the right of battle.
> But although you may desire the land which these people possess, yet yours is the duty to show them justice.
> I forbid you from injustice to those you have found in the land, however you may desire to obtain it.'

This judgment was considered fair by both parties. The Milesians retired to their ships, and waited at a distance of nine waves' length from the land until the signal was given to attack, while the Tuatha Dé Danann, drawn up upon the beach, were ready with their druidical spells to oppose them.

THE CONQUEST OF THE GODS BY MORTALS

The signal was given, and the Milesians bent to their oars. But they had hardly started before they discovered that a strong wind was blowing straight towards them from the shore, so that they could make no progress. At first they thought it might be a natural breeze, but Donn smelt magic in it. He sent a man to climb the mast of his ship, and see if the wind blew as strong at that height as it did at the level of the sea. The man returned, reporting that the air was quite still 'up aloft'. Evidently it was a druidical wind. But Amergin soon coped with it. Lifting up his voice, he invoked the Land of Ireland itself, a power higher than the gods it sheltered.

'I invoke the land of Eriu!
The shining, shining sea!
The fertile, fertile hill!
The wooded vale!
The river abundant, abundant in water!
The fishful, fishful lake!'

In such strain runs the original incantation, one of those magic formulas whose power was held by ancient, and still is held by savage races to reside in their exact consecrated wording rather than in their meaning. To us it sounds nonsense, and so no doubt it did to those who put the old Irish mythical traditions into literary shape; for a later version expands and explains it as follows:

'I implore that we may regain the land of Erin,
We who have come over the lofty waves,
This land whose mountains are great and extensive,
Whose streams are clear and numerous,
Whose woods abound with various fruit,
Its rivers and waterfalls are large and beautiful,
Its lakes are broad and widely spread,

It abounds with fountains on elevated grounds!
May we gain power and dominion over its tribes!
May we have kings of our own ruling at Tara!
May Tara be the regal residence of our many
    succeeding kings!
May the Milesians be the conquerors of its people!
May our ships anchor in its harbours!
May they trade along the coast of Erin!
May Eremon be its first ruling monarch!
May the descendants of Ir and Eber be mighty kings!
I implore that we may regain the land of Erin,
                              I implore!'

The incantation proved effectual. The Land of Ireland was pleased to be propitious, and the druidical wind dropped down.

But success was not quite so easy as they had hoped. Manannán, son of the sea and lord of headlands, shook his magic mantle at them, and hurled a fresh tempest out over the deep. The galleys of the Milesians were tossed helplessly on the waves; many sank with their crews. Donn was among the lost, thus fulfilling Eriu's prophecy, and three other sons of Milé also perished. In the end, a broken remnant, after long beating about the coasts, came to shore at the mouth of the River Boyne. They landed; and Amergin, from the shore, invoked the aid of the sea as he had already done that of the land.

'Sea full of fish! Fertile land! Fish swarming up!
Fish there! Under-wave bird! Great fish!
Crab's hole! Fish swarming up!
Sea full of fish!'

which, being interpreted like the preceding charm seems to have meant:

> 'May the fishes of the sea crowd in shoals to the land
>   for our use!
> May the waves of the sea drive forth to the shore
>   abundance of fish!
> May the salmon swim abundantly into our nets!
> May all kinds of fish come plentifully to us from the sea!
> May its flat-fishes also come in abundance!
> This poem I compose at the sea-shore that fishes may
>   swim in shoals to our coast.'

Then, gathering their forces, they marched on the people of the goddess Danu.

Two battles were fought, the first in Glenn Faisi, a valley of the Slieve Mish Mountains, south of Tralee, and the second at Tailtiu, now called Telltown. In both, the gods were beaten. Their three kings were killed by the three surviving sons of Milé – Mac Cuill by Eber, Mac Cecht by Eremon, and Mac Greiné by the druid Amergin. Defeated and disheartened, they gave in, and, retiring beneath the earth, left the surface of the land to their conquerors.

From this day begins the history of Ireland according to the annalists. Milé's eldest son, Donn, having perished, the kingdom fell by right to the second, Eremon. But Eber, the third son, backed by his followers, insisted upon a partition, and Ireland was divided into two equal parts. At the end of a year, however, war broke out between the brothers; Eber was killed in battle, and Eremon took the sole rule.

VII

THE GODS IN EXILE

But though mortals had conquered gods upon a scale unparalleled in mythology, they had by no means entirely subdued them. Beaten in battle, the people of the goddess Danu had yet not lost their divine attributes, and could use them either to help or hurt. 'Great was the power of the Dagda', says a tract preserved in the Book of Leinster, 'over the sons of Milé, even after the conquest of Ireland; for his subjects destroyed their corn and milk, so that they must needs make a treaty of peace with the Dagda. Not until then, and thanks to his good-will, were they able to harvest corn and drink the milk of their cows.' The basis of this lost treaty seems to have been that the Tuatha Dé Danann, though driven from the soil, should receive homage and offerings from their successors. We are told in the verse *dinnsenchus* of Mag Slecht, that –

> 'Since the rule Of Eremon, the noble man of grace,
> There was worshipping of stones Until the coming of
> good Patrick of Macha'.

Dispossessed of upper earth, the gods had, however, to seek for new homes. A council was convened, but its members were divided between two opinions. One section of them chose to shake the dust of Ireland off its disinherited feet, and seek refuge in a paradise over-seas, situate in some unknown, and, except for favoured mortals, unknowable island of the west, the counterpart in Gaelic myth of the British

> 'island-valley of Avilion; Where falls not hail, or rain, or any snow, Nor ever wind blows loudly; but it lies Deep-meadow'd, happy, fair with orchard-lawns And bowery hollows crown'd with summer sea'

– a land of perpetual pleasure and feasting, described variously as the 'Land of Promise' (*Tir Tairngiré*), the 'Plain of Happiness' (*Mag Mell*), the 'Land of the Living' (*Tir-nam-beo*), the 'Land of the Young' (*Tir-nan-o⁻g*), and 'Breasal's Island' (*Hy-Breasail*). Celtic mythology is full of the beauties and wonders of this mystic country, and the tradition of it has never died out. Hy-Breasail has been set down on old maps as a reality again and again; some pioneers in the Spanish seas thought they had discovered it, and called the land they found 'Brazil'; and it is still said, by lovers of old lore, that a patient watcher, after long gazing westward from the westernmost shores of Ireland or Scotland, may sometimes be lucky enough to catch a glimpse against the sunset of its –

> 'summer isles of Eden lying in dark-purple spheres of sea'.

Of these divine emigrants the principal was Manannán son of Lêr. But, though he had cast in his lot beyond the seas, he did not cease to visit Ireland. An old Irish king, Bran, the son of Febal, met him, according to a seventh-century poem, as Bran journeyed to, and Manannán from, the earthly paradise. Bran was in his boat, and Manannán was driving a chariot over the tops of the waves, and he sang:

> 'Bran deems it a marvellous beauty In his coracle across the clear sea: While to me in my chariot from afar It is a flowery plain on which he rides about.
> 'What is a clear sea For the prowed skiff in which Bran is, That is a happy plain with profusion of flowers To me from the chariot of two wheels.
> 'Bran sees The number of waves beating across the clear sea: I myself see in Mag Mon Red-headed flowers without fault.
> 'Sea-horses glisten in summer As far as Bran has stretched his glance: Rivers pour forth a stream of honey In the land of Manannán son of Lêr
> 'The sheen of the main, on which thou art, The white hue of the sea, on which thou rowest about, Yellow and azure are spread out, It is land, and is not rough.
> 'Speckled salmon leap from the womb Of the white sea, on which thou lookest: They are calves, they are coloured lambs With friendliness, without mutual slaughter.
> 'Though but one chariot-rider is seen
> In Mag Mell of many flowers, There are many steeds on its surface,
>
> Though them thou seest not.
> 'Along the top of a wood has swum
>
> Thy coracle across ridges,

> There is a wood of beautiful fruit
>
> Under the prow of thy little skiff.
> 'A wood with blossom and fruit,
>
> On which is the vine's veritable fragrance;
>
> A wood without decay, without defect,
>
> On which are leaves of a golden hue.'

And, after this singularly poetical enunciation of the philosophical and mystical doctrine that all things are, under their diverse forms, essentially the same, he goes on to describe to Bran the beauties and pleasures of the Celtic Elysium.

But there were others – indeed, the most part – of the gods who refused to expatriate themselves. For these residences had to be found, and the Dagda, their new king, proceeded to assign to each of those who stayed in Ireland a *sídh*. These *sídhe* were barrows, or hillocks, each being the door to an underground realm of inexhaustible splendour and delight, according to the somewhat primitive ideas of the Celts. A description is given of one which the Dagda kept for himself, and out of which his son Angus cheated him, which will serve as a fair example of all. There were apple-trees there always in fruit, and one pig alive and another ready roasted, and the supply of ale never failed. One may still visit in Ireland the *sídhe* of many of the gods, for the spots are known, and the traditions have not died out. To Lêr was given *Sídh Fionnachaidh*, now known as the 'Hill of the White Field', on the top of Slieve Fuad, near Newtown Hamilton, in County Armagh.

Bodb Derg received a *sídh* called by his own name, *Sídh Bodb*, just to the south of Portumna, in Galway. Mider was given the *sídh* of *Bri Leith*, now called Slieve Golry, near Ardagh, in County Longford. Ogma's *sídh* was called *Airceltrai*; to Lugh was assigned *Rodrubân*; Manannán's son, Ilbhreach, received *Sídh Eas Aedha Ruaidh*, now the Mound of Mullachshee, near Ballyshannon, in Donegal; Fionnbharr had *Sídh Meadha*, now 'Knockma', about five miles west of Tuam, where, as present king of the fairies, he is said to live to-day; while the abodes of other gods of lesser fame are also recorded. For himself the Dagda retained two, both near the River Boyne, in Meath, the best of them being the famous Brugh-na-Boyne. None of the members of the Tuatha Dé Danann were left unprovided for, save one.

It was from this time that the Gaelic gods received the name by which the peasantry know them to-day – *Aes Sídhe*, the 'People of the Hills', or, more shortly, the *Sídhe*. Every god, or fairy, is a *Fer-Sídhe*, a 'Man of the Hill'; and every goddess a *Bean-Sídhe*, a 'Woman of the Hill', the banshee of popular legend.

The most famous of such fairy hills are about five miles from Drogheda. They are still connected with the names of the Tuatha Dé Danann, though they are now not called their dwelling-places, but their tombs. On the northern bank of the Boyne stand seventeen barrows, three of which – Knowth, Dowth, and New Grange – are of great size. The last named, largest, and best preserved, is over 300 feet in diameter, and 70 feet high, while its top makes a platform 120 feet across. It has been explored, and Roman coins, gold torques, copper pins, and iron rings and knives have been found in it; but what else it may have once contained will never be known, for, like Knowth and Dowth, it was thoroughly ransacked by Danish spoilers in the ninth century. It is entered by a square doorway, the rims of which are elaborately ornamented with a kind of spiral pattern. This entrance leads to a stone passage, more than 60 feet long, which gradually widens and rises, until it opens into a chamber with a conical dome 20 feet high. On each side of this central chamber is a recess, with a shallow oval stone basin in it. The huge slabs of which the whole is built are decorated upon both the outer and the inner faces with the same spiral pattern as the doorway.

The origin of these astonishing prehistoric monuments is unknown, but they are generally attributed to the race that inhabited Ireland before the Celts. Gazing at marvellous New Grange, one might very well echo the words of the old Irish poet Mac Nia, in the Book of Ballymote:

'Behold the Sídh before your eyes,
It is manifest to you that it is a king's mansion,
Which was built by the firm Dagda,
It was a wonder, a court, an admirable hill.'

It is not, however, with New Grange, or even with Knowth or Dowth, that the Dagda's name is now associated. It is a smaller barrow, nearer to the Boyne, which is known as the 'Tomb of the Dagda'. It has never been opened, and Dr. James Fergusson, the author of *Rude Stone* Monuments, who holds the Tuatha Dé Danann to have been a real people, thinks that 'the bones and armour of the great Dagda may still be found in his honoured grave'. Other Celtic scholars might not be so sanguine, though verses as old as the eleventh century assert that the Tuatha Dé Danann used the brughs for burial. It was about this period that the mythology of Ireland was being rewoven into spurious history. The poem, which is called the 'Chronicles of the Tombs', not only mentions the 'Monument of the Dagda' and the 'Monument of the Morrígú', but also records the last resting-places of Ogma, Etain, Cairpré, Lugh, Boann, and Angus.

We have for the present, however, to consider Angus in a far less sepulchral light. He is, indeed, very much alive in the story to be related. The 'Son of the Young' was absent when the distribution of the *sídhe* was made. When he returned, he came to his father, the Dagda, and demanded one. The Dagda pointed out to him that they had all been given away. Angus protested, but what could be done? By fair means, evidently nothing; but by craft, a great deal. The wily Angus appeared to reconcile himself to fate, and only begged his father to allow him to stay at the *sídh* of Brugh-na-Boyne (New Grange) for a day and a night. The Dagda agreed to this, no doubt congratulating himself on having got out of the difficulty so easily. But when he came to Angus to remind him that the time was up, Angus refused to go. He had been granted, he claimed, day and night, and it is of days and nights that time and eternity are composed; therefore there was no limit to his tenure of the *sídh*. The logic does not seem very convincing to our modern minds, but the Dagda is said to have been satisfied with it. He abandoned the best of his two palaces to his son, who took peaceable possession of it. Thus it got a second name, that of the *Sídh* or *Brugh* of the 'Son of the Young'.

The Dagda does not, after this, play much active part in the history of the people of the goddess Danu. We next hear of a council of gods to elect a fresh ruler. There were five candidates for the vacant throne – Bodb the Red, Mider, Ilbhreach son of Manannán, Lêr, and Angus himself, though the last-named, we are told, had little real desire to rule, as he preferred a life of freedom to the dignities of kingship. The Tuatha Dé Danann went into consultation, and the result of their deliberation was that their choice fell upon Bodb the Red, for three reasons – firstly, for his own sake; secondly, for his father, the Dagda's sake; and thirdly, because he was the Dagda's eldest son. The other competitors approved this choice, except two. Mider refused to give hostages, as was the custom, to Bodb Derg, and fled with his followers to 'a desert country round Mount Leinster', in County Carlow, while Lêr retired in great anger to Sídh Fionnachaidh, declining to recognize or obey the new king.

Why Lêr and Mider should have so taken the matter to heart is difficult to understand, unless it was because they were both among the oldest of the gods. The indifference of Angus is easier to explain. He was the Gaelic Eros, and was busy living up to his character. At this time, the object of his love was a maiden who had visited him one night in a dream, only to vanish when he put out his arms to embrace her. All the next day, we are told, Angus took no food. Upon the following night, the unsubstantial lady again appeared, and played and sang to him. That following day, he also fasted. So things went on for a year, while Angus pined and wasted for love. At last the physicians of the Tuatha Dé Danann guessed his complaint, and told him how fatal it might be to him. Angus asked that his mother Boann might be sent for, and, when she came, he told her his trouble, and implored her help. She went to the Dagda and begged him, if he did not wish to see his son die of unrequited love, a disease that all Diancecht's medicine and Goibniu's magic could not heal, to find the dream-maiden. The Dagda could do nothing himself, but he sent to Bodb the Red, and the new king of the gods sent in turn to the lesser deities of Ireland, ordering all of them to search for her. For a year she could not be found, but at last the disconsolate lover received a message, charging him to come and see if he could recognize the lady of his dreams. Angus came, and knew her at once, even though she was surrounded by thrice fifty attendant nymphs. Her name was Caer, and she was the daughter of Etal Ambuel, who had a *sídh* at Uaman, in Connaught. Bodb the Red demanded her for Angus in marriage, but her father declared that he had no control over her. She was a swan-maiden, he said; and every year, as soon as summer was over, she went with her companions to a lake called 'Dragon-Mouth', and there all of them became swans. But, refusing to be thus put off, Angus waited in patience until the day of the magical change, and then went down to the shore of the lake. There, surrounded by thrice fifty swans, he saw Caer, herself a swan surpassing all the rest in beauty and whiteness. He called to her, proclaiming his passion and his name, and she promised to be his bride, if he too would become a swan. He agreed, and with a word she changed him into swan-shape, and thus they flew side by side to Angus's *sídh*, where they retook the human form, and, no doubt, lived happily as long as could be expected of such changeable immortals as pagan deities.

Meanwhile, the people of the goddess Danu were justly incensed against both Lêr and Mider. Bodb the Red made a yearly war upon Mider in his *sídh*, and many of the divine race were killed on either side. But against Lêr, the new king of the gods refused to move, for there had been a great affection between them. Many times Bodb Derg tried to regain Lêr's friendship by presents and compliments, but for a long time without success.

At last Lêr's wife died, to the sea-god's great sorrow. When Bodb the Red heard the news, he sent a messenger to Lêr, offering him one of his own foster-daughters, Aebh, Aeife, and Ailbhe, the children of Ailioll of Arran. Lêr, touched by this, came to visit Bodb the Red at his *sídh*, and chose Aebh for his wife. 'She is the eldest, so she must be the noblest of them,' he said. They were married, and a great feast made, and Lêr took her back with him to Sídh Fionnachaidh.

Aebh bore four children to Lêr. The eldest was a daughter called Finola, the second was a son called Aed; the two others were twin boys called Fiachra and Conn, but in giving birth to those Aebh died.

Bodb the Red then offered Lêr another of his foster-children, and he chose the second, Aeife. Every year Lêr and Aeife and the four children used to go to Manannán's 'Feast of Age', which was held at each of the *sídhe* in turn. The four children grew up to be great favourites among the people of the goddess Danu.

But Aeife was childless, and she became jealous of Lêr's children; for she feared that he would love them more than he did her. She brooded over this until she began, first to hope for, and then to plot their deaths. She tried to persuade her servants to murder them, but they would not. So she took the four children to Lake Darvra (now called Lough Derravargh in West Meath), and sent them into the water to bathe. Then she made an incantation over them, and touched them, each in turn, with a druidical wand, and changed them into swans.

But, though she had magic enough to alter their shapes, she had not the power to take away their human speech and minds. Finola turned, and threatened her with the anger of Lêr and of Bodb the Red when they came to hear of it. She, however, hardened her heart, and refused to undo what she had done. The children of Lêr, finding their case a hopeless one, asked her how long she intended to keep them in that condition.

'You would be easier in mind,' she said, 'if you had not asked the question; but I will tell you. You shall be three hundred years here, on Lake Darvra; and three hundred years upon the Sea of Moyle, which is between Erin and Alba; and three hundred years more at Irros Domnann and the Isle of Glora in Erris. Yet you shall have two consolations in your troubles; you shall keep your human minds, and yet suffer no grief at knowing that you have been changed into swans, and you shall be able to sing the softest and sweetest songs that were ever heard in the world.'

Then Aeife went away and left them. She returned to Lêr, and told him that the children had fallen by accident into Lake Darvra, and were drowned.

But Lêr was not satisfied that she spoke the truth, and went in haste to the lake, to see if he could find traces of them. He saw four swans close to the shore, and heard them talking to one another with human voices. As he approached, they came out of the water to meet him. They told him what Aeife had done, and begged him to change them back into their own shapes. But Lêr's magic was not so powerful as his wife's, and he could not.

Nor even could Bodb the Red – to whom Lêr went for help, – for all that he was king of the gods. What Aeife had done could not be undone. But she could be punished for it! Bodb ordered his foster-daughter to appear before him, and, when she came, he put an oath on her to tell him truly 'what shape of all others, on the earth, or above the earth, or beneath the earth, she most abhorred, and into which she most dreaded to be transformed'. Aeife was obliged to answer that she most feared to become a demon of the air. So Bodb the Red struck her with his wand, and she fled from them, a shrieking demon.

All the Tuatha Dé Danann went to Lake Darvra to visit the four swans. The Milesians heard of it, and also went; for it was not till long after this that gods and mortals ceased to associate. The visit became a yearly feast. But, at the end of three hundred years, the children of Lêr were compelled to leave Lake Darvra, and go to the Sea of Moyle, to fulfil the second period of their exile.

They bade farewell to gods and men, and went. And, for fear lest they might be hurt by anyone, the Milesians made it law in Ireland that no man should harm a swan, from that time forth for ever.

The children of Lêr suffered much from tempest and cold on the stormy Sea of Moyle, and they were very lonely. Once only during that long three hundred years did they see any of their friends. An embassy of the Tuatha Dé Danann, led by two sons of Bodb the Red, came to look for them, and told them all that had happened in Erin during their exile.

At last that long penance came to an end, and they went to Irros Domnann and Innis Glora for their third stage. And while it was wearily dragging through, Saint Patrick came to Ireland, and put an end to the power of the gods for ever. They had been banned and banished when the children of Lêr found themselves free to return to their old home. Sídh Fionnechaidh was empty and deserted, for Lêr had been killed by Caoilté, the cousin of Finn mac Coul.

So, after long, vain searching for their lost relatives, they gave up hope, and returned to the Isle of Glora. They had a friend there, the Lonely Crane of Inniskea, which has lived upon that island ever since the beginning of the world, and will be still sitting there on the day of judgment. They saw no one else until, one day, a man came to the island. He told them that he was Saint Caemhoc, and that he had heard their story. He brought them to his church, and preached the new faith to them, and they believed on Christ, and consented to be baptised. This broke the pagan spell, and, as soon as the holy water was sprinkled over them, they returned to human shape. But they were very old and bowed – three aged men and an ancient woman. They did not live long after this, and Saint Caemhoc, who had baptised them, buried them all together in one grave.

But, in telling this story, we have leaped nine hundred years – a great space in the history even of gods. We must retrace our steps, if not quite to the days of Eremon and Eber, sons of Milé, and first kings of Ireland, at any rate to the beginning of the Christian era.

At this time Eochaid Airem was high king of Ireland, and reigned at Tara; while, under him, as vassal monarchs, Conchobar mac Nessa ruled over the Red Branch Champions of Ulster; Curoi son of Daire, was king of Munster; Mesgegra was king of Leinster; and Ailell, with his famous queen, Medb, governed Connaught.

Shortly before, among the gods, Angus Son of the Young, had stolen away Etain, the wife of Mider. He kept her imprisoned in a bower of glass, which he carried everywhere with him, never allowing her to leave it, for fear Mider might recapture her. The Gaelic Pluto, however, found out where she was, and was laying plans to rescue her, when a rival of Etain's herself decoyed Angus away from before the pleasant prison-house, and set his captive free. But, instead of returning her to Mider, she changed the luckless goddess into a fly, and threw her into the air, where she was tossed about in great wretchedness at the mercy of every wind.

At the end of seven years, a gust blew her on to the roof of the house of Etair, one of the vassals of Conchobar, who was celebrating a feast. The unhappy fly, who was Etain, was blown down the chimney into the room below, and fell, exhausted, into a golden cup full of beer, which the wife of the master of the house was just going to drink. And the woman drank Etain with the beer.

But, of course, this was not the end of her – for the gods cannot really die, – but only the beginning of a new life. Etain was reborn as the daughter of Etair's wife, no one knowing that she was not of mortal lineage. She grew up to be the most beautiful woman in Ireland.

When she was twenty years old, her fame reached the high king, who sent messengers to see if she was as fair as men reported. They saw her, and returned to the king full of her praises. So Eochaid himself went to pay her a visit. He chose her to be his queen, and gave her a splendid dowry.

It was not till then that Mider heard of her. He came to her in the shape of a young man, beautifully dressed, and told her who she really was, and how she had been his wife among the people of the goddess Danu. He begged her to leave the king, and come with him to his sídh at Bri Leith. But Etain refused with scorn.

'Do you think,' she said, 'that I would give up the high king of Ireland for a person whose name and kindred I do not know, except from his own lips?'

The god retired, baffled for the time. But one day, as King Eochaid sat in his hall, a stranger entered. He was dressed in a purple tunic, his hair was like gold, and his eyes shone like candles.

The king welcomed him.

'But who are you?' he asked; 'for I do not know you.'

'Yet I have known you a long time,' returned the stranger.

'Then what is your name?'

'Not a very famous one. I am Mider of Bri Leith.'

'Why have you come here?'

'To challenge you to a game of chess.'

'I am a good chess-player,' replied the king, who was reputed to be the best in Ireland.

'I think I can beat you,' answered Mider.

'But the chess-board is in the queen's room, and she is asleep,' objected Eochaid.

'It does not matter,' replied Mider. 'I have brought a board with me which can be in no way worse than yours.'

He showed it to the king, who admitted that the boast was true. The chess-board was made of silver set in precious stones, and the pieces were of gold.

'Play!' said Mider to the king.

'I never play without a wager,' replied Eochaid.

'What shall be the stake?' asked Mider.

'I do not care,' replied Eochaid.

'Good!' returned Mider. 'Let it be that the loser pays whatever the winner demands.'

'That is a wager fit for a king,' said Eochaid.

They played, and Mider lost. The stake that Eochaid claimed from him was that Mider and his subjects should make a road through Ireland. Eochaid watched the road being made, and noticed how Mider's followers yoked their oxen, not by the horns, as the Gaels did, but at the shoulders, which was better. He adopted the practice, and thus got his nickname, Airem, that is, 'The Ploughman'.

After a year, Mider returned and challenged the king again, the terms to be the same as before. Eochaid agreed with joy; but, this time, he lost.

'I could have beaten you before, if I had wished,' said Mider, 'and now the stake I demand is Etain, your queen.'

The astonished king, who could not for shame go back upon his word, asked for a year's delay. Mider agreed to return upon that day year to claim Etain. Eochaid consulted with his warriors, and they decided to keep watch through the whole of the day fixed by Mider, and let no one pass in or out of the royal palace till sunset. For Eochaid held that if the fairy king could not get Etain upon that one day, his promise would be no longer binding on him.

So, when the day came, they barred the door and guarded it, but suddenly they saw Mider among them in the hall. He stood beside Etain, and sang this song to her, setting out the pleasures of the homes of the gods under the enchanted hills.

> 'O fair lady! will you come with me
> To a wonderful country which is mine,
> Where the people's hair is of golden hue,
> And their bodies the colour of virgin snow?
> 'There no grief or care is known;
> White are their teeth, black their eyelashes;
> Delight of the eye is the rank of our hosts,
> With the hue of the fox-glove on every cheek.
> 'Crimson are the flowers of every mead,
> Gracefully speckled as the blackbird's egg;
> Though beautiful to see be the plains of Inisfail
> They are but commons compared to our great plains.
> 'Though intoxicating to you be the ale-drink of Inisfail,
> More intoxicating the ales of the great country;
> The only land to praise is the land of which I speak,
> Where no one ever dies of decrepit age. Soft sweet

streams traverse the land;
The choicest of mead and of wine;
Beautiful people without any blemish;
Love without sin, without wickedness.We can see the
   people upon all sides, But by no one can we be
   seen;
The cloud of Adam's transgression it is
That prevents them from seeing us.O lady, should you
   come to my brave land,
It is golden hair that will be on your head;
Fresh pork, beer, new milk, and ale,
You there with me shall have, O fair lady!'

Then Mider greeted Eochaid, and told him that he had come to take away Etain, according to the king's wager. And, while the king and his warriors looked on helplessly, he placed one arm round the now willing woman, and they both vanished. This broke the spell that hung over everyone in the hall; they rushed to the door, but all they could see were two swans flying away.

The king would not, however, yield to the god. He sent to every part of Ireland for news of Etain, but his messengers all came back without having been able to find her. At last, a druid named Dalân learned, by means of ogams carved upon wands of yew, that she was hidden under Mider's sídh of Bri Leith. So Eochaid marched there with an army, and began to dig deep into the abode of the gods of which the 'fairy hill' was the portal. Mider, as terrified as was the Greek god Hades when it seemed likely that the earth would be rent open, and his domains laid bare to the sight, sent out fifty fairy maidens to Eochaid, every one of them having the appearance of Etain. But the king would only be content with the real Etain, so that Mider, to save his *sídh*, was at last obliged to give her up. And she lived with the King of Ireland after that until the death of both of them.

But Mider never forgave the insult. He bided his time for three generations, until Eochaid and Etain had a male descendant. For they had no son, but only a daughter called Etain, like her mother, and this second Etain had a daughter called Messbuachallo, who had a son called Conairé, surnamed 'the Great'. Mider and the gods wove the web of fate round Conairé, so that he and all his men died violent deaths.

VIII

THE IRISH ILIAD

With Eber and Eremon, sons of Milé, and conquerors of the gods, begins a fresh series of characters in Gaelic tradition – the early 'Milesian' kings of Ireland. Though monkish chroniclers have striven to find history in the legends handed down concerning them, they are none the less almost as mythical as the Tuatha Dé Danann. The first of them who has the least appearance of reality is Tigernmas, who is recorded to have reigned a hundred years after the coming of the Milesians. He seems to have been what is sometimes called a 'Culture-king', bearing much the same kind of relation to Ireland as Theseus bore to Athens or Minos to Crete. During his reign, nine new lakes and three new rivers broke forth from beneath the earth to give their waters to Erin. Under his auspices, gold was first smelted, ornaments of gold and silver were first made, and clothes first dyed. He is said to have perished mysteriously with three-fourths of the men of Erin while worshipping Cromm Cruaich on the field of Mag Slecht. In him Mr. Nutt sees, no doubt rightly, the great mythical king who, in almost all national histories, closes the strictly mythological age, and inaugurates a new era of less obviously divine, if hardly less apocryphal characters.

In spite, however, of the worship of the Tuatha Dé Danann instituted by Eremon, we find the early kings and heroes of Ireland walking very familiarly with their gods. Eochaid Airem, high king of Ireland, was apparently reckoned a perfectly fit suitor for the goddess Etain, and proved a far from unsuccessful rival of Mider, the Gaelic Pluto. And adventures of love or war were carried quite as cheerfully among the *sídh* dwellers by Eochaid's contemporaries – Conchobar son of Nessa, King of Ulster, Curoi son of Daire, King of Munster, Mesgegra, King of Leinster, and Ailell and Medb, King and Queen of Connaught.

In spite, however, of the worship of the Tuatha Dé Danann instituted by Eremon, we find the early kings and heroes of Ireland walking very familiarly with their gods. Eochaid Airem, high king of Ireland, was apparently reckoned a perfectly fit suitor for the goddess Etain, and proved a far from unsuccessful rival of Mider, the Gaelic Pluto. And adventures of love or war were carried quite as cheerfully among the *sídh* dwellers by Eochaid's contemporaries – Conchobar son of Nessa, King of Ulster, Curoi son of Daire, King of Munster, Mesgegra, King of Leinster, and Ailell and Medb, King and Queen of Connaught.

All these figures of the second Gaelic cycle (that of the heroes of Ulster, and especially of their great champion, Cuchulainn) lived, according to Irish tradition, at about the beginning of the Christian era. Conchobar, indeed, is said to have expired in a fit of rage on hearing of the death of Christ.

But this is a very transparent monkish interpolation into the original story. A quite different view is taken by most modern scholars, who would see gods and not men in all the legendary characters of the Celtic heroic cycles. Upon such a subject, however, one may legitimately take sides. Were King Conchobar and his Ultonian champions, Finn and his Fenians, Arthur and his Knights once living men round whom the attributes of gods have gathered, or were they ancient deities renamed and stripped of some of their divinity to make them more akin to their human worshippers? History or mythology? A mingling, perhaps, of both. Cuchulainn may have been the name of a real Gaelic warrior, however suspiciously he may now resemble the sun-god, who is said to have been his father. King Conchobar may have been the real chief of a tribe of Irish Celts before he became an adumbration of the Gaelic sky-god. It is the same problem that confronts us in dealing with the heroic legends of Greece and Rome. Were Achilles, Agamemnon, Odysseus, Paris, Æneas gods, demi-gods, or men? Let us call them all alike – whether they be Greek or Trojan heroes, Red Branch Champions, or followers of the Gaelic Finn or the British Arthur – demi-gods. Even so, they stand definitely apart from the older gods who were greater than they were.

We are stretching no point in calling them demi-gods, for they were god-descended. Cuchulainn, the greatest hero of the Ulster cycle, was doubly so; for on his mother's side he was the grandson of the Dagda, while Lugh of the Long Hand is said to have been his father. His mother, Dechtiré, daughter of Maga, the daughter of Angus 'Son of the Young', was half-sister to King Conchobar, and all the other principal heroes were of hardly less lofty descent. It is small wonder that they are described in ancient manuscripts as terrestrial gods and goddesses.

'Terrestrial' they may have been in form, but their acts were superhuman. Indeed, compared with the more modest exploits of the heroes of the '*Iliad*', they were those of giants. Where Greek warriors slew their tens, these Ultonians despatched their hundreds. They came home after such exploits so heated that their cold baths boiled over. When they sat down to meat, they devoured whole oxen, and drank their mead from vats. With one stroke of their favourite swords they beheaded hills for sport. The gods themselves hardly did more, and it is easy to understand that in those old days not only might the sons of gods look upon the daughters of men and find them fair, but immortal women also need not be too proud to form passing alliances with mortal men.

Some of the older deities seem to have already passed out of memory at the time of the compilation of the Ulster cycle. At any rate, they make no appearance in it. Dead Nuada rests in the *grianan* of Aileach; Ogma lies low in *sídh* Airceltrai; while the Dagda, thrust into the background by his son Angus, mixes himself very little in the affairs of Erin. But the Morrígú is no less eager in encouraging human or semi-divine heroes to war than she was when she revived the fainting spirits of the folk of the goddess Danu at the Battle of Moytura. The gods who appear most often in the cycle of the Red Branch of Ulster are the same that have lived on throughout with the most persistent vitality. Lugh the Long-handed, Angus of the Brugh, Mider, Bodb the Red, and Manannán son of Lêr, are the principal deities that move in the background of the stage where the chief parts are now played by mortals. But, to make up for the loss of some of the greater divine figures, the ranks of the gods are being recruited from below. All manner of inferior divinities claim to be members of the tribe of the goddess Danu. The goblins and sprites and demons of the air who shrieked around battles are described collectively as Tuatha Dé Danann.

As for the Fomors, they have lost their distinctive names, though they are still recognized as dwellers beneath the deep, who at times raid upon the coast, and do battle with the heroes over whom Conchobar ruled at Emain Macha.

This seat of his government, the traditional site of which is still marked by an extensive prehistoric entrenchment called Navan

Fort, near Armagh, was the centre of an Ulster that stretched southwards as far as the Boyne, and round its ruler gathered such a galaxy of warriors as Ireland had never seen before, or will again. They called themselves the 'Champions of the Red Branch'; there was not one of them who was not a hero; but they are all dwarfed by one splendid figure – Cuchulainn, whose name means 'Culann's Hound'. Mr. Alfred Nutt calls him 'the Irish Achilles', while Professor Rhys would rather see in him a Heracles of the Gaels. Like Achilles, he was the chosen hero of his people, invincible in battle, and yet 'at once to early death and sorrows doomed beyond the lot of man', while, like Heracles, his life was a series of wonderful exploits and labours. It matters little enough; for the lives of all such mythical heroes must be of necessity somewhat alike.

If Achilles and Heracles were, as some think, personifications of the sun, Cuchulainn is not less so. Most of his attributes, as the old stories record them, are obviously solar symbols. He seemed generally small and insignificant, yet, when he was at his full strength, no one could look him in the face without blinking, while the heat of his constitution melted snow for thirty feet all round him. He turned red and hissed as he dipped his body into its bath – the sea. Terrible was his transformation when sorely oppressed by his enemies, as the sun is by mist, storm, or eclipse. At such times 'among the aërial clouds over his head were visible the virulent pouring showers and sparks of ruddy fire which the seething of his savage wrath caused to mount up above him. His hair became tangled about his head, as it had been branches of a red thorn-bush stuffed into a strongly-fenced gap ... Taller, thicker, more rigid, longer than mast of a great ship was the perpendicular jet of dusky blood which out of his scalp's very central point shot upwards and then was scattered to the four cardinal points; whereby was formed a magic mist of gloom resembling the smoky pall that drapes a regal dwelling, what time a king at nightfall of a winter's day draws near to it.'

So marvellous a being was, of course, of marvellous birth. His mother, Dechtiré, was on the point of being married to an Ulster chieftain called Sualtam, and was sitting at the wedding-feast, when a may-fly flew into her cup of wine and was unwittingly swallowed by her. That same afternoon she fell into a deep sleep, and in her dream the sun-god Lugh appeared to her, and told her that it was he whom she had swallowed, and bore within her. He ordered her and her fifty attendant maidens to come with him at once, and he put upon them the shapes of birds, so that they were not seen to go. Nothing was heard of them again. But one day, months later, a flock of beautiful birds appeared before Emain Macha, and drew out its warriors in their chariots to hunt them.

They followed the birds till nightfall, when they found themselves at the Brugh on the Boyne, where the great gods had their homes. As they looked everywhere for shelter, they suddenly saw a splendid palace. A tall and handsome man, richly dressed, came out and welcomed them and led them in. Within the hall were a beautiful and noble-faced woman and fifty maidens, and on the tables were the richest meats and wines, and everything fit for the needs of warriors. So they rested there the night, and, during the night, they heard the cry of a new-born child. The next morning, the man told them who he was, and that the woman was Conchobar's half-sister Dechtiré, and he ordered them to take the child, and bring it up among the warriors of Ulster. So they brought him back, together with his mother and the maidens, and Dechtiré married Sualtam, and all the chiefs, champions, druids, poets, and lawgivers of Ulster vied with one another in bringing up the mysterious infant.

At first they called him Setanta; and this is how he came to change his name. While still a child, he was the strongest of the boys of Emain Macha, and the champion in their sports. One day he was playing hurley single-handed against all the others, and beating them, when Conchobar the King rode by with his nobles on the way to a banquet given by Culann, the chief smith of the Ultonians. Conchobar called to the boy, inviting him to go with them, and he replied that, when the game was finished, he would follow. As soon as the Ulster champions were in Culann's hall, the smith asked the king's leave to unloose his terrible watch-dog, which was as strong and fierce as a hundred hounds; and Conchobar, forgetting that the boy was to follow them, gave his permission. Immediately the hound saw Setanta coming, it rushed at him, open-mouthed. But the boy flung his playing-ball into its mouth, and then, seizing it by the hind-legs, dashed it against a rock till he had killed it.

The smith Culann was very angry at the death of his dog; for there was no other hound in the world like him for guarding a house and flocks. So Setanta promised to find and train up another one, not less good, for Culann, and, until it was trained, to guard the smith's house as though he were a dog himself. This is why he was called Cuchulainn, that is, 'Culann's Hound'; and Cathbad the Druid prophesied that the time would come when the name would be in every man's mouth.

Not long after this, Cuchulainn overheard Cathbad giving druidical instruction, and one of his pupils asking him what that day would be propitious for. Cathbad replied that, if any young man first took arms on that day, his name would be greater than that of any other hero's, but his life would be short. At once, the boy went to King Conchobar, and demanded arms and a chariot. Conchobar asked him who had put such a thought into his head; and he answered that it was Cathbad the Druid. So Conchobar gave him arms and armour, and sent him out with a charioteer. That evening, Cuchulainn brought back the heads of three champions who had killed many of the warriors of Ulster. He was then only seven years old.

The women of Ulster so loved Cuchulainn after this that the warriors grew jealous, and insisted that a wife should be found for him. But Cuchulainn was very hard to please. He would have only one, Emer, the daughter of Forgall the Wily, the best maiden in Ireland for the six gifts – the gift of beauty, the gift of voice, the gift of sweet speech, the gift of needlework, the gift of wisdom, and the gift of chastity. So he went to woo her, but she laughed at him for a boy. Then Cuchulainn swore by the gods of his people that he would make his name known wherever the deeds of heroes were spoken of, and Emer promised to marry him if he could take her from her warlike kindred.

When Forgall, her father, came to know of this betrothal, he devised a plan to put an end to it. He went to visit King Conchobar at Emain Macha. There he pretended to have heard of Cuchulainn for the first time, and he saw him do all his feats. He said, loud enough to be overheard by all, that if so promising a youth dared to go to the Island of Scathach the Amazon, in the east of Alba, and learn all her warrior-craft, no living man would be able to stand before him. It was hard to reach Scathach's Isle, and still harder to return from it, and Forgall felt certain that, if Cuchulainn went, he would get his death there.

Of course, nothing would now satisfy Cuchulainn but going.

His two friends, Laegaire the Battle-winner and Conall the Victorious, said that they would go with him. But, before they had gone far, they lost heart and turned back. Cuchulainn went on alone, crossing the Plain of Ill-Luck, where men's feet stuck fast, while sharp grasses sprang up and cut them, and through the Perilous Glens, full of devouring wild beasts, until he came to the Bridge of the Cliff, which rose on end, till it stood straight up like a ship's mast, as soon as anyone put foot on it. Three times Cuchulainn tried to cross it, and thrice he failed. Then anger came into his heart, and a magic halo shone round his head, and he did his famous feat of the 'hero's salmon leap', and landed, in one jump, on the middle of the bridge, and then slid down it as it rose up on end.

Scathach was in the *dún*, with her two sons. Cuchulainn went to her, and put his sword to her breast, and threatened to kill her if she would not teach him all her own skill in arms. So he became her pupil, and she taught him all her war-craft. In return, Cuchulainn helped her against a rival queen of the Amazons, called Aoife. He conquered Aoife, and compelled her to make peace with Scathach.

Then he returned to Ireland, and went in a scythed chariot to Forgall's palace. He leaped over its triple walls, and slew everyone who came near him. Forgall met his death in trying to escape Cuchulainn's rage. He found Emer, and placed her in his chariot, and drove away; and, every time that Forgall's warriors came up to them, he turned, and slew a hundred, and put the rest to flight. He reached Emain Macha in safety, and he and Emer were married there.

And so great, after this, were the fame of Cuchulainn's prowess and Emer's beauty that the men and women of Ulster yielded them precedence – him among the warriors and her among the women – in every feast and banquet at Emain Macha.

But all that Cuchulainn had done up to this time was as nothing to the deeds he did in the great war which all the rest of Ireland, headed by Ailill and Medb, King and Queen of Connaught, made upon Ulster, to get the Brown Bull of Cualgne. This Bull was one of two, of fairy descent. They had originally been the swineherds of two of the gods, Bodb, King of the Sídhe of Munster, and Ochall Ochne, King of the Sídhe of Connaught. As swineherds they were in perpetual rivalry; then, the better to carry on their quarrel, they changed themselves into two ravens, and fought for a year; next they turned into water-monsters, which tore one another for a year in the Suir and a year in the Shannon; then they became human again and fought as champions; and ended by changing into eels. One of these eels went into the River Cruind, in Cualgne, in Ulster, where it was swallowed by a cow belonging to Daire of Cualgne, and the other into the spring of Uaran Garad, in Connaught, where it passed into the belly of a cow of Queen Medb's. Thus were born those two famous beasts, the Brown Bull of Ulster and the White-horned Bull of Connaught.

Now the White-horned was of such proud mind that he scorned to belong to a woman, and he went out of Medb's herds into those of her husband Ailill. So that when Ailill and Medb one day, in their idleness, counted up their possessions, to set them off one against the other, although they were equal in every other thing, in jewels and clothes and household vessels, in sheep and horses and swine and cattle, Medb had no one bull that was worthy to be set beside Ailill's White-horned. Refusing to be less in anything than her husband, the proud queen sent heralds, with gifts and compliments, to Daire, asking him to lend her the Brown Bull for a year. Daire would have done so gladly had not one of Medb's messengers been heard boasting in his cups that, if Daire had not lent the Brown Bull of his own free-will, Medb would have taken it. This was reported to Daire, who at once swore that she should never have it. Medb's messenger returned; and the Queen of Connaught, furious at his refusal, vowed that she would take it by force.

She assembled the armies of all the rest of Ireland to go against Ulster, and made Fergus son of Roy, an Ulster champion who had quarrelled with King Conchobar, its leader. They expected to have an easy victory, for the warriors of Ulster were at that time lying under a magic weakness which fell upon them for many days in each year, as the result of a curse laid upon them, long before, by a goddess who had been insulted by one of Conchobar's ancestors. Medb called up a prophetess of her people to foretell victory. 'How do you see our hosts?' asked the queen of the seeress. 'I see crimson on them; I see red,' she replied. 'But the warriors of Ulster are lying in their sickness. Nay, how do you see our men?' 'I see them all crimson; I see them all red,' she repeated. And then she added to the astonished queen, who had expected a quite different foretelling: 'For I see a small man doing deeds of arms, though there are many wounds on his smooth skin; the hero-light shines round his head, and there is victory on his forehead; he is richly clothed, and young and beautiful and modest, but he is a dragon in battle. His appearance and his valour are those of Cuchulainn of Muirthemne; who that "Culann's hound" from Muirthemne may be, I do not know; but I know this, that all our army will be reddened by him. He is setting out for battle; he will hew down your hosts; the slaughter he shall make will be long remembered; there will be many women crying over the bodies mangled by the Hound of the Forge whom I see before me now.'

For Cuchulainn was, for some reason unknown to us, the only man in Ulster who was not subject to the magic weakness, and therefore it fell upon him to defend Ulster single-handed against the whole of Medb's army.

In spite of the injury done him by King Conchobar, Fergus still kept a love for his own country. He had not the heart to march upon the Ultonians without first secretly sending a messenger to warn them. So that, though all the other champions of the Red Branch were helpless, Cuchulainn was watching the marches when the army came.

Now begins the story of the *aristeia* of the Gaelic hero. It is, after the manner of epics, the record of a series of single combats, in each of which Cuchulainn slays his adversary. Man after man comes against him, and not one goes back. In the intervals between these duels, Cuchulainn harasses the army with his sling, slaying a hundred men a day. He kills Medb's pet dog, bird, and squirrel, and creates such terror that no one dares to stir out of the camp. Medb herself has a narrow escape; for one of her serving-women, who puts on her mistress's golden head-dress, is killed by a stone flung from Cuchulainn's sling.

The great queen determines to see with her own eyes this marvellous hero who is holding all her warriors at bay. She sends an envoy, asking him to come and parley with her. Cuchulainn agrees, and, at the meeting, Medb is amazed at his boyish look. She finds it hard to believe that it is this beardless stripling of seventeen who is killing her champions, until the whole army seems as though it were melting away. She offers him her own friendship and great honours and possessions in Connaught if he will forsake Conchobar. He refuses; but she offers it again and again. At last Cuchulainn indignantly declares that the next man who comes with such a message will do so at his peril. One bargain, however, he will make. He is willing to fight one of the men of Ireland every day, and, while the duel lasts, the main army may march on; but, as soon as Cuchulainn has killed his man, it must halt until the next day. Medb agrees to this, thinking it better to lose one man a day than a hundred.

Medb makes the same offer to every famous warrior, to induce him to go against Cuchulainn. The reward for the head of the champion will be the hand of her daughter, Findabair. In spite of this, not one of the aspirants to the princess can stand before Cuchulainn. All perish; and Findabair, when she finds out how she is being promised to a fresh suitor every day, dies of shame. But, while Cuchulainn is engaged in these combats, Medb sends men who scour Ulster for the brown bull, and find him, and drive him, with fifty heifers, into her camp.

Meanwhile the Æs Sídhe, the fairy god-clan, are watching the half-divine, half-mortal hero, amazed at his achievements. His exploits kindle love in the fierce heart of the Morrígú, the great war-goddess. Cuchulainn is awakened from sleep by a terrible shout from the north. He orders his driver, Laeg, to yoke the horses to his chariot, so that he may find out who raised it. They go in the direction from which the sound had come, and meet with a woman in a chariot drawn by a red horse. She has red eyebrows, and a red dress, and a long, red cloak, and she carries a great, gray spear. He asks her who she is, and she tells him that she is a king's daughter, and that she has fallen in love with him through hearing of his exploits. Cuchulainn says that he has other things to think of than love. She replies that she has been giving him her help in his battles, and will still do so; and Cuchulainn answers that he does not need any woman's help. 'Then,' says she, 'if you will not have my love and help, you shall have my hatred and enmity. When you are fighting with a warrior as good as yourself, I will come against you in various shapes and hinder you, so that he shall have the advantage.' Cuchulainn draws his sword, but all he sees is a hoodie crow sitting on a branch. He knows from this that the red woman in the chariot was the great queen of the gods.

The next day, a warrior named Loch went to meet Cuchulainn. At first he refused to fight one who was beardless; so Cuchulainn smeared his chin with blackberry juice, until it looked as though he had a beard. While Cuchulainn was fighting Loch, the Morrígú came against him three times – first as a heifer which tried to overthrow him, and next as an eel which got beneath his feet as he stood in running water, and then as a wolf which seized hold of his right arm. But Cuchulainn broke the heifer's leg, and trampled upon the eel, and put out one of the wolf's eyes, though, every one of these three times, Loch wounded him. In the end, Cuchulainn slew Loch with his invincible spear, the *gae bolg*, made of a sea-monster's bones. The Morrígú came back to Cuchulainn, disguised as an old woman, to have her wounds healed by him, for no one could cure them but he who had made them. She became his friend after this, and helped him.

But the fighting was so continuous that Cuchulainn got no sleep, except just for a while, from time to time, when he might rest a little, with his head on his hand and his hand on his spear and his spear on his knee. So that his father, Lugh the Long-handed, took pity on him and came to him in the semblance of a tall, handsome man in a green cloak and a gold-embroidered silk shirt, and carrying a black shield and a five-pronged spear. He put him into a sleep of three days and three nights, and, while he rested, he laid druidical herbs on to all his wounds, so that, in the end, he rose up again completely healed and as strong as at the very beginning of the war. While he was asleep, the boy-troop of Emain Macha, Cuchulainn's old companions, came and fought instead of him, and slew three times their own number, but were all killed.

It was at this time that Medb asked Fergus to go and fight with Cuchulainn. Fergus answered that he would never fight against his own foster-son. Medb asked him again and again, and at last he went, but without his famous sword. 'Fergus, my guardian,' said Cuchulainn, 'it is not safe for you to come out against me without your sword.' 'If I had the sword,' replied Fergus, 'I would not use it on you.' Then Fergus asked Cuchulainn, for the sake of all he had done for him in his boyhood, to pretend to fight with him, and then give way before him and run away. Cuchulainn answered that he was very loth to be seen running from any man. But Fergus promised Cuchulainn that, if Cuchulainn would run away from Fergus then, Fergus would run away from Cuchulainn at some future time, whenever Cuchulainn wished. Cuchulainn agreed to this, for he knew that it would be for the profit of Ulster. So they fought a little, and then Cuchulainn turned and fled in the sight of all Medb's army. Fergus went back; and Medb could not reproach him any more.

But she cast about to find some other way of vanquishing Cuchulainn. The agreement made had been that only one man a day should be sent against him. But now Medb sent the wizard Calatin with his twenty-seven sons and his grandson all at once, for she said 'they are really only one, for they are all from Calatin's body'. They never missed a throw with their poisoned spears, and every man they hit died, either on the spot or within the week. When Fergus heard of this, he was in great grief, and he sent a man called Fiacha, an exile, like himself, from Ulster, to watch the fight and report how it went. Now Fiacha did not mean to join in it, but when he saw Cuchulainn assailed by twenty-nine at a time, and overpowered, he could not restrain himself. So he drew his sword and helped Cuchulainn, and, between them, they killed Calatin and his whole family.

As a last resource, now, Medb sent for Ferdiad, who was the great champion of the Iberian 'Men of Domnu', who had thrown in their lot with Medb in the war for the Brown Bull. Ferdiad had been a companion and fellow-pupil of Cuchulainn with Scathach, and he did not wish to fight with him. But Medb told him that, if he refused, her satirists should make such lampoons on him that he would die of shame, and his name would be a reproach for ever. She also offered him great rewards and honours, and bound herself in six sureties to keep her promises. At last, reluctantly, he went.

Cuchulainn saw him coming, and went out to welcome him; but Ferdiad said that he had not come as a friend, but to fight. Now Cuchulainn had been Ferdiad's junior and serving-boy in Scathach's Island, and he begged him by the memory of those old times to go back; but Ferdiad said he could not. They fought all day, and neither had gained any advantage by sunset. So they kissed one another, and each went back to his camp. Ferdiad sent half his food and drink to Cuchulainn, and Cuchulainn sent half his healing herbs and medicines to Ferdiad, and their horses were put in the same stable, and their charioteers slept by the same fire. And so it happened on the second day. But at the end of the third day they parted gloomily, knowing that on the morrow one of them must fall; and their horses were not put in the same stall that night, neither did their charioteers sleep at the same fire. On the fourth day, Cuchulainn succeeded in killing Ferdiad, by casting the *gae bolg* at him from underneath. But when he saw that he was dying, the battle-fury passed away, and he took his old companion up in his arms, and carried him across the river on whose banks they had fought, so that he might be with the men of Ulster in his death, and not with the men of Ireland. And he wept over him, and said: 'It was all a game and a sport until Ferdiad came; Oh, Ferdiad! your death will hang over me like a cloud for ever. Yesterday he was greater than a mountain; to-day he is less than a shadow.'

By this time, Cuchulainn was so covered with wounds that he could not bear his clothes to touch his skin, but had to hold them off with hazel-sticks, and fill the spaces in between with grass. There was not a place on him the size of a needle-point that had not a wound on it, except his left hand, which held the shield.

But Sualtam, Cuchulainn's reputed father, had learned what a sore plight his son was in. 'Do I hear the heaven bursting, or the sea running away, or the earth breaking open,' he cried, 'or is it my son's groaning that I hear?' He came to look for him, and found him covered with wounds and blood. But Cuchulainn would not let his father either weep for him or try to avenge him. 'Go, rather,' he said to him, 'to Emain Macha, and tell Conchobar that I can no longer defend Ulster against all the four provinces of Erin without help. Tell him that there is no part of my body on which there is not a wound, and that, if he wishes to save his kingdom, he must make no delay.'

Sualtam mounted Cuchulainn's war-horse, the 'Gray of Battle', and galloped to Emain Macha. Three times he shouted: 'Men are being killed, women carried off, and cattle lifted in Ulster'. Twice he met with no response. The third time, Cathbad the Druid roused himself from his lethargy to denounce the man who was disturbing the king's sleep. In his indignation Sualtam turned away so sharply that the gray steed reared, and struck its rider's shield against his neck with such force that he was decapitated. The startled horse then turned back into Conchobar's stronghold, and dashed through it, Sualtam's severed head continuing to cry out: 'Men are being killed, women carried off, and cattle lifted in Ulster.' Such a portent was enough to rouse the most drowsy. Conchobar, himself again, swore a great oath. 'The heavens are over us, the earth is beneath us, and the sea circles us round, and, unless the heavens fall, with all their stars, or the earth gives way beneath us, or the sea bursts over the land, I will restore every cow to her stable, and every woman to her home.'

He sent messengers to rally Ulster, and they gathered, and marched on the men of Erin. And then was fought such a battle as had never been before in Ireland. First one side, then the other, gave way and rallied again, until Cuchulainn heard the noise of the fight, and rose up, in spite of all his wounds, and came to it.

He called out to Fergus, reminding him how he had bound himself with an oath to run from him when called upon to do so. So Fergus ran before Cuchulainn, and when Medb's army saw their leader running they broke and fled like one man.

But the Brown Bull of Cualgne went with the army into Connaught, and there he met Ailill's bull, the White-horned. And he fought the White-horned, and tore him limb from limb, and carried off pieces of him on his horns, dropping the loins at Athlone and the liver at Trim. Then he went back to Cualgne, and turned mad, killing all who crossed his path, until his heart burst with bellowing, and he fell dead.

This was the end of the great war called *Táin Bó Chuailgné*, the 'Driving of the Cattle of Cooley'.

Yet, wondrous as it was, it was not the most marvellous of Cuchulainn's exploits. Like all the solar gods and heroes of Celtic myth, he carried his conquests into the dark region of Hades. On this occasion the mysterious realm is an island called *Dún Scaith*, that is, the 'Shadowy Town', and though its king is not mentioned by name, it seems likely that he was Mider, and that Dún Scaith is another name for the Isle of Falga, or Man. The story, as a poem relates it, is curiously suggestive of a raid which the powers of light, and especially the sun-gods, are represented as having made upon Hades in kindred British myth. The same loathsome combatants issue out of the underworld to repel its assailants. There was a pit in the centre of Dún Scaith, out of which swarmed a vast throng of serpents. No sooner had Cuchulainn and the heroes of Ulster disposed of these than 'a house full of toads' was loosed upon them – 'sharp, beaked monsters' (says the poem), which caught them by the noses, and these were in turn replaced by fierce dragons. Yet the heroes prevailed and carried off the spoil – three cows of magic qualities and a marvellous cauldron in which was always found an inexhaustible supply of meat, with treasure of silver and gold to boot. They started back for Ireland in a coracle, the three cows being towed behind, with the treasure in bags around their necks. But the gods of Hades raised a storm which wrecked their ship, and they had to swim home. Here Cuchulainn's more than mortal prowess came in useful. We are told that he floated nine men to shore on each of his hands, and thirty on his head, while eight more, clinging to his sides, used him as a kind of life-belt.

After this, came the tragedy of Cuchulainn's career, the unhappy duel in which he killed his only son, not knowing who he was. The story is one common, apparently, to the Aryan nations, for it is found not only in the Gaelic, but in the Teutonic and Persian mythic traditions. It will be remembered that Cuchulainn defeated a rival of Scathach the Amazon, named Aoife, and compelled her to render submission. The hero had also a son by Aoife, and he asked that the boy should be called Conlaoch, and that, when he was of age to travel, he should be sent to Ireland to find his father. Aoife promised this, but, a little later, news came to her that Cuchulainn had married Emer. Mad with jealousy, she determined to make the son avenge her slight upon the father. She taught him the craft of arms until there was no more that he could learn, and sent him to Ireland. Before he started, she laid three geasa upon him. The first was that he was not to turn back, the second that he was never to refuse a challenge, and the third that he was never to tell his name.

He arrived at Dundealgan, Cuchulainn's home, and the warrior Conall came down to meet him, and asked him his name and lineage. He refused to tell them, and this led to a duel, in which Conall was disarmed and humiliated. Cuchulainn next approached him, asked the same question, and received the same answer. 'Yet if I was not under a command,' said Conlaoch, who did not know he was speaking to his father, 'there is no man in the world to whom I would sooner tell it than to yourself, for I love your face.' Even this compliment could not stave off the fight, for Cuchulainn felt it his duty to punish the insolence of this stripling who refused to declare who he was. The fight was a fierce one, and the invincible Cuchulainn found himself so pressed that the 'hero-light' shone round him and transfigured his face. When Conlaoch saw this, he knew who his antagonist must be, and purposely flung his spear slantways that it might not hit his father. But before Cuchulainn understood, he had thrown the terrible *gae bolg*. Conlaoch, dying, declared his name; and so passionate was Cuchulainn's grief that the men of Ulster were afraid that in his madness he might wreak his wrath upon them. They, therefore, called upon Cathbad the Druid to put him under a glamour. Cathbad turned the waves of the sea into the appearance of armed men, and Cuchulainn smote them with his sword until he fell prone from weariness.

It would take too long to relate all the other adventures and exploits of Cuchulainn. Enough has been done if any reader of this chapter should be persuaded by it to study the wonderful saga of ancient Ireland for himself. We must pass on quickly to its tragical close – the hero's death.

Medb, Queen of Connaught, had never forgiven him for keeping back her army from raiding Ulster, and for slaying so many of her friends and allies. So she went secretly to all those whose relations Cuchulainn had killed (and they were many), and stirred them up to revenge.

Besides this, she had sent the three daughters of Calatin the Wizard, born after their father's death at the hands of Cuchulainn, to Alba and to Babylon to learn witchcraft. When they came back they were mistresses of every kind of sorcery, and could make the illusion of battle with an incantation.

And, lest she might fail even then, she waited with patience until the Ultonians were again in their magic weakness, and there was no one to help Cuchulainn but himself.

Lugaid, son of the Curoi, King of Munster whom Cuchulainn had killed for the sake of Blathnat, Mider's daughter, gathered the Munster men; Erc, whose father had also fallen at Cuchulainn's hands, called the men of Meath; the King of Leinster brought out his army; and, with Ailill and Medb and all Connaught, they marched into Ulster again, and began to ravage it.

Conchobar called his warriors and druids into council, to see if they could find some means of putting off war until they were ready to meet it. He did not wish Cuchulainn to go out single-handed a second time against all the rest of Ireland, for he knew that, if the champion perished, the prosperity of Ulster would fall with him for ever. So, when Cuchulainn came to Emain Macha, the king set all the ladies, singers, and poets of the court to keep his thoughts from war until the men of Ulster had recovered from their weakness.

But while they sat feasting and talking in the 'sunny house', the three daughters of Calatin came fluttering down on to the lawn before it, and began gathering grass and thistles and puff-balls and withered leaves, and turning them into the semblance of armies. And, by the same magic, they caused shouts and shrieks and trumpet-blasts and the clattering of arms to be heard all round the house, as though a battle were being fought.

Cuchulainn leaped up, red with shame to think that fighting should be going on without his help, and seized his sword. But Cathbad's son caught him by the arms. All the druids explained to him that what he saw was only an enchantment raised by the children of Calatin to draw him out to his death. But it was as much as all of them could do to keep him quiet while he saw the phantom armies and heard the magic sounds.

So they decided that it would be well to remove Cuchulainn from Emain Macha to *Glean-na-Bodhar*, the 'Deaf Valley', until all the enchantments of the daughters of Calatin were spent. It was the quality of this valley that, if all the men of Ireland were to shout round it at once, no one within it would hear a sound.

But the daughters of Calatin went there too, and again they took thistles and puff-balls and withered leaves, and put on them the appearance of armed men; so that there seemed to be no place outside the whole valley that was not filled with shouting battalions. And they made the illusion of fires all around and the sound of women shrieking. Everyone who heard that outcry was frightened at it, not only the men and women, but even the dogs.

Though the women and the druids shouted back with all the strength of their voices, to drown it they could not keep Cuchulainn from hearing. 'Alas!' he cried, 'I hear the men of Ireland shouting as they ravage the province. My triumph is at an end; my fame is gone; Ulster lies low for ever.'

'Let it pass,' said Cathbad; 'it is only the idle magic noises made by the children of Calatin, who want to draw you out, to put an end to you. Stay here with us, and take no heed of them.'

Cuchulainn obeyed; and the daughters of Calatin went on for a long time filling the air with noises of battle. But they grew tired of it at last; for they saw that the druids and women had outwitted them.

They did not succeed until one of them took the form of a leman of Cuchulainn's, and came to him, crying out that Dundealgan was burnt, and Muirthemne ruined, and the whole province of Ulster ravaged. Then, at last, he was deceived, and took his arms and armour, and, in spite of all that was said to him, he ordered Laeg to yoke his chariot.

Signs and portents now began to gather as thickly round the doomed hero as they did round the wooers in the hall of Odysseus. His famous war-horse, the Gray of Macha, refused to be bridled, and shed large tears of blood. His mother, Dechtiré, brought him a goblet full of wine, and thrice the wine turned into blood as he put it to his lips. At the first ford he crossed, he saw a maiden of the *sídhe* washing clothes and armour, and she told him that it was the clothes and arms of Cuchulainn, who was soon to be dead. He met three ancient hags cooking a hound on spits of rowan, and they invited him to partake of it. He refused, for it was taboo to him to eat the flesh of his namesake; but they shamed him into doing so by telling him that he ate at rich men's tables and refused the hospitality of the poor. The forbidden meat paralysed half his body. Then he saw his enemies coming up against him in their chariots.

Cuchulainn had three spears, of which it was prophesied that each should kill a king. Three druids were charged in turn to ask for these spears; for it was not thought lucky to refuse anything to a druid. The first one came up to where Cuchulainn was making the plain red with slaughter. 'Give me one of those spears,' he said, 'or I will lampoon you.' 'Take it,' replied Cuchulainn, 'I have never yet been lampooned for refusing anyone a gift.' And he threw the spear at the druid, and killed him. But Lugaid, son of Curoi, got the spear, and killed Laeg with it. Laeg was the king of all chariot-drivers.

'Give me one of your spears, Cuchulainn,' said the second druid. 'I need it myself,' he replied. 'I will lampoon the province of Ulster because of you, if you refuse.' 'I am not obliged to give more than one gift in a day,' said Cuchulainn, 'but Ulster shall never be lampooned because of me.' He threw the spear at the druid, and it went through his head. But Erc, King of Leinster, got it, and mortally wounded the Gray of Macha, the king of all horses.

'Give me your spear,' said the third druid. 'I have paid all that is due from myself and Ulster,' replied Cuchulainn. 'I will satirize your kindred if you do not,' said the druid. 'I shall never go home, but I will be the cause of no lampoons there,' answered Cuchulainn, and he threw the spear at the asker, and killed him. But Lugaid threw it back, and it went through Cuchulainn's body, and wounded him to the death.

Then, in his agony, he greatly desired to drink. He asked his enemies to let him go to a lake that lay close by, and quench his thirst, and then come back again. 'If I cannot come back to you, come to fetch me,' he said; and they let him go.

Cuchulainn drank, and bathed, and came out of the water. But he found that he could not walk; so he called to his enemies to come to him. There was a pillar-stone near; and he bound himself to it with his belt, so that he might die standing up, and not lying down. His dying horse, the Gray of Macha, came back to fight for him, and killed fifty men with his teeth and thirty with each of his hoofs. But the 'hero-light' had died out of Cuchulainn's face, leaving it as pale as 'a one-night's snow', and a crow came and perched upon his shoulder.

'Truly it was not upon that pillar that birds used to sit,' said Erc.

Now that they were certain that Cuchulainn was dead, they all gathered round him, and Lugaid cut off his head to take it to Medb. But vengeance came quickly, for Conall the Victorious was in pursuit, and he made a terrible slaughter of Cuchulainn's enemies.

Thus perished the great hero of the Gaels in the twenty-seventh year of his age. And with him fell the prosperity of Emain Macha and of the Red Branch of Ulster.

IX

SOME GAELIC LOVE-STORIES

The heroic age of Ireland was not, however, the mere orgy of battle which one might assume from the previous chapter. It had room for its Helen and its Andromache as well as for its Achilles and its Hector. Its champions could find time to make love as well as war. More than this, the legends of their courtships often have a romantic beauty found in no other early literature. The women have free scope of choice, and claim the respect of their wooers. Indeed, it has been pointed out that the mythical stories of the Celts must have created the chivalrous romances of mediæval Europe. In them, and in no other previous literature, do we find such knightly treatment of an enemy as we see in the story of Cuchulainn and Ferdiad, or such poetic delicacy towards a woman as is displayed in the wooing of Emer. The talk between man and maid when Cuchulainn comes in his chariot to pay his suit to Emer at Forgall's *dún* might, save for its strangeness, almost have come out of some quite modern romance.

'Emer lifted up her lovely face and recognized Cuchulainn, and she said, "May God make smooth the path before you!"'

'"And you," he said, "may you be safe from every harm."'

She asks him whence he has come, and he tells her. Then he questions her about herself.

'I am a Tara of women,' she replies, 'the whitest of maidens, one who is gazed at but who gazes not back, a rush too far to be reached, an untrodden way ... I was brought up in ancient virtues, in lawful behaviour, in the keeping of chastity, in rank equal to a queen, in stateliness of form, so that to me is attributed every noble grace among the hosts of Erin's women.' In more boastful strain Cuchulainn tells of his own birth and deeds. Not like the son of a peasant had he been reared at Conchobar's court, but among heroes and champions, jesters and druids. When he is weakest his strength is that of twenty; alone he will fight against forty; a hundred men would feel safe under his protection. One can imagine Emer's smile as she listens to these braggings. 'Truly,' she says, 'they are goodly feats for a tender boy, but they are not yet those of chariot-chiefs.' Very modern, too, is the way in which she coyly reminds her wooer that she has an elder sister as yet unwed. But, when at last he drives her to the point, she answers him with gentle, but proud decision. Not by words, but by deeds is she to be won. The man she will marry must have his name mentioned wherever the exploits of heroes are spoken of.

'Even as thou hast commanded, so shall all by me be done,' said Cuchulainn.

'And by me your offer is accepted, it is taken, it is granted,' replied Emer.

It seems a pity that, after so fine a wooing, Cuchulainn could not have kept faithful to the bride he won. Yet such is not the way of heroes whom goddesses as well as mortal women conspire to tempt from their loyalty. Fand, the wife of Manannán son of Lêr, deserted by the sea-god, sent her sister Liban to Cuchulainn as an ambassador of love. At first he refused to visit her, but ordered Laeg, his charioteer, to go with Liban to the 'Happy Plain' to spy out the land. Laeg returned enraptured. 'If all Ireland were mine,' he assured his master, 'with supreme rule over its fair inhabitants,

I would give it up without regret to go and live in the place that I have seen.'

So Cuchulainn himself went and stayed a month in the Celtic Paradise with Fand, the fairest woman of the Sídhe. Returning to the land of mortals, he made a tryst with the goddess to meet him again in his own country by the yew-tree at the head of Baile's strand.

But Emer came to hear of it, and went to the meeting-place herself, with fifty of her maidens, each armed with a knife to kill her rival. There she found Cuchulainn, Laeg, and Fand.

'What has led you, Cuchulainn,' said Emer, 'to shame me before the women of Erin and all honourable people? I came under your shelter, trusting in your faithfulness, and now you seek a cause of quarrel with me.'

But Cuchulainn, hero-like, could not understand why his wife should not be content to take her turn with this other woman — surely no unworthy rival, for she was beautiful, and came of the lofty race of gods. We see Emer yield at last, with queenly pathos.

'I will not refuse this woman to you, if you long for her,' she said, for I know that everything that is new seems fair, and everything that is common seems bitter, and everything we have not seems desirable to us, and everything we have we think little of. And yet, Cuchulainn, I was once pleasing to you, and I would wish to be so again.'

Her grief touched him. 'By my word,' he said, 'you are pleasing to me, and will be as long as I live.'

'Then let me be given up,' said Fand. 'It is better that I should be,' replied Emer. 'No,' said Fand; 'it is I who must be given up in the end.

'It is I who will go, though I go with great sorrow. I would rather stay with Cuchulainn than live in the sunny home of the gods.

'O Emer, he is yours, and you are worthy of him! What my hand cannot have, my heart may yet wish well to.

'A sorrowful thing it is to love without return. Better to renounce than not to receive a love equal to one's own.

'It was not well of you, O fair-haired Emer, to come to kill Fand in her misery.'

It was while the goddess and the human woman were contending with one another in self-sacrifice that Manannán, Son of the Sea, heard of Fand's trouble, and was sorry that he had forsaken her. So he came, invisible to all but her alone. He asked her pardon, and she herself could not forget that she had once been happy with the 'horseman of the crested waves', and still might be happy with him again. The god asked her to make her choice between them, and, when she went to him, he shook his mantle between her and Cuchulainn. It was one of the magic properties of Manannán's mantle that those between whom it was shaken could never meet again. Then Fand returned with her divine husband to the country of the immortals; and the druids of Emain Macha gave Cuchulainn and Emer each a drink of oblivion, so that Cuchulainn forgot his love and Emer her jealousy.

The scene of this story takes its name from another, and hardly less beautiful love-tale. The 'yew-tree at the head of Baile's strand' had grown out of the grave of Baile of the Honeyed Speech, and it bore the appearance of Baile's love, Ailinn. This Gaelic Romeo and Juliet were of royal birth: Baile was heir to Ulster, and Ailinn was daughter of the King of Leinster's son. Not by any feud of Montague and Capulet were they parted, however, but by the craft of a ghostly enemy. They had appointed to meet one another at Dundealgan, and Baile, who arrived there first, was greeted by a stranger. 'What news do you bring?' asked Baile. 'None,' replied the stranger, 'except that

Ailinn of Leinster was setting out to meet her lover, but the men of Leinster kept her back, and her heart broke then and there from grief.' When Baile heard this, his own heart broke, and he fell dead on the strand, while the messenger went on the wings of the wind to the home of Ailinn, who had not yet started. 'Whence come you?' she asked him. 'From Ulster, by the shore of Dundealgan, where I saw men raising a stone over one who had just died, and on the stone I read the name of Baile. He had come to meet some woman he was in love with, but it was destined that they should never see one another again in life.' At this news Ailinn, too, fell dead, and was buried; and we are told that an apple-tree grew out of her grave, the apples of which bore the likeness of the face of Baile, while a yew-tree sprung from Baile's grave, and took the appearance of Ailinn. This legend, which is probably a part of the common heritage of the Aryans, is found in folklore over an area which stretches from Ireland to India. The Gaelic version has, however, an ending unknown to the others. The two trees, it relates, were cut down, and made into wands upon which the poets of Ulster and of Leinster cut the songs of the love-tragedies of their two provinces, in *ogam*. But even these mute memorials of Baile and Ailinn were destined not to be divided. After two hundred years, Art the 'Lonely', High-King of Ireland, ordered them to be brought to the hall of Tara, and, as soon as the wands found themselves under the same roof, they all sprang together, and no force or skill could part them again. So the king commanded them to be 'kept, like any other jewel, in the treasury of Tara.'

Neither of these stories, however, has as yet attained the fame of one now to be retold. To many, no doubt, Gaelic romance is summed up in the one word Deirdre. It is the legend of this Gaelic Helen that the poets of the modern Celtic school most love to elaborate, while old men still tell it round the peat-fires of Ireland and the Highlands. Scholar and peasant alike combine to preserve a tradition no one knows how many hundred years old, for it was written down in the twelfth-century Book of Leinster as one of the 'prime stories' which every bard was bound to be able to recite. It takes rank with the 'Fate of the Sons of Tuirenn', and with the 'Fate of the Children of Lêr', as one of the 'Three Sorrowful Stories of Erin'.

So favourite a tale has naturally been much altered and added to in its passage down the generations. But its essential story is as follows: –

King Conchobar of Ulster was holding festival in the house of one of his bards, called Fedlimid, when Fedlimid's wife gave birth to a daughter, concerning whom Cathbad the Druid uttered a prophecy. He foretold that the new-born child would grow up to be the most lovely woman the world had ever seen, but that her beauty would bring death to many heroes, and much peril and sorrow to Ulster. On hearing this, the Red Branch warriors demanded that she should be killed, but Conchobar refused, and gave the infant to a trusted serving-woman, to be hidden in a secret place in the solitude of the mountains, until she was of an age to be his own wife.

So Deirdre (as Cathbad named her) was taken away to a hut so remote from the paths of men that none knew of it save Conchobar. Here she was brought up by a nurse, a fosterer, and a teacher, and saw no other living creatures save the beasts and birds of the hills. Nevertheless, woman-like, she aspired to be loved.

One day, her fosterer was killing a calf for their food, and its blood ran out upon the snowy ground, which brought a black raven swooping to the spot. 'If there were a man,' said Deirdre, 'who had hair of the blackness of that raven, skin of the whiteness of the snow, and cheeks as red as the calf's blood, that is the man whom I would wish to marry me.'

'Indeed there is such a man,' replied her teacher thoughtlessly. 'Naoise, one of the sons of Usnach, heroes of the same race as Conchobar the King.

The curious Deirdre prevailed upon her teacher to bring Naoise to speak with her. When they met she made good use of her time, for she offered Naoise her love, and begged him to take her away from King Conchobar.

Naoise, bewitched by her beauty, consented. Accompanied by his two brothers, Ardan and Ainle, and their followers, he fled with Deirdre to Alba, where they made alliance with one of its kings, and wandered over the land, living by following the deer, and by helping the king in his battles.

The revengeful Conchobar bided his time. One day, as the heroes of the Red Branch feasted together at Emain Macha, he asked them if they had ever heard of a nobler company than their own. They replied that the world could not hold such another. 'Yet', said the king, 'we lack our full tale. The three sons of Usnach could defend the province of Ulster against any other province of Ireland by themselves, and it is a pity that they should still be exiles, for the sake of any woman in the world. Gladly would I welcome them back!'

'We ourselves', replied the Ultonians, 'would have counselled this long ago had we dared, O King!'

'Then I will send one of my three best champions to fetch them,' said Conchobar. 'Either Conall the Victorious, or Cuchulainn, the son of Sualtam, or Fergus, the son of Roy; and I will find out which of those three loves me best.'

First he called Conall to him secretly.

'What would you do, O Conall,' he asked, 'if you were sent to fetch the sons of Usnach, and they were killed here, in spite of your safe-conduct?'

'There is not a man in Ulster,' answered Conall, 'who had hand in it that would escape his own death from me.'

'I see that I am not dearest of all men to you,' replied Conchobar, and, dismissing Conall, he called Cuchulainn, and put the same question to him.

'By my sworn word,' replied Cuchulainn, 'if such a thing happened with your consent, no bribe or blood-fine would I accept in lieu of your own head, O Conchobar.'

'Truly,' said the king, 'it is not you I will send.'

The king then asked Fergus, and he replied that, if the sons of Usnach were slain while under his protection, he would revenge the deed upon anyone who was party to it, save only the king himself.

'Then it is you who shall go,' said Conchobar. 'Set forth to-morrow, and rest not by the way, and when you put foot again in Ireland at the *Dún* of Borrach, whatever may happen to you yourself, send the sons of Usnach forward without delay.'

The next morning, Fergus, with his two sons, Illann the Fair and Buinne the Ruthless Red, set out for Alba in their galley, and reached Loch Etive, by whose shores the sons of Usnach were then living. Naoise, Ainle, and Ardan were sitting at chess when they heard Fergus's shout.

'That is the cry of a man of Erin,' said Naoise.

'Nay,' replied Deirdre, who had forebodings of trouble. 'Do not heed it; it is only the shout of a man of Alba.' But the sons of Usnach knew better, and sent Ardan down to the sea-shore, where he found Fergus and his sons, and gave them greeting, and heard their message, and brought them back with him.

That night Fergus persuaded the sons of Usnach to return with him to Emain Macha. Deirdre, with her 'second sight', implored them to remain in Alba. But the exiles were weary for the sight of their own country, and did not share their companion's fears. As they put out to sea, Deirdre uttered her beautiful 'Farewell to Alba', that land she was never to behold again.

'A lovable land is yon eastern land, Alba, with its marvels. I would not have come hither out of it, Had I not come with Naoise.

'Lovable are Dún-fidga and Duún-finn, Lovable the fortress over them; Dear to the heart Inis Draigende, And very dear is Dún Suibni.

'Caill Cuan! Unto which Ainle would wend, alas! Short the time seemed to me, With Naoise in the region of Alba.

'Glenn Láid! Often I slept there under the cliff; Fish and venison and the fat of the badger Was my portion in Glenn Láid.

'Glenn Masáin! Its garlic was tall, its branches white; We slept a rocking sleep, Over the grassy estuary of Masáin.

'Glenn Etive! Where my first house I raised; Beauteous its wood: – upon rising A cattle-fold for the sun was Glenn Etive …

'Glenn Dá-Rúad! My love to every man who hath it as an heritage! Sweet the cuckoos' note on bending bough, On the peak over Glenn Dá-Rúad.

'Beloved is Draigen, Dear the white sand beneath its waves; I would not have come from it, from the East, Had I not come with my beloved.'

They crossed the sea, and arrived at the *Dún* of Borrach, who bade them welcome to Ireland. Now King Conchobar had sent Borrach a secret command, that he should offer a feast to Fergus on his landing. Strange taboos called *geasa* are laid upon the various heroes of ancient Ireland in the stories; there are certain things that each one of them may not do without forfeiting life or honour; and it was a *geis* upon Fergus to refuse a feast.

Fergus, we are told, 'reddened with anger from crown to sole' at the invitation. Yet he could not avoid the feast. He asked Naoise what he should do, and Deirdre broke in with: 'Do what is asked of you if you prefer to forsake the sons of Usnach for a feast. Yet forsaking them is a good price to pay for it.'

Fergus, however, perceived a possible compromise. Though he himself could not refuse to stop to partake of Borrach's hospitality, he could send Deirdre and the sons of Usnach on to Emain Macha at once, under the safeguard of his two sons, Illann the Fair and Buinne the Ruthless Red. So this was done, albeit to the annoyance of the sons of Usnach and the terror of Deirdre. Visions came to the sorrowful woman; she saw the three sons of Usnach and Illann, the son of Fergus, without their heads; she saw a cloud of blood always hanging over them. She begged them to wait in some safe place until Fergus had finished the feast. But Naoise, Ainle, and Ardan laughed at her fears. They arrived at Emain Macha, and Conchobar ordered the 'Red Branch' palace to be placed at their disposal.

In the evening Conchobar called Levarcham, Deirdre's old teacher, to him. 'Go', he said, 'to the "Red Branch", and see Deirdre, and bring me back news of her appearance, whether she still keeps her former beauty, or whether it has left her.'

So Levarcham came to the 'Red Branch', and kissed Deirdre and the three sons of Usnach, and warned them that Conchobar was preparing treachery. Then she went back to the king, and reported to him that Deirdre's hard life upon the mountains of Alba had ruined her form and face, so that she was no longer worthy of his regard.

At this, Conchobar's jealousy was partly allayed, and he began to doubt whether it would be wise to attack the sons of Usnach. But later on, when he had drunk well of wine, he sent a second messenger to see if what Levarcham had reported about Deirdre was truth.

The messenger, this time a man, went and looked in through a window. Deirdre saw him and pointed him out to Naoise, who flung a chessman at the peering face, and put out one of its eyes. But the man went back to Conchobar, and told him that, though one of his eyes had been struck out, he would gladly have stayed looking with the other, so great was Deirdre's loveliness.

Then Conchobar, in his wrath, ordered the men of Ulster to set fire to the Red Branch House and slay all within it except Deirdre. They flung fire-brands upon it, but Buinne the Ruthless Red came out and quenched them, and drove the assailants back with slaughter. But Conchobar called to him to parley, and offered him a 'hundred' of land and his friendship to desert the sons of Usnach. Buinne was tempted, and fell; but the land given him turned barren that very night in indignation at being owned by such a traitor.

The other of Fergus's sons was of different make. He charged out, torch in hand, and cut down the Ultonians, so that they hesitated to come near the house again. Conchobar dared not offer him a bribe. But he armed his own son, Fiacha, with his own magic weapons, including his shield, the 'Moaner', which roared when its owner was in danger, and sent him to fight Illann.

The duel was a fierce one, and Illann got the better of Fiacha, so that the son of Conchobar had to crouch down beneath his shield, which roared for help. Conall the Victorious heard the roar from far off, and thought that his king must be in peril. He came to the place, and, without asking questions, thrust his spear 'Blue-green' through Illann. The dying son of Fergus explained the situation to Conall, who, by way of making some amends, at once killed Fiacha as well.

After this, the sons of Usnach held their fort till dawn against all Conchobar's host. But, with day, they saw that they must either escape or resign themselves to perish. Putting Deirdre in their centre, protected by their shields, they opened the door suddenly and fled out.

They would have broken through and escaped, had not Conchobar asked Cathbad the Druid to put a spell upon them, promising to spare their lives. So Cathbad raised the illusion of a stormy sea before and all around the sons of Usnach. Naoise lifted Deirdre upon his shoulder, but the magic waves rose higher, until they were all obliged to fling away their weapons and swim.

Then was seen the strange sight of men swimming upon dry land. And, before the glamour passed away, the sons of Usnach were seized from behind, and brought to Conchobar.

In spite of his promise to the druid, the king condemned them to death. None of the men of Ulster would, however, deal the blow. In the end, a foreigner from Norway, whose father Naoise had slain, offered to behead them. Each of the brothers begged to die first, that he might not witness the deaths of the others. But Naoise ended this noble rivalry by lending their executioner the sword called 'The Retaliator', which had been given him by Manannán son of Lêr. They knelt down side by side, and one blow of the sword of the god shore off all their heads.

As for Deirdre, there are varying stories of her death, but most of them agree that she did not survive the sons of Usnach many hours. But, before she died, she made an elegy over them. That it is of a singular pathos and beauty the few verses which there is space to give will show.

> 'Long the day without Usnach's children! It was not mournful to be in their company! Sons of a king by whom sojourners were entertained,
> Three lions from the Hill of the Cave. . . . .
>
> 'Three darlings of the women of Britain, Three hawks of Slieve Gullion, Sons of a king whom valour served, To whom soldiers used to give homage!. . . . .
>
> 'That I should remain after Naoise Let no one in the world suppose: After Ardan and Ainle My time would not be long.

'Ulster's over-king, my first husband, I forsook for Naoise's love. Short my life after them: I will perform their funeral game.

'After them I shall not be alive – Three that would go into every conflict, Three who liked to endure hardships, Three heroes who refused not combats . . . .
. . . .

'O man, that diggest the tomb And puttest my darling from me, Make not the grave too narrow: I shall be beside the noble ones.'

It was a poor triumph for Conchobar. Deirdre in all her beauty had escaped him by death. His own chief followers never forgave it. Fergus, when he returned from Borrach's feast, and found out what had been done, gathered his own people, slew Conchobar's son and many of his warriors, and fled to Ulster's bitterest enemies, Ailill and Medb of Connaught. And Cathbad the Druid cursed both king and kingdom, praying that none of Conchobar's race might ever reign in Emain Macha again.

So it came to pass. The capital of Ulster was only kept from ruin by Cuchulainn's prowess. When he perished, it also fell, and soon became what it is now – a grassy hill.

X

FINN AND THE FENIANS

The epoch of Emain Macha is followed in the annals of ancient Ireland by a succession of monarchs who, though doubtless as mythical as King Conchobar and his court, seem to grow gradually more human. Their line lasts for about two centuries, culminating in a dynasty with which legend has occupied itself more than with its immediate predecessors. This is the one which began, according to the annalists, in AD 177, with the famous Conn 'the Hundred-Fighter', and, passing down to the reign of his even more famous grandson, Cormac 'the Magnificent', is connected with the third Gaelic cycle – that which relates the exploits of Finn and the Fenians. All these kings had their dealings with the national gods. A story contained in a fifteenth-century Irish manuscript, and called 'The Champion's Prophecy', tells how Lugh appeared to Conn, enveloped him in a magic mist, led him away to an enchanted palace, and there prophesied to him the number of his descendants, the length of their reigns, and the manner of their deaths. Another tradition relates how Conn's son, Connla, was wooed by a goddess and borne away, like the British Arthur, in a boat of glass to the Earthly Paradise beyond the sea. Yet another relates Conn's own marriage with Becuma of the Fair Skin, wife of that same Labraid of the Quick Hand on Sword who, in another legend, married Liban, the sister of Fand, Cuchulainn's fairy love. Becuma had been discovered in an intrigue with Gaiar, a son of Manannán, and, banished from the 'Land of Promise', crossed the sea that sunders mortals and immortals to offer her hand to Conn. The Irish king wedded her, but evil came of the marriage. She grew jealous of Conn's other son, Art, and insisted upon his banishment; but they agreed to play chess to decide which should go, and Art won. Art, called 'the Lonely' because he had lost his brother Connla, was king after Conn, but he is chiefly known to legend as the father of Cormac.

Many Irish stories occupy themselves with the fame of Cormac, who is pictured as a great legislator – a Gaelic Solomon. Certain traditions credit him with having been the first to believe in a purer doctrine than the Celtic polytheism, and even with having attempted to put down druidism, in revenge for which a druid called Maelcen sent an evil spirit who placed a salmon-bone crossways in the king's throat, as he sat at meat, and so compassed his death. Another class of stories, however, make him an especial favourite with those same heathen deities. Manannán son of Lêr, was so anxious for his friendship that he decoyed him into fairyland, and gave him a magic branch. It was of silver, and bore golden apples, and, when it was shaken, it made such sweet music that the wounded, the sick, and the sorrowful forgot their pains, and were lulled into deep sleep. Cormac kept this treasure all his life; but, at his death, it returned into the hands of the gods.

King Cormac was a contemporary of Finn mac Coul, whom he appointed head of the *Fianna Eirinn*, more generally known as the 'Fenians'. Around Finn and his men have gathered a cycle of legends which were equally popular with the Gaels of both Scotland and Ireland. We read of their exploits in stories and poems preserved in the earliest Irish manuscripts, while among the peasantry both of Ireland and of the West Highlands their names and the stories connected with them are still current lore. Upon some of these floating traditions, as preserved in folk ballads, MacPherson founded his factitious *Ossian*, and the collection of them from the lips of living men still affords plenty of employment to Gaelic students.

How far Finn and his followers may have been historical personages it is impossible to say. The Irish people themselves have always held that the Fenians were a kind of native militia, and that Finn was their general. The early historical writers of Ireland supported this view. The chronicler Tighernach, who died in 1088, believed in him, and the 'Annals of the Four Masters', compiled between the years 1632 and 1636 from older chronicles, while they ignore King Conchobar and his Red Branch Champions as unworthy of the serious consideration of historians, treat Finn as a real person whose death took place in 283 AD. Even so great a modern scholar as Eugene O'Curry declared in the clearest language that Finn, so far from being 'a merely imaginary or mythical character', was 'an undoubtedly historical personage; and that he existed about the time at which his appearance is recorded in the Annals is as certain as that Julius Caesar lived and ruled at the time stated on the authority of the Roman historians'.

The opinion of more recent Celtic scholars, however, is opposed to this view. Finn's pedigree, preserved in the Book of Leinster, may seem at first to give some support to the theory of his real existence, but, on more careful examination of it, his own name and that of his father equally bewray him. Finn or Fionn, meaning 'fair', is the name of one of the mythical ancestors of the Gaels, while his father's name, Cumhal, signifies the 'sky', and is the same word as Camulus, the Gaulish heaven-god identified by the Romans with Mars. His followers are as doubtfully human as himself. One may compare them with Cuchulainn and the rest of the heroes of Emain Macha. Their deeds are not less marvellous.

Like the Ultonian warriors, they move, too, on equal terms with the gods. 'The Fianna of Erin', says a tract called 'The Dialogue of the Elders', contained in thirteenth and fourteenth-century manuscripts, 'had not more frequent and free intercourse with the men of settled habitation than with the Tuatha Dé Danann'. Angus, Mider, Lêr, Manannán, and Bodb the Red, with their countless sons and daughters, loom as large in the Fenian, or so-called 'Ossianic' stories as do the Fenians themselves. They fight for them, or against them; they marry them, and are given to them in marriage.

A luminous suggestion of Professor Rhys also hints that the Fenians inherited the conduct of that ancient war formerly waged between the Tuatha Dé Danann and the Fomors. The most common antagonists of Finn and his heroes are tribes of invaders from oversea, called in the stories the *Lochlannach*. These 'Men of Lochlann' are usually identified, by those who look for history in the stories of the Fenian cycle, with the invading bands of Norsemen who harried the Irish coasts in the ninth century. But the nucleus of the Fenian tales antedates these Scandinavian raids, and mortal foes have probably merely stepped into the place of those immortal enemies of the gods whose 'Lochlann' was a country, not over the sea – but under it.

The earlier historians of Ireland were as ready with their dates and facts regarding the Fenian band as an institution as with the personality of Finn. It was said to have been first organized by a king called Fiachadh, in 300 BC, and abolished, or rather, exterminated, by Cairbré, the son of Cormac mac Art, in 284 AD. We are told that it consisted of three regiments modelled on the

Roman legion; each of these bodies contained, on a peace footing, three thousand men, but in time of war could be indefinitely strengthened. Its object was to defend the coasts of Ireland and the country generally, throwing its weight upon the side of any prince who happened to be assailed by foreign foes. During the six months of winter, its members were quartered upon the population, but during the summer they had to forage for themselves, which they did by hunting and fishing. Thus they lived in the woods and on the open moors, hardening themselves for battle by their adventurous life. The sites of their enormous camp-fires were long pointed out under the name of the 'Fenians' cooking-places'.

It was not easy to become a member of this famous band. A candidate had to be not only an expert warrior, but a poet and a man of culture as well. He had practically to renounce his tribe; at any rate he made oath that he would neither avenge any of his relatives nor be avenged by them. He put himself under bonds never to refuse hospitality to anyone who asked, never to turn his back in battle, never to insult any woman, and not to accept a dowry with his wife. In addition to all this, he had to pass successfully through the most stringent physical tests. Indeed, as these have come down to us, magnified by the perfervid Celtic imagination, they are of an altogether marvellous and impossible character. An aspirant to the *Fianna Eirinn*, we are told, had first to stand up to his knees in a pit dug for him, his only arms being his shield and a hazel wand, while nine warriors, each with a spear, standing within the distance of nine ridges of land, all hurled their weapons at him at once; if he failed to ward them all off, he was rejected. Should he succeed in this first test, he was given the distance of one tree-length's start, and chased through a forest by armed men; if any of them came up to him and wounded him, he could not belong to the Fenians. If he escaped unhurt, but had unloosed a single lock of his braided hair, or had broken a single branch in his flight, or if, at the end of the run, his weapons trembled in his hands, he was refused. As, besides these tests, he was obliged to jump over a branch as high as his forehead, and stoop under one as low as his knee, while running at full speed, and to pluck a thorn out of his heel without hindrance to his flight, it is clear that even the rank and file of the Fenians must have been quite exceptional athletes.

But it is time to pass on to a more detailed description of these champions. They are a goodly company, not less heroic than the mighty men of Ulster. First comes Finn himself, not the strongest in body of the Fenians, but the truest, wisest, and kindest, gentle to women, generous to men, and trusted by all. If he could help it, he would never let anyone be in trouble or poverty. 'If the dead leaves of the forest had been gold, and the white foam of the water silver, Finn would have given it all away.'

Finn had two sons, Fergus and his more famous brother Ossian. Fergus of the sweet speech was the Fenian's bard, and, also, because of his honeyed words, their diplomatist and ambassador. Yet, by the irony of fate, it is to Ossian, who is not mentioned as a poet in the earliest texts, that the poems concerning the Fenians which are current in Scotland under the name of 'Ossianic Ballads' are attributed. Ossian's mother was Sadb, a daughter of Bodb the Red. A rival goddess changed her into a deer – which explains how Ossian got his name, which means 'fawn'. With such advantages of birth, naturally he was speedy enough to run down a red deer hind and catch her by the ear, though far less swift-footed than his cousin Caoilte, the 'Thin Man'. Neither was he so strong as his own son Oscar, the mightiest of all the Fenians, yet, in his youth, so clumsy that the rest of the band refused to take him with them on their warlike expeditions. They changed their minds, however, when, one day, he followed them unawares, found them giving way before an enemy, and, rushing to their help, armed only with a great log of wood which lay handy on the ground, turned the fortunes of the fight. After this, Oscar was hailed the best warrior of all the Fianna; he was given command of a battalion, and its banner, called the 'Terrible Broom', was regarded as the centre of every battle, for it was never known to retreat a foot. Other prominent Fenians were Goll, son of Morna, at first Finn's enemy but afterwards his follower, a man skilled alike in war and learning. Even though he was one-eyed, we are told that he was much loved by women, but not so much as Finn's cousin, Diarmait O'Duibhne, whose fatal beauty ensnared even Finn's betrothed bride, Grainne. Their comic character was Conan, who is represented as an old, bald, vain, irritable man, as great a braggart as ancient Pistol and as foul-mouthed as Thersites, and yet, after he had once been shamed into activity, a true man of his hands. These are the prime Fenian heroes, the chief actors in its stories.

The Fenian epic begins, before the birth of its hero, with the struggle of two rival clans, each of whom claimed to be the real and only Fianna Eirinn. They were called the Clann Morna, of which Goll mac Morna was head, and the Clann Baoisgne, commanded by Finn's father, Cumhal. A battle was fought at Cnucha, in which Goll killed Cumhal, and the Clann Baoisgne was scattered. Cumhal's wife, however, bore a posthumous son, who was brought up among the Slieve Bloom Mountains secretly, for fear his father's enemies should find and kill him. The boy, who was at first called Deimne, grew up to be an expert hurler, swimmer, runner, and hunter. Later, like Cuchulainn, and indeed many modern savages, he took a second, more personal name. Those who saw him asked who was the 'fair' youth. He accepted the omen, and called himself Deimne Finn.

At length, he wandered to the banks of the Boyne, where he found a soothsayer called Finn the Seer living beside a deep pool near Slane, named 'Fec's Pool', in hope of catching one of the 'salmons of knowledge', and, by eating it, obtaining universal wisdom. He had been there seven years without result, though success had been prophesied to one named 'Finn'. When the wandering son of Cumhal appeared, Finn the Seer engaged him as his servant. Shortly afterwards, he caught the coveted fish, and handed it over to our Finn to cook, warning him to eat no portion of it. 'Have you eaten any of it?' he asked the boy, as he brought it up ready boiled. 'No indeed,' replied Finn; 'but, while I was cooking it, a blister rose upon the skin, and, laying my thumb down upon the blister, I scalded it, and so I put it into my mouth to ease the pain.' The man was perplexed. 'You told me your name was Deimne,' he said; 'but have you any other name?' 'Yes, I am also called Finn.' 'It is enough,' replied his disappointed master. 'Eat the salmon yourself, for you must be the one of whom the prophecy told.' Finn ate the 'salmon of knowledge', and thereafter he had only to put his thumb under his tooth, as he had done when he scalded it, to receive fore-knowledge and magic counsel.

Thus armed, Finn was more than a match for the Clann Morna. Curious legends tell how he discovered himself to his father's old followers, confounded his enemies with his magic, and turned them into faithful servants. Even Goll of the Blows had to submit to his sway. Gradually he welded the two opposing clans into one Fianna, over which he ruled, taking tribute from the kings of

Ireland, warring against the Fomorian 'Lochlannach', destroying every kind of giant, serpent, or monster that infested the land, and at last carrying his mythical conquests over all Europe.

Out of the numberless stories of the Fenian exploits it is hard to choose examples. All are heroic, romantic, wild, fantastic. In many of them the Tuatha Dé Danann play prominent parts. One such story connects itself with an earlier mythological episode already related. The reader will remember how, when the Dagda gave up the kingship of the immortals, five aspirants appeared to claim it; how of these five – Angus, Mider, Lêr, Ilbhreach son of Manannán, and Bodb the Red – the latter was chosen; how Lêr refused to acknowledge him, but was reconciled later; how Mider, equally rebellious, fled to 'desert country round Mount Leinster' in County Carlow; and how a yearly war was waged upon him and his people by the rest of the gods to bring them to subjection. This war was still raging in the time of Finn, and Mider was not too proud to seek his help. One day that Finn was hunting in Donegal, with Ossian, Oscar, Caoilte, and Diarmait, their hounds roused a beautiful fawn, which, although at every moment apparently nearly overtaken, led them in full chase as far as Mount Leinster. Here it suddenly disappeared into a cleft in the hillside. Heavy snow, 'making the forest's branches as it were a withetwist', now fell, forcing the Fenians to seek for some shelter, and they therefore explored the place into which the fawn had vanished. It led to a splendid *sídh* in the hollow of the hill. Entering it, they were greeted by a beautiful goddess-maiden, who told them that it was she, Mider's daughter, who had been the fawn, and that she had taken that shape purposely to lead them there, in the hope of getting their help against the army that was coming to attack the *sídh*. Finn asked who the assailants would be, and was told that they were Bodb the Red with his seven sons, Angus 'Son of the Young' with his seven sons, Lêr of Sídh Fionnechaidh with his twenty-seven sons, and Fionnbharr of Sídh Meadha with his seventeen sons, as well as numberless gods of lesser fame drawn from *sídhe* not only over all Ireland, but from Scotland and the islands as well. Finn promised his aid, and, with the twilight of that same day, the attacking forces appeared, and made their annual assault. They were beaten off, after a battle that lasted all night, with the loss of 'ten men, ten score, and ten hundred'. Finn, Oscar, and Diarmait, as well as most of Mider's many sons, were sorely wounded, but the leech Labhra healed all their wounds.

Sooth to say, the Fenians did not always require the excuse of fairy alliance to start them making war on the race of the hills. One of the so-called 'Ossianic ballads' is entitled 'The Chase of the Enchanted Pigs of Angus of the Brugh'. This Angus is, of course, the 'Son of the Young', and the Brugh that famous *sídh* beside the Boyne out of which he cheated his father, the Dagda. After the friendly manner of gods towards heroes, he invited Finn and a picked thousand of his followers to a banquet at the Brugh. They came to it in their finest clothes, 'goblets went from hand to hand, and waiters were kept in motion'. At last conversation fell upon the comparative merits of the pleasures of the table and of the chase, Angus stoutly contending that 'the gods' life of perpetual feasting' was better than all the Fenian huntings, and Finn as stoutly denying it. Finn boasted of his hounds, and Angus said that the best of them could not kill one of his pigs. Finn angrily replied that his two hounds, Bran and Sgeolan, would kill any pig that trod on dry land. Angus answered that he could show Finn a pig that none of his hounds or huntsmen could catch or kill. Here were the makings of a pretty quarrel among such inflammable creatures as gods and heroes, but the steward of the feast interposed and sent everyone to bed. The next morning, Finn left the Brugh, for he did not want to fight all Angus's fairies with his handful of a thousand men. A year passed before he heard more of it; then came a messenger from Angus, reminding Finn of his promise to pit his men and hounds against Angus's pigs. The Fenians seated themselves on the tops of the hills, each with his favourite hound in leash, and they had not been there long before there appeared on the eastern plain a hundred and one such pigs as no Fenian had ever seen before. Each was as tall as a deer, and blacker than a smith's coals, having hair like a thicket and bristles like ships' masts. Yet such was the prowess of the Fenians that they killed them all, though each of the pigs slew ten men and many hounds. Then Angus complained that the Fenians had murdered his son and many others of the Tuatha Dé Danann, who, indeed, were none other than the pigs whose forms they had taken. There were mighty recriminations on both sides, and, in the end, the enraged Fenians prepared to attack the Brugh on the Boyne. Then only did Angus begin to yield, and, by the advice of Ossian, Finn made peace with him and his fairy folk.

Such are specimens of the tales which go to make up the Fenian cycle of sagas. Hunting is the most prominent feature of them, for the Fenians were essentially a race of mighty hunters. But the creatures of their chase were not always flesh and blood. Enchanters who wished the Fenians ill could always lure them into danger by taking the shape of boar or deer, and many a story begins with an innocent chase and ends with a murderous battle. But out of such struggles the Fenians always emerge successfully, as Ossian is represented proudly boasting, 'through truthfulness and the might of their hands'.

The most famous chase of all is, however, not that of deer or boar, but of a woman and a man, Finn's betrothed wife and his nephew Diarmait. Ever fortunate in war, the Fenian leader found disaster in his love. Wishing for a wife in his old age, he sent to seek Grainne, the daughter of Cormac, the High-King of Ireland. Both King Cormac and his daughter consented, and Finn's ambassadors returned with an invitation to the suitor to come in a fortnight's time to claim his bride. He arrived with his picked band, and was received in state in the great banqueting-hall of Tara. There they feasted, and there Grainne, the king's daughter, casting her eyes over the assembled Fenian heroes, saw Diarmait O'Duibhne.

This Fenian Adonis had a beauty-spot upon his cheek which no woman could see without falling instantly in love with him. Grainne, for all her royal birth, was no exception to this rule. She asked a druid to point her out the principal guests. The druid told her all their names and exploits. Then she called for a jewelled drinking-horn, and, filling it with a drugged wine, sent it round to each in turn, except to Diarmait. None could be so discourteous as to refuse wine from the hand of a princess. All drank, and fell into deep sleep.

Then, rising, she came to Diarmait, told him her passion for him, and asked for its return. 'I will not love the betrothed of my chief,' he replied, 'and, even if I wished, I dare not.' And he praised Finn's virtues, and decried his own fame. But Grainne merely answered that she put him under *geasa* (bonds which no hero could refuse to redeem) to flee with her; and at once went back to her chair before the rest of the company awoke from their slumber.

After the feast, Diarmait went round to his comrades, one by one, and told them of Grainne's love for him, and of the *geasa* she had placed upon him to take her from Tara. He asked each of them what he ought to do. All answered that no hero could break a *geis* put upon him by a woman. He even asked Finn, concealing Grainne's name, and Finn gave him the same counsel as the others. That night, the lovers fled from Tara to the ford of the Shannon at Athlone, crossed it, and came to a place called the 'Wood of the Two Tents', where Diarmait wove a hut of branches for Grainne to shelter in.

Meanwhile Finn had discovered their flight, and his rage knew no bounds. He sent his trackers, the Clann Neamhuain, to follow them. They tracked them to the wood, and one of them climbed a tree, and, looking down, saw the hut, with a strong seven-doored fence built round it, and Diarmait and Grainne inside. When the news came to the Fenians, they were sorry, for their sympathies were with Diarmait and not with Finn. They tried to warn him, but he took no heed; for he had determined to fight and not to flee. Indeed, when Finn himself came to the fence, and called over it to Diarmait, asking if he and Grainne were within, he replied that they were, but that none should enter unless he gave permission.

So Diarmait, like Cuchulainn in the war of Ulster against Ireland, found himself matched single-handed against a host. But, also like Cuchulainn, he had a divine helper. The favourite of the Tuatha Dé Danann, he had been the pupil of Manannán son of Lêr in the 'Land of Promise', and had been fostered by Angus of the Brugh. Manannán had given him his two spears, the 'Red Javelin' and the 'Yellow Javelin', and his two swords, the 'Great Fury' and the 'Little Fury'. And now Angus came to look for his foster-son, and brought with him the magic mantle of invisibility used by the gods. He advised Diarmait and Grainne to come out wrapped in the cloak, and thus rendered invisible. Diarmait still refused to flee, but asked Angus to protect Grainne. Wrapping the magic mantle round her, the god led the princess away unseen by any of the Fenians.

By this time, Finn had posted men outside all the seven doors in the fence. Diarmait went to each of them in turn. At the first, were Ossian and Oscar with the Clann Baoisgne. They offered him their protection. At the second, were Caoilte and the Clann Ronan, who said they would fight to the death for him. At the third, were Conan and the Clann Morna, also his friends. At the fourth, stood Cuan with the Fenians of Munster, Diarmait's native province. At the fifth, were the Ulster Fenians, who also promised him protection against Finn. But at the sixth, were the Clann Neamhuain, who hated him; and at the seventh, was Finn himself.

'It is by your door that I will pass out, O Finn,' cried Diarmait. Finn charged his men to surround Diarmait as he came out, and kill him. But he leaped the fence, passing clean over their heads, and fled away so swiftly that they could not follow him. He never halted till he reached the place to which he knew Angus had taken Grainne. The friendly god left them with a little sage advice: never to hide in a tree with only one trunk; never to rest in a cave with only one entrance; never to land on an island with only one channel of approach; not to eat their supper where they had cooked it, nor to sleep where they had supped, and, where they had slept once, never to sleep again. With these Red-Indian-like tactics, it was some time before Finn discovered them.

However, he found out at last where they were, and sent champions with venomous hounds to take or kill them. But Diarmait conquered all who were sent against him.

Yet still Finn pursued, until Diarmait, as a last hope of escape, took refuge under a magic quicken-tree, which bore scarlet fruit, the ambrosia of the gods. It had grown from a single berry dropped by one of the Tuatha Dé Danann, who, when they found that they had carelessly endowed mortals with celestial and immortal food, had sent a huge, one-eyed Fomor called Sharvan the Surly to guard it, so that no man might eat of its fruit. All day, this Fomor sat at the foot of the tree, and, all night, he slept among its branches, and so terrible was his appearance that neither the Fenians nor any other people dared to come within several miles of him.

But Diarmait was willing to brave the Fomor in the hope of getting a safe hiding-place for Grainne. He came boldly up to him, and asked leave to camp and hunt in his neighbourhood. The Fomor told him surlily that he might camp and hunt where he pleased, so long as he refrained from taking any of the scarlet berries. So Diarmait built a hut near a spring; and he and Grainne lived there, killing the wild animals for food.

But, unhappily, Grainne conceived so strong a desire to eat the quicken berries that she felt that she must die unless her wish could be gratified. At first she tried to hide this longing, but in the end she was forced to tell her companion. Diarmait had no desire to quarrel with the Fomor; so he went to him and told the plight that Grainne was in, and asked for a handful of the berries as a gift.

But the Fomor merely answered: 'I swear to you that if nothing would save the princess and her unborn child except my berries, and if she were the last woman upon the earth, she should not have any of them.' Whereupon Diarmait fought the Fomor, and, after much trouble, killed him.

It was reported to Finn that the guardian of the magic quicken-tree lived no longer, and he guessed that Diarmait must have killed him; so he came down to the place with seven battalions of the Fenians to look for him. By this time, Diarmait had abandoned his own hut and taken possession of that built by the Fomor among the branches of the magic quicken. He was sitting in it with Grainne when Finn and his men came and camped at the foot of the tree, to wait till the heat of noon had passed before beginning their search.

To beguile the time, Finn called for his chess-board and challenged his son Ossian to a game. They played until Ossian had only one more move.

'One move would make you a winner,' said Finn to him, 'but I challenge you and all the Fenians to guess it.'

Only Diarmait, who had been looking down through the branches upon the players, knew the move. He could not resist dropping a berry on to the board, so deftly that it hit the very chessman which Ossian ought to move in order to win. Ossian took the hint, moved it, and won. A second and a third game were played; and in each case the same thing happened. Then Finn felt sure that the berries that had prompted Ossian must have been thrown by Diarmait.

He called out, asking Diarmait if he were there, and the Fenian hero, who never spoke an untruth, answered that he was. So the quicken-tree was surrounded by armed men, just as the fenced hut in the woods had been. But, again, things happened in the same way; for Angus of the Brugh took away Grainne wrapped in the invisible magic cloak, while Diarmait, walking to the end of a thick branch, cleared the circle of Fenians at a bound, and escaped untouched.

This was the end of the famous 'Pursuit'; for Angus came as ambassador to Finn, urging him to become reconciled to the fugitives, and all the best of the Fenians begged Finn to consent. So Diarmait and Grainne were allowed to return in peace.

But Finn never really forgave, and, soon after, he urged Diarmait to go out to the chase of the wild boar of Benn Gulban. Diarmait killed the boar without getting any hurt; for, like the Greek Achilles, he was invulnerable, save in his heel alone. Finn, who knew this, told him to measure out the length of the skin with his bare feet. Diarmait did so. Then Finn, declaring that he had measured it wrongly, ordered him to tread it again in the opposite direction. This was against the lie of the bristles; and one of them pierced Diarmait's heel, and inflicted a poisoned and mortal wound.

This 'Pursuit of Diarmait and Grainne', which has been told at such length, marks in some degree the climax of the Fenian power, after which it began to decline towards its end. The friends of Diarmait never forgave the treachery with which Finn had compassed his death. The ever-slumbering rivalry between Goll and his Clann Morna and Finn and his Clann Baoisgne began to show itself as open enmity. Quarrels arose, too, between the Fenians and the High-Kings of Ireland, which culminated at last in the annihilation of the Fianna at the battle of Gabhra.

This is said to have been fought in AD 284. Finn himself had perished a year before it, in a skirmish with rebellious Fenians at the Ford of Brea on the Boyne. King Cormac the Magnificent, Grainne's father, was also dead. It was between Finn's grandson Oscar and Cormac's son Cairbré that war broke out. This mythical battle was as fiercely waged as that of Arthur's last fight at Camlan. Oscar slew Cairbré, and was slain by him. Almost all the Fenians fell, as well as all Cairbré's forces.

Only two of the greater Fenian figures survived. One was Caoilte, whose swiftness of foot saved him at the end when all was lost. The famous story, called the 'Dialogue of the Elders', represents him discoursing to St. Patrick, centuries after, of the Fenians' wonderful deeds. Having lost his friends of the heroic age, he is said to have cast in his lot with the Tuatha Dé Danann. He fought in a battle, with Ilbhreach son of Manannán, against Lêr himself, and killed the ancient sea-god with his own hand. The tale represents him taking possession of Lêr's fairy palace of Sídh Fionnechaidh, after which we know no more of him, except that he has taken rank in the minds of the Irish peasantry as one of, and a ruler among, the Sídhe.

The other was Ossian, who did not fight at Gabhra, for, long before, he had taken the great journey which most heroes of mythology take, to that bourne from which no ordinary mortal ever returns. Like Cuchulainn, it was upon the invitation of a goddess that he went. The Fenians were hunting near Lake Killarney when a lady of more than human beauty came to them, and told them that her name was Niamh, daughter of the Son of the Sea. The Gaelic poet, Michael Comyn, who, in the eighteenth century, rewove the ancient story into his own words, describes her in just the same way as one of the old bards would have done:

'A royal crown was on her head; And a brown mantle of precious silk, Spangled with stars of red gold, Covering her shoes down to the grass.

'A gold ring was hanging down From each yellow curl of her golden hair; Her eyes, blue, clear, and cloudless, Like a dew-drop on the top of the grass.

'Redder were her cheeks than the rose, Fairer was her visage than the swan upon the wave, And more sweet was the taste of her balsam lips Than honey mingled thro' red wine.

'A garment, wide, long, and smooth Covered the white steed, There was a comely saddle of red gold, And her right hand held a bridle with a golden bit.

'Four shoes well-shaped were under him, Of the yellow gold of the purest quality; A silver wreath was on the back of his head, And there was not in the world a steed better.'

Such was Niamh of the Golden Hair, Manannán's daughter; and it is small wonder that, when she chose Ossian from among the sons of men to be her lover, all Finn's supplications could not keep him. He mounted behind her on her fairy horse, and they rode across the land to the sea-shore, and then over the tops of the waves. As they went, she described the country of the gods to him in just the same terms as Manannán himself had pictured it to Bran, son of Febal, as Mider had painted it to Etain, and as everyone that went there limned it to those that stayed at home on earth.

'It is the most delightful country to be found Of greatest repute under the sun; Trees drooping with fruit and blossom, And foliage growing on the tops of boughs.

'Abundant, there, are honey and wine, And everything that eye has beheld, There will not come decline on thee with lapse of time.

Death or decay thou wilt not see.'

As they went they saw wonders. Fairy palaces with bright sun-bowers and lime-white walls appeared on the surface of the sea. At one of these they halted, and Ossian, at Niamh's request, attacked a fierce Fomor who lived there, and set free a damsel of the Tuatha Dé Danann whom he kept imprisoned. He saw a hornless fawn leap from wave to wave, chased by one of those strange hounds of Celtic myth which are pure white, with red ears. At last they reached the 'Land of the Young', and there Ossian dwelt with Niamh for three hundred years before he remembered Erin and the Fenians. Then a great wish came upon him to see his own country and his own people again, and Niamh gave him leave to go, and mounted him upon a fairy steed for the journey. One thing alone she made him swear – not to let his feet touch earthly soil. Ossian promised, and reached Ireland on the wings of the wind. But, like the children of Lêr at the end of their penance, he found all changed. He asked for Finn and the Fenians, and was told that they were the names of people who had lived long ago, and whose deeds were written of in old books. The Battle of Gabhra had been fought, and St. Patrick had come to Ireland, and made all things new. The very forms of men had altered; they seemed dwarfs compared with the giants of his day. Seeing three hundred of them trying in vain to raise a marble slab, he rode up to them in contemptuous kindness, and lifted it with one hand. But, as he did so, the golden saddle-girth broke with the strain, and he touched the earth with his feet. The fairy horse vanished, and Ossian rose from the ground, no longer divinely young and fair and strong, but a blind, gray-haired, withered old man.

A number of spirited ballads tell how Ossian, stranded in his old age upon earthly soil, unable to help himself or find his own food, is taken by St. Patrick into his house to be converted. The saint paints to him in the brightest colours the heaven which may be his own if he will but repent, and in the darkest the hell in which he tells him his old comrades now lie in anguish. Ossian replies to the saint's arguments, entreaties, and threats in language which is extraordinarily frank. He will not believe that heaven could be closed to the Fenians if they wished to enter it, or that God himself would not be proud to claim friendship with Finn. And if it be not so, what is the use to him of eternal life where there is no hunting, or wooing fair women, or listening to the songs and tales of bards? No, he will go to the Fenians, whether they sit at the feast or in the fire; and so he dies as he had lived.

XI

THE DECLINE AND FALL OF THE GODS

In spite, however, of the wide-spread popularity of the ballads that took the form of dialogues between Ossian and Patrick, certain traditions say that the saint succeeded in converting the hero. Caoilté, the other great surviving Fenian, was also represented as having gladly exchanged his pagan lore for the faith and salvation offered him. We may see the same influence on foot in the later legends concerning the Red Branch Champions. It was the policy of the first Christianizers of Ireland to describe the loved heroes of their still half-heathen flocks as having handed in their submission to the new creed. The tales about Conchobar and Cuchulainn were amended, to prove that those very pagan personages had been miraculously brought to accept the gospel at the last. An entirely new story told how the latter hero was raised from the dead by Saint Patrick that he might bear witness of the truth of Christianity to Laogaire the Second, King of Ireland, which he did with such fervour and eloquence that the sceptical monarch was convinced.

Daring attempts were also made to change the Tuatha Dé Danann from pagan gods into Christian saints, but these were by no means so profitable as the policy pursued towards the more human-seeming heroes. With one of them alone, was success immediate and brilliant. Brigit, the goddess of fire, poetry, and the hearth, is famous to-day as Saint Bridget, or Bride. Most popular of all the Irish saints, she can still be easily recognized as the daughter of the Dagda. Her Christian attributes, almost all connected with fire, attest her pagan origin. She was born at sunrise; a house in which she dwelt blazed into a flame which reached to heaven; a pillar of fire rose from her head when she took the veil; and her breath gave new life to the dead. As with the British goddess Sul, worshipped at Bath, who – the first-century Latin writer Solinus tells us – 'ruled over the boiling springs, and at her altar there flamed a perpetual fire which never whitened into ashes, but hardened into a stony mass', the sacred flame on her shrine at Kildare was never allowed to go out. It was extinguished once, in the thirteenth century, but was relighted, and burnt with undying glow until the suppression of the monasteries by Henry the Eighth. This sacred fire might not be breathed on by the impure human breath. For nineteen nights it was tended by her nuns, but on the twentieth night it was left untouched, and kept itself alight miraculously. With so little of her essential character and ritual changed, it is small wonder that the half-pagan, half-Christian Irish gladly accepted the new saint in the stead of the old goddess.

Doubtless a careful examination of Irish hagiology would result in the discovery of many other saints whose names and attributes might render them suspect of previous careers as pagan gods. But their acceptation was not sufficiently general to do away with the need of other means of counteracting the still living influence of the Gaelic Pantheon. Therefore a fresh school of euhemerists arose to prove that the gods were never even saints, but merely worldly men who had once lived and ruled in Erin. Learned monks worked hard to construct a history of Ireland from the Flood downwards. Mr. Eugene O'Curry has compiled from the various pedigrees they elaborated, and inserted into the books of Ballymote, Lecan, and Leinster an amazing genealogy which shows how, not merely the Tuatha Dé Danann, but also the Fir Bolgs, the Fomors, the Milesians, and the races of Partholon and Nemed were descended from Noah. Japhet, the patriarch's son, was the father of Magog, from whom came two lines, the first being the Milesians, while the second branched out into all the other races.

Having once worked the gods, first into universal history, and then into the history of Ireland, it was an easy matter to supply them with dates of birth and death, local habitations, and places of burial. We are told with precision exactly how long Nuada, the Dagda, Lugh, and the others reigned at Tara. The barrows by the Boyne provided them with comfortable tombs. Their enemies, the Fomors, became real invaders who were beaten in real battles. Thus it was thought to make plain prose of their divinities.

It is only fair, however, to these early euhemerists to say that they have their modern disciples. There are many writers, of recognized authority upon their subjects, who, in dealing with the history of Ireland or the composition of the British race, claim to find real peoples in the tribes mentioned in Gaelic myth. Unfortunately, the only point they agree upon is the accepted one – that the 'Milesians' were Aryan Celts. They are divided upon the question of the 'Fir Bolgs', in whom some see the pre-Aryan tribes, while others, led astray by the name, regard them as Belgic Gauls; and over the really mythological races they run wild. In the Tuatha Dé Danann are variously found Gaels, Picts, Danes, Scandinavians, Ligurians, and Finns, while the Fomors rest under the suspicion of having been Iberians, Moors, Romans, Finns, Goths, or Teutons. As for the people of Partholon and Nemed, they have even been explained as men of the Palæolithic Age. This chaos of opinion was fortunately avoided by the native annalists, who had no particular views upon the question of race, except that everybody came from 'Spain'.

Of course there were dissenters from this prevailing mania for euhemerization. As late as the tenth century, a poet called Eochaid O'Flynn, writing of the Tuatha Dé Danann, at first seems to hesitate whether to ascribe humanity or divinity to them, and at last frankly avows their godhead. In his poem, preserved in the Book of Ballymote, he says:–

> 'Though they came to learned Erinn Without buoyant, adventurous ships, No man in creation knew Whether they were of the earth or of the sky.
>
> 'If they were diabolical demons, They came from that woeful expulsion; If they were of a race of tribes and nations, If they were human, they were of the race of Beothach.'

Then he enumerates them in due succession, and ends by declaring:

> 'Though I have treated of these deities in their order, Yet I have not adored them'.

One may surmise with probability that the common people agreed rather with the poet than with the monk. Pious men in monasteries might write what they liked, but mere laymen would not be easily persuaded that their cherished gods had never been anything more than men like themselves. Probably they said little, but acted in secret according to their inherited ideas. Let it be granted, for the sake of peace, that Goibniu was only a man; none the less, his name was known to be uncommonly effective in an incantation. This applied equally to Diancecht, and invocations to both of them are contained in some verses which an eighth-century Irish monk wrote on the margin of a manuscript still preserved at St. Gall, in Switzerland. Some prescriptions of Diancecht's have come down to us, but it must be admitted that they hardly differ from those current among ordinary mediæval physicians. Perhaps, after that unfortunate spilling of the herbs that grew out of Miach's body, he had to fall back upon empirical research. He invented a porridge for 'the relief of ailments of the body, as cold, phlegm, throat cats, and the presence of living things in the body, as worms'; it was compounded of hazel buds, dandelion, chickweed, sorrel, and oatmeal; and was to be taken every morning and evening. He also prescribed against the effects of witchcraft and the fourteen diseases of the stomach.

Goibniu, in addition to his original character as the divine smith and sorcerer, gained a third reputation among the Irish as a great builder and bridge-maker. As such he is known as the Gobhan Saer, that is, Goibniu the Architect, and marvellous tales, current all over Ireland attest his prowess.

> 'Men call'd him Gobhan Saer, and many a tale Yet lingers in the by-ways of the land Of how he cleft the rock, or down the vale Led the bright river, child-like, in his hand: Of how on giant ships he spread great sail, And many marvels else by him first plann'd',

writes a poet of modern Ireland. Especially were the 'round towers' attributed to him, and the Christian clerics appropriated his popularity by describing him as having been the designer of their churches. He used, according to legend, to wander over the country, clad, like the Greek Hephaestus, whom he resembles, in working dress, seeking commissions and adventures. His works remain in the cathedrals and churches of Ireland; and, with regard to his adventures, many strange legends are still, or were until very recently, current upon the lips of old people in remote parts of Ireland.

Some of these are, as might have been expected, nothing more than half-understood recollections of the ancient mythology. In them appear as characters others of the old, yet not quite forgotten gods – Lugh, Manannán, and Balor – names still remembered as those of long-past druids, heroes, and kings of Ireland in the misty olden time.

One or two of them are worth retelling. Mr. William Larminie, collecting folk-tales in Achill Island, took one from the lips of an aged peasant which tells in its confused way what might almost be called the central incident of Gaelic mythology, the mysterious birth of the sun-god from demoniac parentage, and his eventual slaying of his grandfather when he came to full age.

Gobhan the Architect and his son, young Gobhan, runs the tale, were sent for by Balor of the Blows to build him a palace. They built it so well that Balor decided never to let them leave his kingdom alive, for fear they should build another one equally good for someone else. He therefore had all the scaffolding removed from round the palace while they were still on the top, with the intention of leaving them up there to die of hunger. But, when they discovered this, they began to destroy the roof, so that Balor was obliged to let them come down.

He, none the less, refused to allow them to return to Ireland. The crafty Gobhan, however, had his plan ready. He told Balor that the injury that had been done to the palace roof could not be repaired without special tools, which he had left behind him at home. Balor declined to let either old Gobhan or young Gobhan go back to fetch them; but he offered to send his own son. Gobhan gave Balor's son directions for the journey. He was to travel until he came to a house with a stack of corn at the door. Entering it, he would find a woman with one hand and a child with one eye.

Balor's son found the house, and asked the woman for the tools. She expected him; for it had been arranged between Gobhan and his wife what should be done, if Balor refused to let him return. She took Balor's son to a huge chest, and told him that the tools were at the bottom of it, so far down that she could not reach them, and that he must get into the chest, and pick them up himself. But, as soon as he was safely inside, she shut the lid on him, telling him that he would have to stay there until his father allowed old Gobhan and young Gobhan to come home with their pay. And she sent the same message to Balor himself.

There was an exchange of prisoners, Balor giving the two Gobhans their pay and a ship to take them home, and Gobhan's wife releasing Balor's son. But, before the two builders went, Balor asked them whom he should now employ to repair his palace. Old Gobhan told him that, next to himself, there was no workman in Ireland better than one Gavidjeen Go.

When Gobhan got back to Ireland, he sent Gavidjeen Go to Balor. But he gave him a piece of advice – to accept as pay only one thing: Balor's gray cow, which would fill twenty barrels at one milking. Balor agreed to this, but, when he gave the cow to Gavidjeen Go to take back with him to Ireland, he omitted to include her byre-rope, which was the only thing that would keep her from returning to her original owner.

The gray cow gave so much trouble to Gavidjeen Go by her straying, that he was obliged to hire military champions to watch her during the day and bring her safely home at night. The bargain made was that Gavidjeen Go should forge the champion a sword for his pay, but that, if he lost the cow, his life was to be forfeited.

At last, a certain warrior called Cian was unlucky enough to let the cow escape. He followed her tracks down to the sea-shore and right to the edge of the waves, and there he lost them altogether. He was tearing his hair in his perplexity, when he saw a man rowing a coracle. The man, who was no other than Manannán son of Lêr, came in close to the shore, and asked what was the matter.

Cian told him.

'What would you give to anyone who would take you to the place where the gray cow is?' asked Manannán.

'I have nothing to give,' replied Cian.

'All I ask,' said Manannán, 'is half of whatever you gain before you come back.'

Cian agreed to that willingly enough, and Manannán told him to get into the coracle. In the wink of an eye, he had landed him in Balor's kingdom, the realm of the cold, where they roast no meat, but eat their food raw. Cian was not used to this diet, so he lit himself a fire, and began to cook some food. Balor saw the fire, and came down to it, and he was so pleased that he appointed Cian to be his fire-maker and cook.

Now Balor had a daughter, of whom a druid had prophesied that she would, some day, bear a son who would kill his grandfather. Therefore, like Acrisius, in Greek legend, he shut her up in a tower, guarded by women, and allowed her to see no man but himself. One day, Cian saw Balor go to the tower. He waited until he had come back, and then went to explore. He had the gift of opening locked doors and shutting them again after him. When he got inside, he lit a fire, and this novelty so delighted Balor's daughter that she invited him to visit her again. After this – in the Achill islander's quaint phrase – 'he was ever coming there, until a child happened to her.' Balor's daughter gave the baby to Cian to take away. She also gave him the byre-rope which belonged to the gray cow.

Cian was in great danger now, for Balor had found out about the child. He led the gray cow away with the rope to the sea-shore, and waited for Manannán. The Son of Lêr had told Cian that, when he was in any difficulty, he was to think of him, and he would at once appear. Cian thought of him now, and, in a moment, Manannán appeared with his coracle. Cian got into the boat, with the baby and the gray cow, just as Balor, in hot pursuit, came down to the beach.

Balor, by his incantations, raised a great storm to drown them; but Manannán, whose druidism was greater, stilled it. Then Balor turned the sea into fire, to burn them; but Manannán put it out with a stone.

When they were safe back in Ireland, Manannán asked Cian for his promised reward.

'I have gained nothing but the boy, and I cannot cut him in two, so I will give him to you whole,' he replied.

'That is what I was wanting all the time,' said Manannán; 'when he grows up, there will be no champion equal to him.'

So Manannán baptized the boy, calling him 'the Dul-Dauna'. This name, meaning 'Blind-Stubborn', is certainly a curious corruption of the original *Ioldanach* 'Master of all Knowledge'. When the boy had grown up, he went one day to the sea-shore. A ship came past, in which was a man. The traditions of

Donnybrook Fair are evidently prehistoric, for the boy, without troubling to ask who the stranger was, took a dart 'out of his pocket', hurled it, and hit him. The man in the boat happened to be Balor. Thus, in accordance with the prophecy, he was slain by his grandson, who, though the folk-tale does not name him, was obviously Lugh.

Another version of the same legend, collected by the Irish scholar O'Donovan on the coast of Donegal, opposite Balor's favourite haunt, Tory Island, is interesting as completing the one just narrated. In this folk-tale, Goibniu is called Gavida, and is made one of three brothers, the other two being called Mac Kineely and Mac Samthainn. They were chiefs of Donegal, smiths and farmers, while Balor was a robber who harassed the mainland from his stronghold on Tory Island. The gray cow belonged to Mac Kineely, and Balor stole it. Its owner determined to be revenged, and, knowing the prediction concerning Balor's death at the hands of an as yet unborn grandson, he persuaded a kindly fairy to spirit him in female disguise to Tor Mor, where Balor's daughter, who was called Ethnea, was kept imprisoned. The result of this expedition was not merely the one son necessary to fulfil the prophecy, but three. This apparent superfluity was fortunate; for Balor drowned two of them, the other being picked out of the sea by the same fairy who had been incidentally responsible for his birth, and handed over to his father, Mac Kineely, to be brought up. Shortly after this, Balor managed to capture Mac Kineely, and, in retaliation for the wrong done him, chopped off his head upon a large white stone, still known locally as the 'Stone of Kineely'. Satisfied with this, and quite unaware that one of his daughter's children had been saved from death, and was now being brought up as a smith by Gavida, Balor went on with his career of robbery, varying it by visits to the forge to purchase arms. One day, being there during Gavida's absence, he began boasting to the young assistant of how he had compassed Mac Kineely's death. He never finished the story, for Lugh – which was the boy's name – snatched a red-hot iron from the fire, and thrust it into Balor's eye, and through his head.

Thus, in these two folk-tales, gathered in different parts of Ireland, at different times, by different persons, survives quite a mass of mythological detail only to be found otherwise in ancient manuscripts containing still more ancient matter. Crystallized in them may be found the names of six members of the old Gaelic Pantheon, each filling the same part as of old. Goibniu has not lost his mastery of smithcraft; Balor is still the Fomorian king of the cold regions of the sea; his daughter Ethniu becomes, by Cian, the mother of the sun-god; Lugh, who still bears his old title of *Ioldanach*, though it is strangely corrupted into a name meaning almost the exact opposite, is still fostered by Manannán, Son of the Sea, and in the end grows up to destroy his grandfather by a blow in the one vulnerable place, his death-dealing eye. Perhaps, too, we may claim to see a genuine, though jumbled tradition, in the Fomor-like deformities of Gobhan's wife and child, and in the story of the gray cow and her byre-rope, which recalls that of the Dagda's black-maned heifer, Ocean.

The memories of the peasantry still hold many stories of Lugh, as well as of Angus, and others of the old gods. But, next to the Gobhan Saer, the one whose fame is still greatest is that ever-potent and ever-popular figure, the great Manannán.

The last, perhaps, to receive open adoration, he is represented by kindly tradition as having been still content to help and watch over the people who had rejected and ceased to worship him. Up to the time of St. Columba, he was the special guardian of Irishmen in foreign parts, assisting them in their dangers and bringing them home safe. For the peasantry, too, he caused favourable weather and good crops. His fairy subjects tilled the ground while men slept. But this is said to have come to an end at last. Saint Columba, having broken his golden chalice, gave it to a servant to get repaired. On his way, the servant was met by a stranger, who asked him where he was going. The man told him, and showed him the chalice. The stranger breathed upon it, and, at once, the broken parts reunited. Then he begged him to return to his master, give him the chalice, and tell him that Manannán son of Lêr, who had mended it, desired to know in very truth whether he would ever attain paradise. 'Alas,' said the ungrateful saint, 'there is no forgiveness for a man who does such works as this!' The servant went back with the answer, and Manannán, when he heard it, broke out into indignant lament. 'Woe is me, Manannán mac Lêr! for years I've helped the Catholics of Ireland, but I'll do it no more, till they're as weak as water. I'll go to the gray waves in the Highlands of Scotland.'

And there he remained. For, unless the charming stories of Miss Fiona Macleod are mere beautiful imaginings and nothing more, he is not unknown even to-day among the solitary shepherds and fishers of 'the farthest Hebrides'. In the *Contemporary Review* for October, 1902, she tells how an old man of four-score years would often be visited in his shieling by a tall, beautiful stranger, with a crest on his head, 'like white canna blowing in the wind, but with a blueness in it', and 'a bright, cold, curling flame under the soles of his feet'. The man told him many things, and prophesied to him the time of his death. Generally, the stranger's hands were hidden in the folds of the white cloak he wore, but, once, he moved to touch the shepherd, who saw then that his flesh was like water, with sea-weed floating among the bones. So that Murdo MacIan knew that he could be speaking with none other than the Son of the Sea.

Nor is he yet quite forgotten in his own Island of Man, of which local tradition says he was the first inhabitant. He is also described as its king, who kept it from invasion by his magic. He would cause mists to rise at any moment and conceal the island, and by the same glamour he could make one man seem like a hundred, and little chips of wood which he threw into the water to appear like ships of war. It is no wonder that he held his kingdom against all-comers, until his sway was ended, like that of the other Gaelic gods, by the arrival of Saint Patrick. After this, he seems to have declined into a traditionary giant who used to leap from Peel Castle to Contrary Head for exercise, or hurl huge rocks, upon which the mark of his hand can still be seen. It is said that he took no tribute from his subjects, or worshippers except bundles of green rushes, which were placed every Midsummer Eve upon two mountain peaks, one called Warrefield in olden days, but now South Barrule, and the other called Man, and not now to be identified. His grave, which is thirty yards long, is pointed out, close to Peel Castle. The most curious legend connected with him, however, tells us that he had three legs, on which he used to travel at a great pace. How this was done may be seen from the arms of the island, on which are pictured his three limbs, joined together, and spread out like the spokes of a wheel.

An Irish tradition tells us that, when Manannán left Ireland for Scotland, the vacant kingship of the gods or fairies was taken by one Mac Moineanta; to the great grief of those who had known Manannán. Perhaps this great grief led to Mac Moineanta's being deposed, for the present king of the Irish fairies is Finvarra, the same Fionnbharr to whom the Dagda allotted the *sídh* of Meadha after the conquest of the Tuatha Dé Danann by the Milesians, and who takes a prominent part in the Fenian stories. So great is the persistence of tradition in Ireland that this hill of Meadha, now spelt Knockma, is still considered to be the abode of him and his queen, Onagh. Numberless stories are told about Finvarra, including, of course, that very favourite Celtic tale of the stolen bride, and her recapture from the fairies by the siege and digging up of the *sídh* in which she was held prisoner. Finvarra, like Mider of Bri Leith, carried away a human Etain – the wife, not of a high king, but of an Irish lord. The modern Eochaid Airem, having heard an invisible voice tell him where he was to look for his lost bride, gathered all his workmen and labourers and proceeded to demolish Knockma. Every day they almost dug it up, but every night the breach was found to have been repaired by fairy workmen of Finvarra's. This went on for three days, when the Irish lord thought of the well-known device of sanctifying the work of excavation by sprinkling the turned-up earth with salt. Needless to say, it succeeded. Finvarra gave back the bride, still in the trance into which he had thrown her; and the deep cut into the fairy hill still remains to furnish proof to the incredulous.

Finvarra does not always appear, however, in such unfriendly guise. He was popularly reputed to have under his special care the family of the Kirwans of Castle Hacket, on the northern slope of Knockma. Owing to his benevolent influence, the castle cellars never went dry, nor did the quality of the wine deteriorate. Besides the wine-cellar, Finvarra looked after the stables, and it was owing to the exercise that he and his fairy followers gave the horses by night that Mr. John Kirwan's racers were so often successful on the Curragh. That such stories could have passed current as fact, which they undoubtedly did, is excellent proof of how late and how completely a mythology may survive among the uncultured.

Finvarra rules to-day over a wide realm of fairy folk. Many of these, again, have their own vassal chieftains, forming a tribal hierarchy such as must have existed in the Celtic days of Ireland. Finvarra and Onagh are high king and queen, but, under them, Cliodna is tributary queen of Munster, and rules from a *sídh* near Mallow in County Cork, while, under her again, are Aoibhinn, queen of the fairies of North Munster, and Ainé, queen of the fairies of South Munster. These names form but a single instance. A map of fairy Ireland could without much difficulty be drawn, showing, with almost political exactness, the various kingdoms of the Sídhe.

Far less easy, however, would be the task of ascertaining the origin and lineage of these fabled beings. Some of them can still be traced as older gods and goddesses. In the eastern parts of Ireland, Badb and her sisters have become 'banshees' who wail over deaths not necessarily found in battle. Aynia, deemed the most powerful fairy in Ulster, and Ainé, queen of South Munster, are perhaps the same person, the mysterious and awful goddess once adored as Anu, or Danu. Of the two, it is Ainé who especially seems to carry on the traditions of the older Anu, worshipped, according to the 'Choice of Names', in Munster as a goddess of prosperity and abundance. Within living memory, she was propitiated by a magical ritual upon every Saint John's Eve, to ensure fertility during the coming year. The villagers round her *sídh* of Cnoc Ainé (Knockainy) carried burning bunches of hay or straw upon poles to the top of the hill, and thence dispersed among the fields, waving these torches over the crops and cattle. This fairy, or goddess was held to be friendly, and, indeed, more than friendly, to men. Whether or not she were the mother of the gods, she is claimed as first ancestress by half a dozen famous Irish families.

Among her children was the famous Earl Gerald, offspring of her alliance with the fourth Earl of Desmond, known as 'The Magician'. As in the well-known story of the Swan-maidens, the magician-earl is said to have stolen Ainé's cloak while she was bathing, and refused to return it unless she became his bride. But, in the end, he lost her. Ainé had warned her husband never to show surprise at anything done by their son; but a wonderful feat which he performed made the earl break this condition, and Ainé was obliged, by fairy law, to leave him. But, though she had lost her husband, she was not separated from her son, who was received into the fairy world after his death, and now lives under the surface of Lough Gur, in County Limerick, waiting, like the British Arthur, for the hour to strike in which he shall lead forth his warriors to drive the foreigners from Ireland. But this will not be until, by riding round the lake once in every seventh year, he shall have worn his horse's silver shoes as thin as a cat's ear.

Not only the tribe of Danu, but heroes of the other mythical cycles swell the fairy host to-day. Donn, son of Milé, who was drowned before ever he set foot on Irish soil, lives at 'Donn's House', a line of sand-hills in the Dingle Peninsula of Kerry, and, as late as the eighteenth century, we find him invoked by a local poet, half in jest, no doubt, but still, perhaps also a little in earnest. The heroes of Ulster have no part in fairyland; but their enemy, Medb, is credited with queenly rule among the Sídhe, and is held by some to have been the original of 'Queen Mab'. Caoilté, last of the Fenians, was, in spite of his leanings towards Christianity, enrolled among the Tuatha Dé Danann, but none of his kin are known there, neither Ossian, nor Oscar, nor even Finn himself. Yet not even to merely historical mortals are the gates of the gods necessarily closed. The Barry, chief of the barony of Barrymore, is said to inhabit an enchanted palace in Knockthierna, one of the Nagles Hills. The not less traditionally famous O'Donaghue, whose domain was near Killarney, now dwells beneath the waters of that lake, and may still be seen, it is said, upon May Day.

But besides these figures, which can be traced in mythology or history, and others who, though all written record of them has perished, are obviously of the same character, there are numerous beings who suggest a different origin from that of the Aryan-seeming fairies. They correspond to the elves and trolls of Scandinavian, or the silenoi and satyrs of Greek myth. Such is the Leprechaun, who makes shoes for the fairies, and knows where hidden treasures are; the Gan Ceanach, or 'love-talker', who fills the ears of idle girls with pleasant fancies when, to merely mortal ideas, they should be busy with their work; the Pooka, who leads travellers astray, or, taking the shape of an ass or mule, beguiles them to mount upon his back to their discomfiture; the Dulachan, who rides without a head; and other friendly or malicious sprites. Whence come they? A possible answer suggests itself. Preceding the Aryans, and surviving the Aryan conquest all over Europe, was a large non-Aryan population, which must have had its own gods, who would retain their worship, be revered by successive generations, and remain rooted to the soil. May not these uncouth and half-developed Irish Leprechauns, Pookas, and Dulachans, together with the Scotch Cluricanes, Brownies, and their kin, be no 'creations of popular fancy', but the dwindling figures of those darker gods of 'the dark Iberians'?

THE BRITISH GODS AND THEIR STORIES

XII

THE GODS OF THE BRITONS

The descriptions and the stories of the British gods have hardly come down to us in so ample or so compact a form as those of the deities of the Gaels, as they are preserved in the Irish and Scottish manuscripts. They have also suffered far more from the sophistications of the euhemerist. Only in the 'Four Branches of the Mabinogi' do the gods of the Britons appear in anything like their real character of supernatural beings, masters of magic, and untrammelled by the limitations which hedge in mortals. Apart from those four fragments of mythology, and from a very few scattered references in the early Welsh poems, one must search for them under strange disguises. Some masquerade as kings in Geoffrey of Monmouth's more than apocryphal *Historia Britonum*. Others have received an undeserved canonization, which must be stripped from them before they can be seen in their true colours. Others, again, were adopted by the Norman-French romancers, and turned into the champions of chivalry now known as Arthur's Knights of the Round Table. But, however disguised, their real nature can still be discerned. The Gaels and the Britons were but two branches of one race – the Celtic. In many of the gods of the Britons we shall recognize, with names alike and attributes the same, the familiar features of the Gaelic Tuatha Dé Danann.

The British gods are sometimes described as divided into three families – the 'Children of Dôn', the 'Children of Nudd', and the

'Children of Llyr'. But these three families are really only two; for Nudd, or Lludd, as he is variously called, is himself described as a son of Beli, who was the husband of the goddess Dôn. There can be no doubt that Dôn herself is the same divine personage as Danu, the mother of the Tuatha Dé Danann, and that Beli is the British equivalent of the Gaelic Bilé, the universal Dis Pater who sent out the first Gaels from Hades to take possession of Ireland. With the other family, the 'Children of Llyr', we are equally on familiar ground; for the British Llyr can be none other than the Gaelic sea-god Lêr. These two families or tribes are usually regarded as in opposition, and their struggles seem to symbolize in British myth that same conflict between the powers of heaven, light, and life and of the sea, darkness, and death which are shadowed in Gaelic mythology in the battles between the Tuatha Dé Danann and the Fomors.

For the children of Dôn were certainly gods of the sky. Their names are writ large in heaven. The glittering W which we call 'Cassiopeia's Chair' was to our British ancestors *Llys Dôn*, or 'Dôn's Court'; our 'Northern Crown' was *Caer Arianrod*, the 'Castle of Arianrod', Dôn's daughter; while the 'Milky Way' was the 'Castle of Gwydion', Dôn's son. More than this, the greatest of her children, the Nudd or Lludd whom some make the head of a dynasty of his own, was the Zeus alike of the Britons and of the Gaels. His epithet of *Llaw Ereint*, that is, 'of the Hand of Silver', proves him the same personage as Nuada the 'Silver-Handed'. The legend which must have existed to explain this peculiarity has been lost on British ground, but it was doubtless the same as that told of the Irish god. With it, and, no doubt, much else, has disappeared any direct account of battles fought by him as sky-god against Fomor-like enemies. But, under the faint disguise of a king of Britain, an ancient Welsh tale records how he put an end to three supernatural 'plagues' which oppressed his country. In addition to this, we find him under his name of Nudd described in a Welsh Triad as one of 'the three generous heroes of the Isle of Britain', while another makes him the owner of twenty-one thousand milch cows – an expression which must, to the primitive mind, have implied inexhaustible wealth. Both help us to the conception of a god of heaven and battle, triumphant, and therefore rich and liberal.

More tangible evidence is, however, not lacking to prove the wide-spread nature of his worship. A temple dedicated to him in Roman times under the name of Nodens, or Nudens, has been discovered at Lydney, on the banks of the Severn. The god is pictured on a plaque of bronze as a youthful deity, haloed like the sun, and driving a four-horsed chariot. Flying spirits, typifying the winds, accompany him; while his power over the sea is symbolized by attendant Tritons. This was in the west of Britain, while, in the east, there is good reason to believe that he had a shrine overlooking the Thames. Tradition declares that St. Paul's Cathedral occupies the site of an ancient pagan temple; while the spot on which it stands was called, we know from Geoffrey of Monmouth, 'Parth Lludd' by the Britons, and 'Ludes Geat' by the Saxons.

Great, however, as he probably was, Lludd, or Nudd occupies less space in Welsh story, as we have it now, than his son. Gwyn ap Nudd has outlived in tradition almost all his supernatural kin. Professor Rhys is tempted to see in him the British equivalent of the Gaelic Finn mac Cumhail. The name of both alike means 'white'; both are sons of the heaven-god; both are famed as hunters. Gwyn, however, is more than that; for his game is man. In the early Welsh poems, he is a god of battle and of the dead, and, as such, fills the part of a *psychopompos*, conducting the slain into Hades, and there ruling over them. In later, semi-Christianized story he is described as 'Gwyn, son of Nudd, whom God has placed over the brood of devils in Annwn, lest they should destroy the present race'. Later again, as paganism still further degenerated, he came to be considered as king of the *Tylwyth Teg*, the Welsh fairies, and his name as such has hardly yet died out of his last haunt, the romantic vale of Neath. He is the wild huntsman of Wales and the West of England, and it is his pack which is sometimes heard at chase in waste places by night.

In his earliest guise, as a god of war and death, he is the subject of a poem in dialogue contained in the Black Book of Caermarthen. Obscure, like most of the ancient Welsh poems, it is yet a spirited production, and may be quoted here as a favourable specimen of the poetry of the early Cymri. In it we shall see mirrored perhaps the clearest figure of the British Pantheon, the 'mighty hunter', not of deer, but of men's souls, riding his demon horse, and cheering on his demon hound to the fearful chase. He knows when and where all the great warriors fell, for he gathered their souls upon the field of battle, and now rules over them in Hades, or upon some 'misty mountain-top'. It describes a mythical prince, named Gwyddneu Garanhir, known to Welsh legend as the ruler of a lost country now covered by the waters of Cardigan Bay, asking protection of the god, who accords it, and then relates the story of his exploits:

Gwyddneu.
> A bull of conflict was he, active in dispersing an
> arrayed army,
> The ruler of hosts, indisposed to anger,

Blameless and pure his conduct in protecting life.

Gwyn.

Against a hero stout was his advance, The ruler of hosts, disposer of wrath, There will be protection for thee since thou askest it.

Gwyddneu.

For thou hast given me protection How warmly wert thou welcomed! The hero of hosts, from what region thou comest?

Gwyn.

I come from battle and conflict With a shield in my hand; Broken is the helmet by the pushing of spears.

Gwyddneu.

I will address thee, exalted man, With his shield in distress. Brave man, what is thy descent?

Gwyn.

Round-hoofed is my horse, the torment of battle, Fairy am I called, Gwyn the son of Nudd, The lover of Creurdilad, the daughter of Lludd.

Gwyddneu.

Since it is thou, Gwyn, an upright man, From thee there is no concealing: I am Gwyddneu Garanhir.

Gwyn.

Hasten to my ridge, the Tawë abode; Not the nearest Tawë name I to thee, But that Tawë which is the farthest. Polished is my ring, golden my saddle and bright: To my sadness I saw a conflict before Caer Vandwy. Before Caer Vandwy a host I saw, Shields were shattered and ribs broken; Renowned and splendid was he who made the assault.

Gwyddneu.

> Gwyn, son of Nudd, the hope of armies, Quicker would legions fall before the hoofs Of thy horse than broken rushes to the ground.

Gwyn.

> Handsome my dog, and round-bodied, And truly the best of dogs; Dormarth was he, which belonged to Maelgwyn.

Gwyddneu.

> Dormarth with the ruddy nose! what a gazer Thou art upon me because I notice Thy wanderings on Gwibir Vynyd.

Gwyn.

> I have been in the place where was killed Gwendoleu, The son of Ceidaw, the pillar of songs, When the ravens screamed over blood. I have been in the place where Brân was killed, The son of Iweridd, of far extending fame, When the ravens of the battle-field screamed. I have been where Llacheu was slain, The son of Arthur, extolled in songs, When the ravens screamed over blood. I have been where Meurig was killed,The son of Carreian, of honourable fame,When the ravens screamed over flesh. I have been where Gwallawg was killed, The son of Goholeth, the accomplished, The resister of Lloegyr, the son of Lleynawg. I have been where the soldiers of Britain were slain, From the east to the north: I am the escort of the grave. I have been where the soldiers of Britain were slain, From the east to the south: I am alive, they in death!

A line in this poem allows us to see Gwyn in another and less sinister rôle. 'The lover of Creurdilad, the daughter of Lludd,' he calls himself; and an episode in the mythical romance of 'Kulhwch and Olwen', preserved in the Red Book of Hergest, gives the details of his courtship. Gwyn had as rival a deity called Gwyrthur ap Greidawl, that is 'Victor, son of Scorcher'. These two waged perpetual war for Creurdilad, or Creudylad, each in turn stealing her from the other, until the matter was referred to Arthur, who decided that Creudylad should be sent back to her father, and that Gwyn and Gwyrthur 'should fight for her every first of May, from henceforth until the day of doom, and that whichever of them should then be conqueror should have the maiden'. What satisfaction this would be to the survivor of what might be somewhat flippantly described as, in two senses, the longest engagement on record, is not very clear; but its mythological interpretation appears fairly obvious. In Gwyn, god of death and the underworld, and in the solar deity, Gwyrthur, we may see the powers of darkness and sunshine, of winter and summer, in contest, each alternately winning and losing a bride who would seem to represent the spring with its grain and flowers. Creudylad, whom the story of 'Kulhwch and Olwen' calls 'the most splendid maiden in the three islands of the mighty and in the three islands adjacent', is, in fact, the British Persephoné. As the daughter of Lludd, she is child of the shining sky. But a different tradition must have made her a daughter of Llyr, the sea-god; for her name as such passed, through Geoffrey of Monmouth, to Shakespeare, in whose hands she became that pathetic figure, Cordelia in 'King Lear'. It may not be altogether unworthy of notice, though perhaps it is only a coincidence, that in some myths the Greek Persephoné is made a daughter of Zeus and in others of Poseidon.

Turning from the sky-god and his son, we find others of Dôn's children to have been the exponents of those arts of life which early races held to have been taught directly by the gods to men. Dôn herself had a brother, Mâth, son of a mysterious Mâthonwy, and recognizable as a benevolent ruler of the underworld akin to Beli, or perhaps that god himself under another title, for the name Mâth, which means 'coin, money, treasure', recalls that of Plouton, the Greek god of Hades, in his guise of possessor and giver of metals. It was a belief common to the Aryan races that wisdom, as well as wealth, came originally from the underworld; and we find Mâth represented, in the Mabinogi bearing his name, as handing on his magical lore to his nephew and pupil Gwydion, who, there is good reason to believe, was the same divine personage whom the Teutonic tribes worshipped as 'Woden' and 'Odin'. Thus equipped, Gwydion son of Dôn became the druid of the gods, the 'master of illusion and phantasy', and, not only that, but the teacher of all that is useful and good, the friend and helper of mankind, and the perpetual fighter against niggardly underworld powers for the good gifts which they refused to allow out of their keeping. Shoulder to shoulder with him in this 'holy war' of culture against ignorance, and light against darkness, stood his brothers Amaethon, god of agriculture, and Govannan, a god of smithcraft identical with the Gaelic Giobniu. He had also a sister called Arianrod, or 'Silver Circle', who, as is common in mythologies, was not only his sister, but also his wife. So Zeus wedded Heré; and, indeed, it is difficult to say where otherwise the partners of gods are to come from. Of this connection two sons were born at one birth – Dylan and Lieu, who are considered as representing the twin powers of darkness and light. With darkness the sea was inseparably connected by the Celts, and, as soon as the dark twin was born and named, he plunged headlong into his native element. 'And immediately when he was in the sea,' says the Mabinogi of Mâth, son of Mâthonwy, 'he took its nature, and swam as well as the best fish that was therein. And for that reason was he called Dylan, the Son of the Wave. Beneath him no wave ever broke.' He was killed with a spear at last by his uncle, Govannan, and, according to the bard Taliesin, the waves of Britain, Ireland, Scotland, and the Isle of Man wept for him. Beautiful legends grew up around his death. The clamour of the waves dashing upon the beach is the expression of their longing to avenge their son. The sound of the sea rushing up the mouth of the River Conway is still known as 'Dylan's death-groan'. A small promontory on the Carnarvonshire side of the Menai Straits, called *Pwynt Maen Tylen*, or *Pwynt Maen Dulan*, preserves his name.

The other child of Gwydion and Arianrod grew up to become the British sun-god, Lleu Llaw Gyffes, the exact counterpart of the Gaelic Lugh Lamh-fada, 'Light the Long-handed'. Like all solar deities, his growth was rapid. When he was a year old, he seemed to be two years; at the age of two, he travelled by himself; and when he was four years old, he was as tall as a boy of eight, and was his father's constant companion.

One day, Gwydion took him to the castle of Arianrod – not her castle in the sky, but her abode on earth, the still-remembered site of which is marked by a patch of rocks in the Menai Straits, accessible without a boat only during the lowest spring and autumn tides. Arianrod had disowned her son, and did not recognize him when she saw him with Gwydion. She asked who he was, and was much displeased when told.

She demanded to know his name, and, when Gwydion replied that he had as yet received none, she 'laid a destiny upon' him, after the fashion of the Celts, that he should be without a name until she chose to bestow one on him herself.

To be without a name was a very serious thing to the ancient Britons, who seem to have held the primitive theory that the name and the soul are the same. So Gwydion cast about to think by what craft he might extort from Arianrod some remark from which he could name their son. The next day, he went down to the sea-shore with the boy, both of them disguised as cordwainers. He made a boat out of sea-weed by magic, and some beautifully-coloured leather out of some dry sticks and sedges. Then they sailed the boat to the port of Arianrod's castle, and, anchoring it where it could be seen, began ostentatiously to stitch away at the leather. Naturally, they were soon noticed, and Arianrod sent someone out to see who they were and what they were doing. When she found that they were shoemakers, she remembered that she wanted some shoes. Gwydion, though he had her measure, purposely made them, first too large, and then too small. This brought Arianrod herself down to the boat to be fitted.

While Gwydion was measuring Arianrod's foot for the shoes, a wren came and stood upon the deck. The boy took his bow and arrow, and hit the wren in the leg – a favourite shot of Celtic 'crack' archers, at any rate in romance. The goddess was pleased to be amiable and complimentary. 'Truly,' said she, 'the lion aimed at it with a steady hand.' It is from such incidents that primitive people take their names, all the world over. The boy had got his. 'It is no thanks to you,' said Gwydion to Arianrod, 'but now he has a name. And a good name it is. He shall be called Llew Llaw Gyffes.'

This name of the sun-god is a good example of how obsolete the ancient pagan tradition had become before it was put into writing. The old word *Lleu*, meaning 'light', had passed out of use, and the scribe substituted for a name that was unintelligible to him one like it which he knew, namely *Llew*, meaning 'lion'. The word *Gyffes* seems also to have suffered change, and to have meant originally not 'steady', but 'long'.

At any rate, Arianrod was defeated in her design to keep her son nameless. Neither did she even get her shoes; for, as soon as he had gained his object, Gwydion allowed the boat to change back into sea-weed, and the leather to return to sedge and sticks. So, in her anger, she put a fresh destiny on the boy, that he should not take arms till she herself gave them him.

Gwydion, however, took Lleu to Dinas Dinllev his castle, which still stands at the edge of the Menai Straits, and brought him up as a warrior. As soon as he thought him old enough to have arms, he took him with him again to Caer Arianrod. This time, they were disguised as bards. Arianrod received them gladly, heard Gwydion's songs and tales, feasted them, and prepared a room for them to sleep in.

The next morning, Gwydion got up very early, and prepared his most powerful incantations. By his druidical arts he made it seem as if the whole country rang with the shouts and trumpets of an army, and he put a glamour over everyone, so that they saw the bay filled with ships. Arianrod came to him in terror, asking what could be done to protect the castle. 'Give us arms,' he replied, 'and we will do the best we can.' So Arianrod's maidens armed Gwydion, while Arianrod herself put arms on Lleu. By the time she had finished, all the noises had ceased, and the ships had vanished. 'Let us take our arms off again,' said Gwydion; 'we shall not need them now.' 'But the army is all round the castle!' cried Arianrod. 'There was no army,' answered Gwydion; 'it was only an illusion of mine to cause you to break your prophecy and give our son arms. And now he has got them, without thanks to you.' 'Then I will lay a worse destiny on him,' cried the infuriated goddess. 'He shall never have a wife of the people of this earth.' 'He shall have a wife in spite of you,' said Gwydion.

So Gwydion went to Mâth, his uncle and tutor in magic, and between them they made a woman out of flowers by charms and illusion. 'They took the blossoms of the oak, and the blossoms of the broom, and the blossoms of the meadow-sweet, and produced from them a maiden, the fairest and most graceful that man ever saw.' They called her Blodeuwedd (Flower-face), and gave her to Lleu as his wife. And they gave Lleu a palace called Mur y Castell, near Bala Lake.

All went well until, one day, Gronw Pebyr, one of the gods of darkness, came by, hunting, and killed the stag at nightfall near Lieu's castle. The sun-god was away upon a visit to Mâth, but Blodeuwedd asked the stranger to take shelter with her. That night they fell in love with one another, and conspired together how Lleu might be put away. When Lleu came back from Mâth's court, Blodeuwedd, like a Celtic Dalilah, wormed out of him the secret of how his life was preserved. He told her that he could only die in one way; he could not be killed either inside or outside a house, either on horseback or on foot, but that if a spear that had been a year in the making, and which was never worked upon except during the sacrifice on Sunday, were to be cast at him as he stood beneath a roof of thatch, after having just bathed, with one foot upon the edge of the bath and the other upon a buck goat's back, it would cause his death. Blodeuwedd piously thanked Heaven that he was so well protected, and sent a messenger to her paramour, telling him what she had learned. Gronw set to work on the spear; and in a year it was ready. When she knew this, Blodeuwedd asked

Lleu to show her exactly how it was he could be killed.

Lleu agreed; and Blodeuwedd prepared the bath under the thatched roof, and tethered the goat by it. Lleu bathed, and then stood with one foot upon the edge of the bath, and the other upon the goat's back. At this moment, Gronw, from an ambush, flung the spear, and hit Lleu, who, with a terrible cry, changed into an eagle, and flew away. He never came back; and Gronw took possession of both his wife and his palace.

But Gwydion set out to search everywhere for his son. At last, one day, he came to a house in North Wales where the man was in great anxiety about his sow; for as soon as the sty was opened, every morning, she rushed out, and did not return again till late in the evening. Gwydion offered to follow her, and, at dawn, the man took him to the sty, and opened the door. The sow leaped forth, and ran, and Gwydion ran after her. He tracked her to a brook between Snowdon and the sea, still called Nant y Llew, and saw her feeding underneath an oak. Upon the top of the tree there was an eagle, and, every time it shook itself, there fell off it lumps of putrid meat, which the sow ate greedily. Gwydion suspected that the eagle must be Lleu. So he sang this verse:

> 'Oak that grows between the two banks; Darkened is
> the sky and hill! Shall I not tell him by his wounds,
> That this is Lleu?'

The eagle, on hearing this, came half-way down the tree. So Gwydion sang:

> 'Oak that grows in upland ground, Is it not wetted by
> the rain? Has it not been drenched By nine score

tempests? It bears in its branches Lleu Llaw Gyffes.'

The eagle came slowly down until it was on the lowest branch. Gwydion sang:

'Oak that grows beneath the steep; Stately and majestic is its aspect! Shall I not speak it? That Lleu will come to my lap?'

Then the eagle came down, and sat on Gwydion's knee. Gwydion struck it with his magic wand, and it became Lleu again, wasted to skin and bone by the poison on the spear.

Gwydion took him to Mâth to be healed, and left him there, while he went to Mur y Castell, where Blodeuwedd was. When she heard that he was coming, she fled. But Gwydion overtook her, and changed her into an owl, the bird that hates the day. A still older form of this probably extremely ancient myth of the sun-god – the savage and repulsive details of which speak of a hoary antiquity – makes the chase of Blodeuwedd by Gwydion to have taken place in the sky, the stars scattered over the Milky Way being the traces of it. As for her accomplice, Lleu would accept no satisfaction short of Gronw's submitting to stand exactly where Lleu had stood, to be shot at in his turn. To this he was obliged to agree; and Lleu killed him.

There are two other sons of Beli and Dôn of whom so little is recorded that it would hardly be worth while mentioning them, were it not for the wild poetry of the legend connected with them. The tale, put into writing at a time when all the gods were being transfigured into simple mortals, tells us that they were two kings of Britain, brothers. One starlight night they were walking together.

'See,' said Nynniaw to Peibaw, 'what a fine, wide-spreading field I have.' 'Where is it?' asked Peibaw. 'There,' replied Nynniaw; 'the whole stretch of the sky, as far as the eye reaches.' 'Look then,' returned Peibaw, 'what a number of cattle I have grazing on your field.' 'Where are they?' asked Nynniaw. 'All the stars that you can see,' replied Peibaw, 'every one of them of fiery-coloured gold, with the moon for a shepherd over them.' 'They shall not feed on my field,' cried Nynniaw. 'They shall,' exclaimed Peibaw. 'They shall not,' cried Nynniaw, 'They shall,' said Peibaw. 'They shall not,' Nynniaw answered; and so they went on, from contradiction to quarrel, and from private quarrel to civil war, until the armies of both of them were destroyed, and the two authors of the evil were turned by God into oxen for their sins.

Last of the children of Dôn, we find a goddess called Penardun, of whom little is known except that she was married to the sea-god Llyr. This incident is curious, as forming a parallel to the Gaelic story which tells of intermarriage between the Tuatha Dé Danann and the Fomors. Brigit, the Dagda's daughter, was married to Bress, son of Elathan, while Cian, the son of Diancecht, wedded Ethniu, the daughter of Balor. So, in this kindred mythology, a slender tie of relationship binds the gods of the sky to the gods of the sea.

The name *Llyr* is supposed, like its Irish equivalent Lêr, to have meant 'the Sea'. The British sea-god is undoubtedly the same as the Gaelic; indeed, the two facts that he is described in Welsh literature as Llyr Llediath, that is, 'Llyr of the Foreign Dialect', and is given a wife called Iweridd (Ireland), suggest that he may have been borrowed by the Britons from the Gaels later than any mythology common to both. As a British god, he was the far-off original of Shakespeare's 'King Lear'. The chief city of his worship is still called after him, Leicester, that is, Llyr-cestre, in still earlier days, Caer Llyr.

Llyr, we have noticed, married two wives, Penardun and Iweridd. By the daughter of Dôn he had a son called Manawyddan, who is identical with the Gaelic Manannán mac Lir. We know less of his character and attributes than we do of the Irish god; but we find him equally a ruler in that Hades or Elysium which the Celtic mind ever connected with the sea. Like all the inhabitants. of that other world, he is at once a master of magic and of the useful arts, which he taught willingly to his friends. To his enemies, however, he could show a different side of his character. A triad tells us that –

'The achievement of Manawyddan the Wise,
After lamentation and fiery wrath, Was the constructing
of the bone-fortress of Oeth and Anoeth',

which is described as a prison made, in the shape of a bee-hive, entirely of human bones mortared together, and divided into innumerable cells, forming a kind of labyrinth. In this ghastly place he immured those whom he found trespassing in Hades; and among his captives was no less a person than the famous Arthur.

'Ireland' bore two children to Llyr: a daughter called Branwen and a son called Brân. The little we know of Branwen of the 'Fair Bosom' shows her as a goddess of love – child, like the Greek Aphrodité, of the sea. Brân, on the other hand, is, even more clearly than Manawyddan, a dark deity of Hades. He is represented as of colossal size, so huge, in fact, that no house or ship was big enough to hold him. He delighted in battle and carnage, like the hoodie-crow or raven from which he probably took his name, but he was also the especial patron of bards, minstrels, and musicians, and we find him in one of the poems ascribed to Taliesin claiming to be himself a bard, a harper, a player on the crowth, and seven-score other musicians all at once. His son was called Caradawc the Strong-armed, who, as the British mythology crumbled, became confounded with the historical Caratacus, known popularly as 'Caractacus'.

Both Brân and Manawyddan were especially connected with the Swansea peninsula. The bone-fortress of Oeth and Anoeth was placed by tradition in Gower. That Brân was equally at home there may be proved from the Morte Darthur, in which store-house of forgotten and misunderstood mythology Brân of Gower survives as 'King Brandegore'.

Such identification of a mere mortal country with the other world seems strange enough to us, but to our Celtic ancestors it was a quite natural thought. All islands – and peninsulas, which, viewed from an opposite coast, probably seemed to them islands – were deemed to be pre-eminently homes of the dark Powers of Hades. Difficult of access, protected by the turbulent and dangerous sea, sometimes rendered quite invisible by fogs and mists and, at other times, looming up ghostlily on the horizon, often held by the remnant of a hostile lower race, they gained a mystery and a sanctity from the law of the human mind which has always held the unknown to be the terrible. The Cornish Britons, gazing from the shore, saw Gower and Lundy, and deemed them outposts of the over-sea Other World. To the Britons of Wales, Ireland was no human realm, a view reciprocated by the Gaels, who saw Hades in Britain, while the Isle of Man was a little Hades common to them both. Nor even was the sea always necessary to sunder the world of ghosts from that of 'shadow-casting men'. Glastonbury

Tor, surrounded by almost impassable swamps, was one of the especial haunts of Gwyn ap Nudd. The Britons of the north held that beyond the Roman wall and the vast Caledonian wood lived ghosts and not men. Even the Roman province of Demetia – called by the Welsh Dyfed, and corresponding, roughly, to the modern County of Pembrokeshire – was, as a last stronghold of the aborigines, identified with the mythic underworld.

As such, Dyfed was ruled by a local tribe of gods, whose greatest figures were Pwyll, 'Head of Annwn' (the Welsh name for Hades), with his wife Rhiannon, and their son Pryderi. These beings are described as hostile to the children of Dôn, but friendly to the race of Llyr. After Pwyll's death or disappearance, his widow Rhiannon becomes the wife of Manawyddan. In a poem of Taliesin's we find Manawyddan and Pryderi joint-rulers of Hades, and warders of that magic cauldron of inspiration which the gods of light attempted to steal or capture, and which became famous afterwards as the 'Holy Grail'. Another of their treasures were the 'Three Birds of Rhiannon', which, we are told in an ancient book, could sing the dead to life and the living into the sleep of death. Fortunately they sang seldom. 'There are three things,' says a Welsh triad, 'which are not often heard: the song of the birds of Rhiannon, a song of wisdom from the mouth of a Saxon, and an invitation to a feast from a miser.'

Nor is the list of British gods complete without mention of Arthur, though most readers will be surprised to find him in such company. The genius of Tennyson, who drew his materials mostly from the Norman-French romances, has stereotyped the popular conception of Arthur as a king of early Britain who fought for his fatherland and the Christian faith against invading Saxons. Possibly there may, indeed, have been a powerful British chieftain bearing that typically Celtic name, which is found in Irish legend as Artur, one of the sons of Nemed who fought against the Fomors, and on the Continent as Artaius, a Gaulish deity whom the Romans identified with Mercury, and who seems to have been a patron of agriculture. But the original Arthur stands upon the same ground as Cuchulainn and Finn. His deeds are mythical, because superhuman. His companions can be shown to have been divine. Some we know were worshipped in Gaul. Others are children of Dôn, of Llyr, and of Pwyll, dynasties of older gods to whose head Arthur seems to have risen, as his cult waxed and theirs waned. Stripped of their godhead, and strangely transformed, they fill the pages of romance as Knights of the Table Round.

These deities were the native gods of Britain. Many others are, however, mentioned upon inscriptions found in our island, but these were almost all exotic and imported. Imperial Rome brought men of diverse races among her legions, and these men brought their gods. Scattered over Britain, but especially in the north, near the Wall, we find evidence that deities of many nations – from Germany to Africa, and from Gaul to Persia – were sporadically worshipped. Most of these foreign gods were Roman, but a temple at Eboracum (now York) was dedicated to Serapis, and Mithras, the Persian sun-god, was also adored there; while at Corbridge, in Northumberland (the ancient Corspitium), there have been found altars to the Tyrian Hercules and to Astarte. The war-god was also invoked under many strange names – as 'Cocidius' by a colony of Dacians in Cumberland; as Toutates, Camulus, Coritiacus, Belatucador, Alator, Loucetius, Condates, and Rigisamos by men of different countries. A goddess of war was worshipped at Bath under the name of Nemetona. The hot springs of the same town were under the patronage of a divinity called Sul, identified by the Romans with Minerva, and she was helped by a god of medicine described on a dedicatory tablet as 'Sol Apollo Anicetus'. Few of these 'strange gods', however, seem to have taken hold of the imagination of the native Britons. Their worshippers did not proselytize, and their general influence was probably about equal to that of an Evangelical Church in a Turkish town. The sole exceptions to this rule are where the foreign gods are Gaulish; but in several instances it can be proved that they were not so much of Roman, as of original Celtic importation. The warlike heaven-god Camulus appears in Gaelic heroic myth as Cumhal, the father of Finn, and in British mythical history as Coel, a duke of Caer Coelvin (known earlier as Camulodunum, and now as Colchester), who seized the crown of Britain, and spent his short reign in a series of battles. The name of the sun-god Maponos is found alike upon altars in Gaul and Britain, and in Welsh literature as Mabon, a follower of Arthur; while another Gaulish sun-god, Belinus, who had a splendid temple at Bajocassos (the modern Bayeux), though not mentioned in the earliest British mythology, as its scattered records have come down to us, must have been connected with Brân; for we find in Geoffrey of Monmouth's History 'King Belinus' as brother of 'King Brennius', and in the Morte Darthur 'Balin' as brother of 'Balan'. A second-century Greek writer gives an account of a god of eloquence worshipped in Gaul under the name of Ogmios, and represented as equipped like Heracles, a description which exactly corresponds to the conception of the Gaelic Ogma, at once patron of literature and writing and professional strong man of the Tuatha Dé Danann. Nemetona, the war-goddess worshipped at Bath, was probably the same as Nemon, one of Nuada's Valkyr-wives, while a broken inscription to *athubodva*, which probably stood, when intact, for *Cathubodva*, may well have been addressed to the Gaulish equivalent of Badb Catha, the 'War-fury'. Lugh, or Lleu, was also widely known on the Continent as Lugus. Three important towns – Laon, Leyden, and Lyons – were all anciently called after him *Lugu-dunum* (Lugus' town), and at the last and greatest of these a festival was still held in Roman times upon the sun-god's day – the first of August – which corresponded to the *Lugnassad* (Lugh's commemoration) held in ancient Ireland. Brigit, the Gaelic Minerva, is also found in Britain as Brigantia, tutelary goddess of the Brigantes, a Northern tribe, and in Eastern France as Brigindo, to whom Iccavos, son of Oppianos, made a dedicatory offering of which there is still record.

Other, less striking agreements between the mythical divine names of the Insular and Continental Celts might be cited. These recorded should, however, prove sufficiently that Gaul, Gael, and Briton shared in a common heritage of mythological names and ideas, which they separately developed into three superficially different, but essentially similar cults.

XIII

THE ADVENTURES OF THE GODS OF HADES

It is with the family of Pwyll, deities connected with the southwest corner of Wales, called by the Romans Demetia, and by the Britons Dyfed, and, roughly speaking, identical with the modern county of Pembrokeshire, that the earliest consecutive accounts of the British gods begin. The first of the Four Branches of the Mabinogi tell us how 'Pwyll, Prince of Dyfed', gained the right to be called *Pen Annwn*, the 'Head of Hades'. Indeed, it almost seems as if it had been deliberately written to explain how the same person could be at once a mere mortal prince, however legendary, and a ruler in the mystic Other World, and so to reconcile two conflicting traditions. But to an earlier age than that in which the legend was put into a literary shape, such forced reconciliation would not have been needed; for the two legends would not have been considered to conflict. When Pwyll, head of Annwn, was a mythic person whose tradition was still alive, the unexplored, rugged, and savage country of Dyfed, populated by the aboriginal Iberians whom the Celt had driven into such remote districts, appeared to those who dwelt upon the eastern side of its dividing river, the Tawë, at least a dependency of Annwn, if not that weird realm itself. But, as men grew bolder, the frontier was crossed, and Dyfed entered and traversed, and found to be not so unlike other countries. Its inhabitants, if not of Celtic race, were yet of flesh and blood. So that, though the province still continued to bear to a late date the names of the 'Land of Illusion' and the 'Realm of Glamour', it was no longer deemed to be Hades itself. That fitful and shadowy country had folded its tents, and departed over or under seas.

The story of 'Pwyll, Prince of Dyfed', tells us how there was war in Annwn between its two kings – or between two, perhaps, of its many chieftains. Arawn ('Silver-Tongue') and Havgan ('Summer-White') each coveted the dominions of the other. In the continual contests between them, Arawn was worsted, and in despair he visited the upper earth to seek for a mortal ally.

At this time Pwyll, Prince of Dyfed, held his court at Narberth. He had, however, left his capital upon a hunting expedition to Glyn Cûch, known to-day as a valley upon the borders of the two counties of Pembroke and Carmarthen. Like so many kings of European and Oriental romance, when an adventure is at hand, he became separated from his party, and was, in modern parlance, 'thrown out'. He could, however, still hear the music of his hounds, and was listening to them, when he also distinguished the cry of another pack coming towards him. As he watched and listened, a stag came into view; and the strange hounds pulled it down almost at his feet. At first Pwyll hardly looked at the stag, he was so taken up with gazing at the hounds, for 'of all the hounds that he had seen in the world, he had never seen any that were like unto these. For their hair was of a brilliant shining white, and their ears were red; and as the whiteness of their bodies shone, so did the redness of their ears glisten.' They were, indeed, though Pwyll does not seem to have known it, of the true Hades breed – the snow-white, red-eared hounds we meet in Gaelic legends, and which are still said to be sometimes heard and seen scouring the hills of Wales by night. Seeing no rider with the hounds, Pwyll drove them away from the dead stag, and called up his own pack to it.

While he was doing this, a man 'upon a large, light-gray steed, with a hunting-horn round his neck, and clad in garments of gray woollen in the fashion of a hunting garb' appeared, and rated Pwyll for his unsportsmanlike conduct. 'Greater discourtesy,' said he, 'I never saw than your driving away my dogs after they had killed the stag, and calling your own to it. And though I may not be revenged upon you for this, I swear that I will do you more damage than the value of a hundred stags.'

Pwyll expressed his contrition, and, asking the new-comer's name and rank, offered to atone for his fault. The stranger told his name – Arawn, a king of Annwn – and said that Pwyll could gain his forgiveness only in one way, by going to Annwn instead of him, and fighting for him with Havgan. Pwyll agreed to do this, and the King of Hades put his own semblance upon the mortal prince, so that not a person in Annwn – not even Arawn's own wife – would know that he was not that king. He led him by a secret path into Annwn, and left him before his castle, charging him to return to the place where they had first met, at the end of a year from that day. On the other hand, Arawn took on Pwyll's shape, and went to Narberth.

No one in Annwn suspected Pwyll of being anyone else than their king. He spent the year in ruling the realm, in hunting, minstrelsy, and feasting. Both by day and night, he had the company of Arawn's wife, the most beautiful woman he had ever yet seen, but he refrained from taking advantage of the trust placed in him. At last the day came when he was to meet Havgan in single combat. One blow settled it; for Pwyll, Havgan's destined conqueror, thrust his antagonist an arm's and a spear's length over the crupper of his horse, breaking his shield and armour, and mortally wounding him. Havgan was carried away to die, and Pwyll, in the guise of Arawn, received the submission of the dead king's subjects, and annexed his realm. Then he went back to Glyn Cûch, to keep his tryst with Arawn.

They retook their own shapes, and each returned to his own kingdom. Pwyll learned that Dyfed had never been ruled so well, or been so prosperous, as during the year just passed. As for the King of Hades, he found his enemy gone, and his domains extended. And when he caressed his wife, she asked him why he did so now, after the lapse of a whole year. So he told her the truth, and they both agreed that they had indeed got a true friend in Pwyll.

After this, the kings of Annwn and Dyfed made their friendship strong between them. From that time forward, says the story, Pwyll was no longer called Prince of Dyfed, but Pen Annwn, 'the Head of Hades'.

The second mythological incident in the Mabinogi of Pwyll, Prince of Dyfed, tells how the Head of Hades won his wife, Rhiannon, thought by Professor Rhys to have been a goddess either of the dawn or of the moon. There was a mound outside Pwyll's palace at Narberth which had a magical quality. To anyone who sat upon it there happened one of two things: either he received wounds and blows, or else he saw a wonder. One day, it occurred to Pwyll that he would like to try the experience of the mound. So he went and sat upon it.

No unseen blows assailed Pwyll, but he had not been sitting long upon the mound before he saw, coming towards him, 'a lady on a pure-white horse of large size, with a garment of shining gold around her', riding very quietly. He sent a man on foot to ask her who she was, but, though she seemed to be moving so slowly, the man could not come up to her. He failed utterly to overtake her, and she passed on out of sight.

The next day, Pwyll went again to the mound. The lady appeared, and, this time, Pwyll sent a horseman. At first, the horseman only ambled along at about the same pace at which the lady seemed to be going; then, failing to get near her, he urged his horse into a gallop. But, whether he rode slow or fast, he could come no closer to the lady than before, although she seemed to the eyes of those who watched to have been going only at a foot's pace.

The day after that, Pwyll determined to accost the lady himself. She came at the same gentle walk, and Pwyll at first rode easily, and then at his horse's topmost speed, but with the same result, or lack of it. At last, in despair, he called to the mysterious damsel to stop. 'I will stop gladly,' said she, 'and it would have been better for your horse if you had asked me before.' She told him that her name was Rhiannon, daughter of Heveydd the Ancient. The nobles of her realm had determined to give her in marriage against her will, so she had come to seek out Pwyll, who was the man of her choice. Pwyll was delighted to hear this, for he thought that she was the most beautiful lady he had ever seen. Before they parted, they had plighted troth, and Pwyll had promised to appear on that day twelvemonth at the palace of her father, Heveydd. Then she vanished, and Pwyll returned to Narberth.

At the appointed time, Pwyll went to visit Heveydd the Ancient, with a hundred followers. He was received with much welcome, and the disposition of the feast put under his command, as the Celts seem to have done to especially honoured guests. As they sat at meat, with Pwyll between Rhiannon and her father, a tall auburn-haired youth came into the hall, greeted Pwyll, and asked a boon of him. 'Whatever boon you may ask of me,' said Pwyll thoughtlessly, 'if it is in my power, you shall have it.' Then the suitor threw off all disguise, called the guests to witness Pwyll's promise, and claimed Rhiannon as his bride. Pwyll was dumb. 'Be silent as long as you will,' said the masterful Rhiannon; 'never did a man make worse use of his wits than you have done.' 'Lady,' replied the amazed Pwyll, 'I knew not who he was.' 'He is the man to whom they would have given me against my will,' she answered, 'Gwawl, the son of Clûd. You must bestow me upon him now, lest shame befall you.' 'Never will I do that,' said Pwyll. 'Bestow me upon him,' she insisted, 'and I will cause that I shall never be his.' So Pwyll promised Gwawl that he would make a feast that day year, at which he would resign Rhiannon to him.

The next year, the feast was made, and Rhiannon sat by the side of her unwelcome bridegroom. But Pwyll was waiting outside the palace, with a hundred men in ambush. When the banquet was at its height, he came into the hall, dressed in coarse, ragged garments, shod with clumsy old shoes, and carrying a leather bag. But the bag was a magic one, which Rhiannon had given to her lover, with directions as to its use. Its quality was that, however much was put into it, it could never be filled. 'I crave a boon,' he said to Gwawl. 'What is it?' Gwawl replied. 'I am a poor man, and all I ask is to have this bag filled with meat.' Gwawl granted what he said was 'a request within reason', and ordered his followers to fill the bag. But the more they put into it, the more room in it there seemed to be. Gwawl was astonished, and asked why this was. Pwyll replied that it was a bag that could never be filled until someone possessed of lands and riches should tread the food down with both his feet. 'Do this for the man,' said Rhiannon to Gwawl. 'Gladly I will,' replied he, and put both his feet into the bag. But no sooner had he done so than Pwyll slipped the bag over Gwawl's head, and tied it up at the mouth. He blew his horn, and all his followers came in. 'What have you got in the bag?' asked each one in turn. 'A badger,' replied Pwyll. Then each, as he received Pwyll's answer, kicked the bag, or hit it with a stick. 'Then,' says the story, 'was the game of "Badger in the Bag" first played.'

Gwawl, however, fared better than we suspect that the badger usually did; for Heveydd the Ancient interceded for him. Pwyll willingly released him, on condition that he promised to give up all claim to Rhiannon, and renounced all projects of revenge. Gwawl consented, and gave sureties, and went away to his own country to have his bruises healed.

This country of Gwawl's was, no doubt, the sky; for he was evidently a sun-god. His name bewrays him; for the meaning of 'Gwawl' is 'light'. It was one of the hours of victory for the dark powers, such as were celebrated in the Celtic calendar by the Feast of Samhain, or Summer End.

There was no hindrance now to the marriage of Pwyll and Rhiannon. She became his bride, and returned with him to Dyfed.

For three years, they were without an heir, and the nobles of Dyfed became discontented. They petitioned Pwyll to take another wife instead of Rhiannon. He asked for a year's delay. This was granted, and, before the end of the year, a son was born. But, on the night of his birth, the six women set to keep watch over Rhiannon all fell asleep at once; and when they woke up, the boy had vanished. Fearful lest their lives should be forfeited for their neglect, they agreed to swear that Rhiannon had eaten her child.

They killed a litter of puppies, and smeared some of the blood on Rhiannon's face and hands, and put some of the bones by her side. Then they awoke her with a great outcry, and accused her. She swore that she knew nothing of the death of her son, but the women persisted that they had seen her devour him, and had been unable to prevent it. The druids of that day were not sufficiently practical anatomists to be able to tell the bones of a child from those of a dog, so they condemned Rhiannon upon the evidence of the women. But, even now, Pwyll would not put her away; so she was assigned a penance. For seven years, she was to sit by a horse-block outside the gate, and offer to carry visitors into the palace upon her back. 'But it rarely happened,' says the Mabinogi, 'that any would permit her to do so.'

Exactly what had become of Rhiannon's child seems to have been a mystery even to the writer of the Mabinogi. It was, at any rate, in some way connected with the equally mysterious disappearance on every night of the first of May – Beltaine, the Celtic sun-festival – of the colts foaled by a beautiful mare belonging to Teirnyon Twryv Vliant, one of Pwyll's vassals. Every May-day night, the mare foaled, but no one knew what became of the colt. Teirnyon decided to find out. He caused the mare to be taken into a house, and there he watched it, fully armed. Early in the night, the colt was born. Then there was a great noise, and an arm with claws came through the window, and gripped the colt's mane. Teirnyon hacked at the arm with his sword, and cut it off. Then he heard wailing, and opened the door, and found a baby in swaddling clothes, wrapped in a satin mantle. He took it up and brought it to his wife, and they decided to adopt it. They called the boy Gwri Wallt Euryn, that is 'Gwri of the Golden Hair'.

The older the boy grew, the more it seemed to Teirnyon that he became like Pwyll. Then he remembered that he had found him upon the very night that Rhiannon lost her child. So he consulted with his wife, and they both agreed that the baby they had so mysteriously found must be the same that Rhiannon had so mysteriously lost. And they decided that it would not be right for them to keep the son of another, while so good a lady as Rhiannon was being punished wrongfully.

So, the very next day, Teirnyon set out for Narberth, taking the boy with him. They found Rhiannon sitting, as usual, by the gate, but they would not allow her to carry them into the palace on her back. Pwyll welcomed them; and that evening, as they sat at supper, Teirnyon told his hosts the story from beginning to end. And he presented her son to Rhiannon.

As soon as everyone in the palace saw the boy, they admitted that he must be Pwyll's son. So they adopted him with delight; and Pendaran Dyfed, the head druid of the kingdom, gave him a new name. He called him 'Pryderi', meaning 'trouble', from the first word that his mother had uttered when he was restored to her. For she had said: '*Trouble* is, indeed, at an end for me, if this be true'.

XIV

THE WOOING OF BRANWEN AND THE BEHEADING OF BRÂN

In the second of the 'Four Branches', Pryderi, come to man's estate, and married to a wife called Kicva, appears as a guest or vassal at the court of a greater god of Hades than himself – Brân, the son of the sea-god Llyr. The children of Llyr – Brân, with his sister Branwen of the 'Fair Bosom' and his half-brother Manawyddan, as well as two sons of Manawyddan's mother, Penardun, by an earlier marriage, were holding court at *Twr Branwen*, 'Branwen's Tower', now called Harlech. As they sat on a cliff, looking over the sea, they saw thirteen ships coming from Ireland. The fleet sailed close under the land, and Brân sent messengers to ask who they were, and why they had come. It was replied that they were the vessels of Matholwch, King of Ireland, and that he had come to ask Brân for his sister Branwen in marriage. Brân consented, and they fixed upon Aberffraw, in Anglesey, as the place at which to hold the wedding feast. Matholwch and his fleet went there by sea, and Brân and his host by land. When they arrived, and met, they set up pavilions; for 'no house could ever hold the blessed Brân'. And there Branwen became the King of Ireland's bride.

These relations were not long, however, allowed to be friendly. Of the two other sons of Llyr's wife, Penardun, the mother of Manawyddan, one was called Nissyen, and the other, Evnissyen.

Nissyen was a lover of peace, and would always 'cause his family to be friends when their wrath was at the highest', but Evnissyen 'would cause strife between his two brothers when they were most at peace'. Now Evnissyen was enraged because his consent had not been asked to Branwen's marriage. Out of spite at this, he cut off the lips, ears, eyebrows, and tails of all Matholwch's horses.

When the King of Ireland found this out, he was very indignant at the insult. But Brân sent an embassy to him twice, explaining that it had not been done by his consent or with his knowledge. He appeased Matholwch by giving him a sound horse in place of every one that Evnissyen had mutilated, as well as a staff of silver as large and tall as Matholwch himself, and a plate of gold as broad as Matholwch's face. To these gifts he also added a magic cauldron brought from Ireland. Its property was that any slain man who was put into it was brought to life again, except that he lost the use of speech. The King of Ireland accepted this recompense for the insult done him, renewed his friendship with the children of Llyr, and sailed away with Branwen to Ireland.

Before a year was over, Branwen bore a son. They called him Gwern, and put him out to be foster-nursed among the best men of Ireland. But, during the second year, news came to Ireland of the insult that Matholwch had received in Britain. The King of Ireland's foster-brothers and near relations insisted that he should revenge himself upon Branwen. So the queen was compelled to serve in the kitchen, and, every day, the butcher gave her a box upon the ear. That this should not become known to Brân, all traffic was forbidden between Ireland and Britain. This went on for three years.

But, in the meantime, Branwen had reared a tame starling, and she taught it to speak, and tied a letter of complaint to the root of its wing, and sent it off to Britain. At last it found Brân, whom its mistress had described to it, and settled upon his shoulder, ruffling its wings. This exposed the letter, and Brân read it. He sent messengers to one hundred and forty-four countries, to raise an army to go to Ireland. Leaving his son Caradawc, with seven others, in charge of Britain, he started – himself wading through the sea, while his men went by ship.

No one in Ireland knew that they were coming until the royal swineherds, tending their pigs near the sea-shore, beheld a marvel. They saw a forest on the surface of the sea – a place where certainly no forest had been before – and, near it, a mountain with a lofty ridge on its top, and a lake on each side of the ridge. Both the forest and the mountain were swiftly moving towards Ireland. They informed Matholwch, who could not understand it, and sent messengers to ask Branwen what she thought it might be. 'It is the men of the Island of the Mighty,' said she, 'who are coming here because they have heard of my ill-treatment. The forest that is seen on the sea is made of the masts of ships. The mountain is my brother Brân, wading into shoal water; the lofty ridge is his nose, and the two lakes, one on each side of it, are his eyes.'

The men of Ireland were terrified. They fled beyond the Shannon, and broke down the bridge over it. But Brân lay down across the river, and his army walked over him to the opposite side.

Matholwch now sent messengers suing for peace. He offered to resign the throne of Ireland to Gwern, Branwen's son and Brân's nephew. 'Shall I not have the kingdom myself?' said Brân, and would not hear of anything else. So the counsellors of Matholwch advised him to conciliate Brân by building him a house so large that it would be the first house that had ever held him, and, in it, to hand over the kingdom to his will. Brân consented to accept this, and the vast house was built.

It concealed treachery. Upon each side of the hundred pillars of the house was hung a bag, and in the bag was an armed man, who was to cut himself out at a given signal. But Evnissyen came into the house, and seeing the bags there, suspected the plot. 'What is in this bag?' he said to one of the Irish, as he came up to the first one. 'Meal,' replied the Irishman. Then Evnissyen kneaded the bag in his hands, as though it really contained meal, until he had killed the man inside; and he treated all of them in turn in the same way.

A little later, the two hosts met in the house. The men of Ireland came in on one side, and the men of Britain on the other, and met at the hearth in the middle, and sat down. The Irish court did homage to Brân, and they crowned Gwern, Branwen's son, King of Ireland in place of Matholwch. When the ceremonies were over, the boy went from one to another of his uncles, to make acquaintance with them. Brân fondled and caressed him, and so did Manawyddan, and Nissyen. But when he came to Evnissyen, the wicked son of Penardun seized the child by the feet, and dropped him head first into the great fire.

When Branwen saw her son killed, she tried to leap into the flames after him, but Brân held her back. Then every man armed himself, and such a tumult was never heard in one house before. Day after day they fought; but the Irish had the advantage, for they had only to plunge their dead men into the magic cauldron to bring them back to life. When Evnissyen knew this, he saw a way of atoning for the misfortunes his evil nature had brought upon Britain. He disguised himself as an Irishman, and lay upon the floor as if dead, until they put him into the cauldron. Then he stretched himself, and, with one desperate effort, burst both the cauldron and his own heart.

Thus things were made equal again, and in the next battle the men of Britain killed all the Irish. But of themselves there were only seven left unhurt – Pryderi; Manawyddan; Gluneu, the son of Taran; Taliesin the Bard; Ynawc; Grudyen, the son of Muryel; and Heilyn, the son of Gwynn the Ancient.

Brân himself was wounded in the foot with a poisoned dart, and was in agony. So he ordered his seven surviving followers to cut off his head, and to take it to the White Mount in London, and bury it there, with the face towards France. He prophesied how they would perform the journey. At Harlech they would be feasting seven years, the birds of Rhiannon singing to them all the time, and Brân's own head conversing with them as agreeably as when it was on his body. Then they would be fourscore years at Gwales. All this while, Brân's head would remain uncorrupted, and would talk so pleasantly that they would forget the flight of time. But, at the destined hour, someone would open a door which looked towards Cornwall, and, after that, they could stay no longer, but must hurry to London to bury the head.

So the seven beheaded Brân, and set off, taking Branwen also with them. They landed at the mouth of the River Alaw, in Anglesey. Branwen first looked back towards Ireland, and then forward towards Britain. 'Alas.' she cried, 'that I was ever born! two islands have been destroyed because of me.' Her heart broke with sorrow, and she died. An old Welsh poem says, with a touch of real pathos:

'Softened were the voices in the brakes Of the wondering birds On seeing the fair body. Will there not be relating again Of that which befel the paragon At the stream of Amlwch?'

'They made her a four-sided grave,' says the Mabinogi, 'and buried her upon the banks of the Alaw.' The traditional spot has always borne the name of *Ynys Branwen*, and, curiously enough, an urn was found there, in 1813, full of ashes and half-burnt bones, which certain enthusiastic local antiquaries saw 'every reason to suppose' were those of the fair British Aphrodité herself.

The seven went on towards Harlech, and, as they journeyed, they met men and women who gave them the latest news. Caswallawn, a son of Beli, the husband of Dôn, had destroyed the ministers left behind by Brân to take care of Britain. He had made himself invisible by the help of a magic veil, and thus had killed all of them except Pendaran Dyfed, foster-father of Pryderi, who had escaped into the woods, and Caradawc son of Brân, whose heart had broken from grief. Thus he had made himself king of the whole island in place of Manawyddan, its rightful heir now that Brân was dead.

However, the destiny was upon the seven that they should go on with their leader's head. They went to Harlech and feasted for seven years, the three birds of Rhiannon singing them songs compared with which all other songs seemed unmelodious. Then they spent fourscore years in the Isle of Gwales, eating and drinking, and listening to the pleasant conversation of Brân's head. The 'Entertaining of the Noble Head' this eighty years' feast was called. Brân's head, indeed, is almost more notable in British mythology than Brân before he was decapitated. Taliesin and the other bards invoke it repeatedly as *Urddawl Ben* (the 'Venerable Head') and *Uther Ben* (the 'Wonderful Head').

But all pleasure came to an end when Heilyn, the son of Gwynn, opened the forbidden door, like Bluebeard's wife, 'to know if that was true which was said concerning it'. As soon as they looked towards Cornwall, the glamour that had kept them merry for eighty-seven years failed, and left them as grieved about the death of their lord as though it had happened that very day. They could not rest for sorrow, but went at once to London, and laid the now dumb and corrupting head in its grave on Tower Hill, with its face turned towards France, to watch that no foe came from foreign lands to Britain. There it reposed until, ages afterwards, Arthur, in his pride of heart, dug it up, 'as he thought it beneath his dignity to hold the island otherwise than by valour'. Disaster, in the shape of

'the godless hosts
Of heathen swarming o'er the Northern sea',

came of this disinterment; and therefore it is called, in a triad, one of the 'Three Wicked Uncoverings of Britain'.

XV

THE WAR OF ENCHANTMENTS

Manawyddan was now the sole survivor of the family of Llyr. He was homeless and landless. But Pryderi offered to give him a realm in Dyfed, and his mother, Rhiannon, for a wife. The lady, her son explained, was still not uncomely, and her conversation was pleasing. Manawyddan seems to have found her attractive, while Rhiannon was not less taken with the son of Llyr. They were wedded, and so great became the friendship of Pryderi and Kicva, Manawyddan and Rhiannon, that the four were seldom apart.

One day, after holding a feast at Narberth, they went up to the same magic mound where Rhiannon had first met Pwyll. As they sat there, thunder pealed, and immediately a thick mist sprang up, so that not one of them could see the other. When it cleared, they found themselves alone in an uninhabited country. Except for their own castle, the land was desert and untilled, without sign of dwelling, man, or beast. One touch of some unknown magic had utterly changed the face of Dyfed from a rich realm to a wilderness.

Manawyddan and Pryderi, Rhiannon and Kicva traversed the country on all sides, but found nothing except desolation and wild beasts. For two years they lived in the open upon game and honey.

During the third year, they grew weary of this wild life, and decided to go into Lloegyr, and support themselves by some handicraft. Manawyddan could make saddles, and he made them so well that soon no one in Hereford, where they had settled, would buy from any saddler but himself. This aroused the enmity of all the other saddlers, and they conspired to kill the strangers. So the four went to another city.

Here they made shields, and soon no one would purchase a shield unless it had been made by Manawyddan and Pryderi. The shield-makers became jealous, and again a move had to be made.

But they fared no better at the next town, where they practised the craft of cordwainers, Manawyddan shaping the shoes and Pryderi stitching them. So they went back to Dyfed again, and occupied themselves in hunting.

One day, the hounds of Manawyddan and Pryderi roused a white wild boar. They chased it till they came to a castle at a place where both the huntsmen were certain that no castle had been before. Into this castle went the boar, and the hounds after it. For some time, Manawyddan and Pryderi waited in vain for their return. Pryderi then proposed that he should go into the castle, and see what had become of them. Manawyddan tried to dissuade him, declaring that whoever their enemy was who had laid Dyfed waste had also caused the appearance of this castle. But Pryderi insisted upon entering.

In the castle, he found neither the boar nor his hounds, nor any trace of man or beast. There was nothing but a fountain in the centre of the castle floor, and, on the brink of the fountain, a beautiful golden bowl fastened to a marble slab by chains.

Pryderi was so pleased with the beauty of the bowl that he put out his hands and took hold of it. Whereupon his hands stuck to the bowl, so that he could not move from where he stood.

Manawyddan waited for him till the evening, and then returned to the palace, and told Rhiannon. She, more daring than her husband, rebuked him for cowardice, and went straight to the magic castle. In the court she found Pryderi, his hands still glued to the bowl and his feet to the slab. She tried to free him, but became fixed, herself, and, with a clap of thunder and a fall of mist, the castle vanished with its two prisoners.

Manawyddan was now left alone with Kicva, Pryderi's wife. He calmed her fears, and assured her of his protection. But they had lost their dogs, and could not hunt any more, so they set out together to Lloegyr, to practise again Manawyddan's old trade of cordwainer. A second time, the envious cordwainers conspired to kill them, so they were obliged to return to Dyfed.

But Manawyddan took back a burden of wheat with him to Narberth, and sowed three crofts, all of which sprang up abundantly. When harvest time came, he went to look at his first croft, and found it ripe. 'I will reap this to-morrow,' he said. But in the morning he found nothing but the bare straw. Every ear had been taken away.

So he went to the next croft, which was also ripe. But, when he came to cut it, he found it had been stripped like the first. Then he knew that whoever had wasted Dyfed, and carried off Rhiannon and Pryderi, was also at work upon his wheat.

The third croft was also ripe, and over this one he determined to keep watch. In the evening he armed himself and waited. At midnight he heard a great tumult, and, looking out, saw a host of mice coming. Each mouse bit off an ear of wheat and ran off with it. He rushed among them, but could only catch one, which was more sluggish than the rest. This one he put into his glove, and took it back, and showed it to Kicva.

'To-morrow I will hang it,' he said. 'It is not a fit thing for a man of your dignity to hang a mouse,' she replied. 'Nevertheless will I do so,' said he. 'Do so then,' said Kicva.

The next morning, Manawyddan went to the magic mound, and set up two forks on it, to make a gallows. He had just finished, when a man dressed like a poor scholar came towards him, and greeted him.

'What are you doing, Lord?' he said.

'I am going to hang a thief,' replied Manawyddan.

'What sort of a thief? I see an animal like a mouse in your hand, but a man of rank like yours should not touch so mean a creature. Let it go free.'

'I caught it robbing me,' replied Manawyddan, 'and it shall die a thief's death.'

'I do not care to see a man like you doing such a thing,' said the scholar. 'I will give you a pound to let it go.'

'I will not let it go,' replied Manawyddan, 'nor will I sell it.'

'As you will, Lord. It is nothing to me,' returned the scholar. And he went away.

Manawyddan laid a cross-bar along the forks. As he did so, another man came by, a priest riding on a horse. He asked Manawyddan what he was doing, and was told. 'My lord,' he said, 'such a reptile is worth nothing to buy, but rather than see you degrade yourself by touching it, I will give you three pounds to let it go.'

'I will take no money for it,' replied Manawyddan. 'It shall be hanged.'

'Let it be hanged,' said the priest, and went his way.

Manawyddan put the noose round the mouse's neck, and was just going to draw it up, when he saw a bishop coming, with his whole retinue.

'Thy blessing, Lord Bishop,' he said.

'Heaven's blessing upon you,' said the bishop. 'What are you doing?'

'I am hanging a thief,' replied Manawyddan. 'This mouse has robbed me.'

'Since I happen to have come at its doom, I will ransom it,' said the bishop. 'Here are seven pounds. Take them, and let it go.'

'I will not let it go,' replied Manawyddan.

'I will give you twenty-four pounds of ready money if you will let it go,' said the bishop.

'I would not, for as much again,' replied Manawyddan.

'If you will not free it for that,' said the bishop, 'I will give you all my horses and their baggage to let it go.'

'I will not,' replied Manawyddan.

'Then name your own price,' said the bishop.

'That offer I accept,' replied Manawyddan. 'My price is that Rhiannon and Pryderi be set free.'

'They shall be set free,' replied the bishop.

'Still I will not let the mouse go,' said Manawyddan.

'What more do you ask?' exclaimed the bishop. 'That the charm be removed from Dyfed,' replied Manawyddan.

'It shall be removed,' promised the bishop. 'So set the mouse free.'

'I will not,' said Manawyddan, 'till I know who the mouse is.'

'She is my wife,' replied the bishop, 'and I am called Llwyd, the son of Kilcoed, and I cast the charm over Dyfed, and upon Rhiannon and Pryderi, to avenge Gwawl son of Clûd for the game of "badger in the bag" which was played on him by Pwyll, Head of Annwn. It was my household that came in the guise of mice and took away your corn. But since my wife has been caught, I will restore Rhiannon and Pryderi and take the charm off Dyfed if you will let her go.'

'I will not let her go,' said Manawyddan, 'until you have promised that there shall be no charm put upon Dyfed again.'

'I will promise that also,' replied Llwyd. 'So let her go.'

'I will not let her go,' said Manawyddan, 'unless you swear to take no revenge for this hereafter.'

'You have done wisely to claim that,' replied Llwyd. 'Much trouble would else have come upon your head because of this. Now I swear it. So set my wife free.'

'I will not,' said Manawyddan, 'until I see Rhiannon and Pryderi.'

Then he saw them coming towards him; and they greeted one another.

'Now set my wife free,' said the bishop.

'I will, gladly,' replied Manawyddan. So he released the mouse, and Llwyd struck her with a wand, and turned her into 'a young woman, the fairest ever seen'.

And when Manawyddan looked round him, he saw Dyfed tilled and cultivated again, as it had formerly been.

The powers of light had, this time, the victory. Little by little, they increased their mastery over the dominion of darkness, until we find the survivors of the families of Llyr and Pwyll mere vassals of Arthur.

XVI

THE VICTORIES OF LIGHT OVER DARKNESS

The powers of light were, however, by no means invariably successful in their struggles with the powers of darkness. Even Gwydion son of Dôn had to serve his apprenticeship to misfortune. Assailing Caer Sidi – Hades under one of its many titles, – he was caught by Pwyll and Pryderi, and endured a long imprisonment. The sufferings he underwent made him a bard – an ancient Celtic idea which one can still see surviving in the popular tradition that whoever dares to spend a night alone either upon the chair of the Giant Idris (the summit of Cader Idris, in Merionethshire), or under the haunted Black Stone of Arddu, upon the Llanberis side of Snowdon, will be found in the morning either inspired or mad. How he escaped we are not told; but the episode does not seem to have quenched his ardour against the natural enemies of his kind.

Helped by his brother, Amaethon, god of agriculture, and his son, Lleu, he fought the Battle of Godeu, or 'the Trees', an exploit which is not the least curious of Celtic myths. It is known also as the Battle of Achren, or Ochren, a name for Hades of unknown meaning, but appearing again in the remarkable Welsh poem which describes the 'Spoiling of Annwn' by Arthur. The King of Achren was Arawn; and he was helped by Brân, who apparently had not then made his fatal journey to Ireland. The war was made to secure three boons for man – the dog, the deer, and the lapwing, all of them creatures for some reason sacred to the gods of the nether world.

Gwydion was this time not alone, as he apparently was when he made his first unfortunate reconnaissance of Hades. Besides his brother and his son, he had an army which he raised for the purpose. For a leader of Gwydion's magical attainments there was no need of standing troops. He could call battalions into being with a charm, and dismiss them when they were no longer needed. The name of the battle shows what he did on this occasion; and the bard Taliesin adds his testimony:

'I have been in the battle of Godeu, with Lieu and
    Gwydion,
They changed the forms of the elementary trees
    and sedges'.

In a poem devoted to it he describes in detail what happened. The trees and grasses, he tells us, hurried to the fight: the alders led the van, but the willows and the quickens came late, and the birch, though courageous, took long in arraying himself; the elm stood firm in the centre of the battle, and would not yield a foot; heaven and earth trembled before the advance of the oak-tree, that stout door-keeper against an enemy; the heroic holly and the hawthorn defended themselves with their spikes; the heather kept off the enemy on every side, and the broom was well to the front, but the fern was plundered, and the furze did not do well; the stout, lofty pine, the intruding pear-tree, the gloomy ash, the bashful chestnut-tree, the prosperous beech, the long-enduring poplar, the scarce plum-tree, the shelter-seeking privet and woodbine, the wild, foreign laburnum; 'the bean, bearing in its shade an army of phantoms'; rose-bush, raspberry, ivy, cherry-tree, and medlar – all took their parts.

In the ranks of Hades there were equally strange fighters. We are told of a hundred-headed beast, carrying a formidable battalion under the root of its tongue and another in the back of its head; there was a gaping black toad with a hundred claws; and a crested snake of many colours, within whose flesh a hundred souls were tormented for their sins – in fact, it would need a Doré or a Dante to do justice to this weird battle between the arrayed magics of heaven and hell.

It was magic that decided its fate. There was a fighter in the ranks of Hades who could not be overcome unless his antagonist guessed his name – a peculiarity of the terrene gods, remarks Professor Rhys, which has been preserved in our popular fairy tales. Gwydion guessed the name, and sang these two verses: –

'Sure-hoofed is my steed impelled by the spur; The high sprigs of alder are on thy shield; Brân art thou called, of the glittering branches!

'Sure-hoofed is my steed in the day of battle: The high sprigs of alder are on thy hand: *Brân* . . . by the branch thou bearest Has Amaethon the Good prevailed!'

Thus the power of the dark gods was broken, and the sons of Dôn retained for the use of men the deer, the dog, and the lapwing, stolen from that underworld, whence all good gifts came.

It was always to obtain some practical benefit that the gods of light fought against the gods of darkness. The last and greatest of Gwydion's raids upon Hades was undertaken to procure – pork!

Gwydion had heard that there had come to Dyfed some strange beasts, such as had never been seen before. They were called 'pigs' or 'swine', and Arawn, King of Annwn, had sent them as a gift to Pryderi son of Pwyll. They were small animals, and their flesh was said to be better than the flesh of oxen. He thought it would be a good thing to get them, either by force or fraud, from the dark powers. Mâth son of Mâthonwy, who ruled the children of Dôn from his Olympus of Caer Dathyl, gave his consent, and Gwydion set off, with eleven others, to Pryderi's palace. They disguised themselves as bards, so as to be received by Pryderi, and Gwydion, who was 'the best teller of tales in the world', entertained the Prince of Dyfed and his court more than they had ever been entertained by any story-teller before. Then he asked Pryderi to grant him a boon – the animals which had come from Annwn. But Pryderi had pledged his word to Arawn that he would neither sell nor give away any of the new creatures until they had increased to double their number, and he told the disguised Gwydion so.

'Lord,' said Gwydion, 'I can set you free from your promise. Neither give me the swine at once, nor yet refuse them to me altogether, and to-morrow I will show you how.'

He went to the lodging Pryderi had assigned him, and began to work his charms and illusions. Out of fungus he made twelve gilded shields, and twelve horses with gold harness, and twelve black greyhounds with white breasts, each wearing a golden collar and leash. And these he showed to Pryderi.

'Lord,' said he, 'there is a release from the word you spoke last evening concerning the swine – that you may neither give them nor sell them. You may exchange them for something which is better. I will give you these twelve horses with their gold harness, and these twelve greyhounds with their gold collars and leashes, and these twelve gilded shields for them.'

Pryderi took counsel with his men, and agreed to the bargain. So Gwydion and his followers took the swine and went away with them, hurrying as fast as they could, for Gwydion knew that the illusion would not last longer than a day. The memory of their journey was long kept up; every place where they rested between Dyfed and Caer Dathyl is remembered by a name connecting it with pigs. There is a Mochdrev ('Swine's Town') in each of the three counties of Cardiganshire, Montgomeryshire, and Denbighshire, and a Castell y Moch ('Swine's Castle') near Mochnant ('Swine's Brook'), which runs through part of the two latter counties. They shut up the pigs in safety, and then assembled all Mâth's army; for the horses and hounds and shields had returned to fungus, and Pryderi, who guessed Gwydion's part in it, was coming northward in hot haste.

There were two battles – one at Maenor Penardd, near Conway, and the other at Maenor Alun, now called Coed Helen, near Caernarvon. Beaten in both, Pryderi fell back upon Nant Call, about nine miles from Caernarvon. Here he was again defeated with great slaughter, and sent hostages, asking for peace and a safe retreat.

This was granted by Mâth; but, none the less, the army of the sons of Dôn insisted on following the retreating host, and harassing it. So Pryderi sent a complaint to Mâth, demanding that, if there must still be war, Gwydion, who had caused all the trouble, should fight with him in single combat.

Gwydion agreed, and the champions of light and darkness met face to face. But Pryderi was the waning power, and he fell before the strength and magic of Gwydion. 'And at Maen Tyriawc, above Melenryd, was he buried, and there is his grave', says the Mabinogi, though the ancient Welsh poem, called the 'Verses of the Graves of the Warriors', assigns him a different resting-place.

This decisive victory over Hades and its kings was the end of the struggle, until it was renewed, with still more complete success, by one greater than Gwydion – the invincible Arthur.

XVII

THE MYTHOLOGICAL 'COMING OF ARTHUR'

The 'Coming of Arthur', his sudden rise into prominence, is one of the many problems of the Celtic mythology. He is not mentioned in any of the Four Branches of the Mabinogi, which deal with the races of British gods equivalent to the Gaelic Tuatha Dé Danann. The earliest references to him in Welsh literature seem to treat him as merely a warrior-chieftain, no better, if no worse, than several others, such as 'Geraint, a tributary prince of Devon', immortalized both by the bards and by Tennyson. Then, following upon this, we find him lifted to the extraordinary position of a king of gods, to whom the old divine families of Dôn, of Llyr, and of Pwyll pay unquestioned homage. Triads tell us that Lludd – the Zeus of the older Pantheon – was one of Arthur's 'Three Chief War-Knights', and Arawn, King of Hades, one of his 'Three Chief Counselling Knights'. In the story called the 'Dream of Rhonabwy', in the Red Book of Hergest, he is shown as a leader to whom are subject those we know to have been of divine race – sons of Nudd, of Llyr, of Brân, of Govannan, and of Arianrod. In another 'Red Book' tale, that of 'Kulhwch and Olwen', even greater gods are his vassals. Amaethon son of Dôn, ploughs for him, and Govannan son of Dôn, rids the iron, while two other sons of Beli, Nynniaw and Peibaw, 'turned into oxen on account of their sins', toil at the yoke, that a mountain may be cleared and tilled and the harvest reaped in one day. He assembles his champions to seek the 'treasures of Britain'; and Manawyddan son of Llyr, Gwyn son of Nudd, and Pryderi son of Pwyll rally round him at his call.

The most probable, and only adequate explanation, is given by Professor Rhys, who considers that the fames of two separate Arthurs have been accidentally confused, to the exceeding renown of a composite, half-real, half-mythical personage into whom the two blended. One of these was a divine Arthur, a god more or less widely worshipped in the Celtic world – the same, no doubt, whom an *ex voto* inscription found in south-eastern France calls *Mercurius Artaius*. The other was a human Arthur, who held among the Britons the post which, under Roman domination, had been called *Comes Britanniæ*. This 'Count of Britain' was the supreme military authority; he had a roving commission to defend the country against foreign invasion; and under his orders were two slightly subordinate officers, the *Dux Britanniarum* (Duke of the Britains), who had charge of the northern wall, and the *Comes Littoris Saxonici* (Count of the Saxon Shore), who guarded the south-eastern coasts. The Britons, after the departure of the Romans, long kept intact the organization their conquerors had built up; and it seems reasonable to believe that this post of leader in war was the same which early Welsh literature describes as that of 'emperor', a title given to Arthur alone among the British heroes. The fame of Arthur the Emperor blended with that of Arthur the God, so that it became conterminous with the area over which we have traced Brythonic settlement in Great Britain. Hence the many disputes, ably, if unprofitably, conducted, over 'Arthurian localities' and the sites of such cities as Camelot, and of Arthur's twelve great battles. Historical elements doubtless coloured the tales of

Arthur and his companions, but they are none the less as essentially mythic as those told of their Gaelic analogues – the Red Branch Heroes of Ulster and the Fenians.

Of those two cycles, it is with the latter that the Arthurian legend shows most affinity. Arthur's position as supreme war-leader of Britain curiously parallels that of Finn's as general of a 'native Irish militia'. His 'Round Table' of warriors also reminds one of Finn's Fenians sworn to adventure. Both alike battle with human and superhuman foes.

Both alike harry Europe, even to the walls of Rome. The love-story of Arthur, his wife Gwynhwyvar (Guinevere), and his nephew Medrawt (Mordred), resembles in several ways that of Finn, his wife Grainne, and his nephew Diarmait. In the stories of the last battles of Arthur and of the Fenians, the essence of the kindred myth still subsists, though the actual exponents of it slightly differ. At the fight of Camlan, it was Arthur and Medrawt themselves who fought the final duel. But in the last stand of the Fenians at Gabhra, the original protagonists have given place to their descendants and representatives. Both Finn and Cormac were already dead. It is Oscar, Finn's grandson, and Cairbré, Cormac's son, who fight and slay each other. And again, just as Arthur was thought by many not to have really died, but to have passed to 'the island valley of Avilion', so a Scottish legend tells us how, ages after the Fenians, a man, landing by chance upon a mysterious western island, met and spoke with Finn mac Coul. Even the alternative legend, which makes Arthur and his warriors wait under the earth in a magic sleep for the return of their triumph, is also told of the Fenians.

But these parallels, though they illustrate Arthur's pre-eminence, do not show his real place among the gods. To determine this, we must examine the ranks of the older dynasties carefully, to see if any are missing whose attributes this new-comer may have inherited. We find Lludd and Gwyn, Arawn, Pryderi, and Manawyddan side by side with him under their own names. Among the children of Dôn are Amaethon and Govannan. But here the list stops, with a notable omission. There is no mention, in later myth, of Gwydion. That greatest of the sons of Dôn has fallen out, and vanished without a sign.

Singularly enough, too, the same stories that were once told of Gwydion are now attached to the name of Arthur. So that we may assume, with Professor Rhys, that Arthur, the prominent god of a new Pantheon, has taken the place of Gwydion in the old. A comparison of Gwydion-myths and Arthur-myths shows an almost exact correspondence in everything but name.

Like Gwydion, Arthur is the exponent of culture and of arts. Therefore we see him carrying on the same war against the underworld for wealth and wisdom that Gwydion and the sons of Dôn waged against the sons of Llyr, the Sea, and of Pwyll, the Head of Hades.

Like Gwydion, too, Arthur suffered early reverses. He failed, indeed, even where his prototype had succeeded. Gwydion, we know from the Mabinogi of Mâth, successfully stole Pryderi's pigs, but Arthur was utterly baffled in his attempt to capture the swine of a similar prince of the underworld, called March son of Meirchion. Also as with Gwydion, his earliest reconnaissance of Hades was disastrous, and led to his capture and imprisonment. Manawyddan son of Llyr, confined him in the mysterious and gruesome bone-fortress of Oeth and Anoeth, and there he languished for three days and three nights before a rescuer came in the person of Goreu, his cousin. But, in the end, he triumphed.

A Welsh poem, ascribed to the bard Taliesin, relates, under the title 'The Spoiling of Annwn', an expedition of Arthur and his followers into the very heart of that country, from which he appears to have returned (for the verses are somewhat obscure) with the loss of almost all his men, but in possession of the object of his quest – the magic cauldron of inspiration and poetry.

Taliesin tells the story as an eye-witness. He may well have done so; for it was his boast that from the creation of the world he had allowed himself to miss no event of importance. He was in Heaven, he tells us, when Lucifer fell, and in the Court of Dôn before Gwydion was born; he had been among the constellations both with Mary Magdalene and with the pagan goddess Arianrod; he carried a banner before Alexander, and was chief director of the building of the Tower of Babel; he saw the fall of Troy and the founding of Rome; he was with Noah in the Ark, and he witnessed the destruction of Sodom and Gomorrah; and he was present both at the Manger of Bethlehem and at the Cross of Calvary. But, unfortunately, Taliesin, as a credible personage, rests under exactly the same disabilities as Arthur himself. It is not denied by scholars that there was a real Taliesin, a sixth-century bard to whom were attributed, and who may have actually composed, some of the poems in the Book of Taliesin. But there was also another Taliesin, whom mythical poet of the British Celts, Professor Rhys is inclined to equate with the Gaelic Ossian. The traditions of the two mingled, endowing the historic Taliesin with the god-like attributes of his predecessor, and clothing the mythical Taliesin with some of the actuality of his successor.

It is regrettable that our bard did not at times sing a little less incoherently, for his poem contains the fullest description that has come down to us of the other world as the Britons conceived it.

Apparently the numerous names, all different and some now untranslatable, refer to the same place, and they must be collated to form a right idea of what Annwn was like. With the exception of an obviously spurious last verse, here omitted, the poem is magnificently pagan, and quite a storehouse of British mythology.

> 'I will praise the Sovereign, supreme Lord of the land, Who hath extended his dominion over the shore of the world. Stout was the prison of Gweir, in Caer Sidi, Through the spite of Pwyll and Pryderi: No one before him went into it. The heavy blue chain firmly held the youth, And before the spoils of Annwn woefully he sang, And thenceforth till doom he shall remain a bard Thrice enough to fill Prydwen we went into it; Except seven, none returned from Caer Sidi.
>
> 'Am I not a candidate for fame, to be heard in song In Caer Pedryvan, four times revolving? The first word from the cauldron, when was it spoken?
>
> 'By the breath of nine maidens it was gently warmed. Is it not the cauldron of the chief of Annwn? What is its fashion? A rim of pearls is round its edge.
> It will not cook the food of a coward or one forsworn. A sword flashing bright will be raised to him, And left in the hand of Lleminawg. And before the door of the gate of Uffern the lamp was burning. When we went with Arthur – a splendid labour! – Except seven, none returned from Caer Vedwyd.

'Am I not a candidate for fame, to be heard in song In Caer Pedryvan, in the Isle of the Strong Door, Where twilight and pitchy darkness meet together,
And bright wine is the drink of the host? Thrice enough to fill Prydwen we went on the sea Except seven, none returned from Caer Rigor.

'I will not allow much praise to the leaders of literature. Beyond Caer Wydyr they saw not the prowess of Arthur; Three-score hundreds stood on the walls; It was hard to converse with their watchman. Thrice enough to fill Prydwen we went with Arthur; Except seven, none returned from Caer Golud.

'I will not allow much praise to the spiritless. They know not on what day, or who caused it, Or in what hour of the serene day Cwy was born, Or who caused that he should not go to the dales of Devwy. They know not the brindled ox with the broad head-band,
Whose yoke is seven-score handbreadths. When we went with Arthur, of mournful memory, Except seven, none returned from Caer Vandwy.

'I will not allow much praise to those of drooping courage, They know not on what day the chief arose, Nor in what hour of the serene day the owner was born, Nor what animal they keep, with its head of silver. When we went with Arthur, of anxious striving,
Except seven, none returned from Caer Ochren'.

Many of the allusions of this poem will perhaps never be explained. We know no better than the 'leaders of literature' whom the vainglorious Taliesin taunted with their ignorance and lack of spirit in what hour Cwy was born, or even who he was, much less who prevented him from going to the dales of Devwy, wherever they may have been. We are in the dark as much as they were with regard to the significance of the brindled ox with the broad head-band, and of the other animal with the silver head. But the, earlier portion of the poem is, fortunately, clearer, and it gives glimpses of a grandeur of savage imagination. The strong-doored, foursquare fortress of glass, manned by its dumb, ghostly sentinels, spun round in never-ceasing revolution, so that few could find its entrance; it was pitch-dark save for the twilight made by the lamp burning before its circling gate; feasting went on there, and revelry, and in its centre, choicest of its many riches, was the pearl-rimmed cauldron of poetry and inspiration, kept bubbling by the breaths of nine British pythonesses, so that it might give forth its oracles. To this scanty information we may add a few lines, also by Taliesin, and contained in a poem called 'A Song Concerning the Sons of Llyr ab Brochwel Powys':–

'Perfect is my chair in Caer Sidi:
Plague and age hurt not him who's in it –
They know, Manawyddan and Pryderi.
Three organs round a fire sing before it,
And about its points are ocean's streams
And the abundant well above it –
Sweeter than white wine the drink in it.'

Little is, however, added by it to our knowledge. It reminds us that Annwn was surrounded by the sea – 'the heavy blue chain' which held Gweir so firmly; – it informs us that the 'bright wine' which was 'the drink of the host' was kept in a well; it adds to the revelry the singing of the three organs; it makes a point that its inhabitants were freed from age and death; and, last of all, it shows us, as we might have expected, the ubiquitous Taliesin as a privileged resident of this delightful region. We have two clues as to where the country may have been situated. Lundy Island, off the coast of Devonshire, was anciently called *Ynys Wair*, the 'Island of Gweir', or Gwydion. The Welsh translation of the *Seint Greal*, an Anglo-Norman romance embodying much of the old mythology, locates its 'Turning Castle' – evidently the same as Caer Sidi – in the district around and comprising Puffin Island off the coast of Anglesey. But these are slender threads by which to tether to firm ground a realm of the imagination.

With Gwydion, too, have disappeared the whole of the characters connected with him in that portion of the Mabinogi of Mâth, Son of Mâthonwy, which recounts the myth of the birth of the sun-god. Neither Mâth himself, nor Lieu Llaw Gyffes, nor Dylan, nor their mother, Arianrod, play any more part; they have vanished as completely as Gwydion. But the essence of the myth of which they were the figures remains intact. Gwydion was the father by his sister Arianrod, wife of a waning heaven-god called Nwyvre (Space), of twin sons, Lieu, a god of light, and Dylan, a god of darkness; and we find this same story woven into the very innermost texture of the legend of Arthur. The new Arianrod, though called 'Morgawse' by Sir Thomas Malory, and 'Anna' by Geoffrey of Monmouth, is known to earlier Welsh myth as 'Gwyar'. She was the sister of Arthur and the wife of the sky-god, Lludd, and her name, which means 'shed blood' or 'gore', reminds us of the relationship of the Morrígú, the war-goddess of the Gaels, to the heaven-god Nuada. The new Lleu Llaw Gyffes is called Gwalchmei, that is, the 'Falcon of May', and the new Dylan is Medrawt, at once Arthur's son and Gwalchmei's brother, and the bitterest enemy of both.

Besides these 'old friends with new faces', Arthur brings with him into prominence a fresh Pantheon, most of whom also replace the older gods of the heavens and earth and the regions under the earth. The Zeus of Arthur's cycle is called Myrddin, who passed into the Norman-French romances as 'Merlin'. All the myths told of him bear witness to his high estate. The first name of Britain, before it was inhabited, was, we learn from a triad, *Clas Myrddin*, that is, 'Myrddin's Enclosure'. He is given a wife whose attributes recall those of the consorts of Nuada and Lludd. She is described as the only daughter of Coel – the British name of the Gaulish *Camulus*, a god of war and the sky – and was called Elen Lwyddawg, that is, 'Elen, Leader of Hosts'. Her memory is still preserved in Wales in connection with ancient roadways; such names as *Ffordd Elen* ('Elen's Road') and *Sarn Elen* ('Elen's Causeway') seem to show that the paths on which armies marched were ascribed or dedicated to her. As Myrddin's wife, she is credited with having founded the town of Carmarthen (*Caer Myrddin*), as well as the 'highest fortress in Arvon', which must have been the site near Beddgelert still called *Dinas Emrys*, the 'Town of Emrys', one of Myrddin's epithets or names.

Professor Rhys is inclined to credit Myrddin, or, rather, the British Zeus under whatever name, with having been the god especially worshipped at Stonehenge. Certainly this impressive temple, ever unroofed and open to the sun and wind and rain of heaven, would seem peculiarly appropriate to a British supreme god of light and sky. Neither are we quite without documentary evidence which will allow us to connect it with him. Geoffrey of Monmouth, whose historical fictions usually conceal mythological facts, relates that the stones which compose it were erected by Merlin. Before that, they had stood in Ireland, upon a hill which Geoffrey calls 'Mount Killaraus', and which can be identified as the same spot known to Irish legend as the 'Hill of Uisnech', and, still earlier, connected with Balor. According to British tradition, the primeval giants who first colonized Ireland had brought them from their original home on 'the farthest coast of Africa', on account of their miraculous virtues; for any water in which they were bathed became a sovereign remedy either for sickness or for wounds. By the order of Aurelius, a half-real, half-mythical king of Britain, Merlin brought them thence to England, to be set up on Salisbury Plain as a monument to the British chieftains treacherously slain by Hengist and his Saxons. With this scrap of native information about Stonehenge we may compare the only other piece we have – the account of the classic Diodorus, who called it a temple of Apollo. At first, these two statements seem to conflict. But it is far from unlikely that the earlier Celtic settlers in Britain made little or no religious distinction between sky and sun. The sun-god, as a separate personage, seems to have been the conception of a comparatively late age. Celtic mythology allows us to be present, as it were, at the births both of the Gaelic Lugh Lamhfada and the British Lleu Llaw Gyffes.

Even the well-known story of Myrddin's, or Merlin's final imprisonment in a tomb of airy enchantment – 'a tour withouten walles, or withoute eny closure' – reads marvellously like a myth of the sun 'with all his fires and travelling glories round him'. Encircled, shielded, and made splendid by his atmosphere of living light, the Lord of Heaven moves slowly towards the west, to disappear at last into the sea (as one local version of the myth puts it), or on to a far-off island (as another says), or into a dark forest (the choice of a third). When the myth became finally fixed, it was Bardsey Island, off the extreme westernmost point of Caernarvonshire, that was selected as his last abode. Into it he went with nine attendant bards, taking with him the 'Thirteen Treasures of Britain', thenceforth lost to men. Bardsey Island no doubt derives its name from this story; and what is probably an allusion to it is found in a first-century Greek writer called Plutarch, who describes a grammarian called Demetrius as having visited Britain, and brought home an account of his travels. He mentioned several uninhabited and sacred islands off our coasts which he said were named after gods and heroes, but there was one especially in which Cronos was imprisoned with his attendant deities, and Briareus keeping watch over him as he slept; 'for sleep was the bond forged for him'. Doubtless this disinherited deity, whom the Greek, after his fashion, called 'Cronos', was the British heaven- and sun-god, after he had descended into the prison of the west.

Among other new-comers is Kai, who, as Sir Kay the Seneschal, fills so large a part in the later romances. Purged of his worst offences, and reduced to a surly butler to Arthur, he is but a shadow of the earlier Kai who murdered Arthur's son Llacheu, and can only be acquitted, through the obscurity of the poem that relates the incident, of having also carried off, or having tried to carry off, Arthur's wife, Gwynhwyvar. He is thought to have been a personification of fire, upon the strength of a description given of him in the mythical romance of 'Kulhwch and Olwen'. 'Very subtle', it says, 'was Kai. When it pleased him he could render himself as tall as the highest tree in the forest. And he had another peculiarity – so great was the heat of his nature, that, when it rained hardest, whatever he carried remained dry for a handbreadth above and a handbreadth below his hand; and when his companions were coldest, it was to them as fuel with which to light their fire.'

Another personage who owes his prominence in the Arthurian story to his importance in Celtic myth was March son of Meirchion, whose swine Arthur attempted to steal, as Gwydion had done those of Pryderi. In the romances, he has become the cowardly and treacherous Mark, king, according to some stories, of Cornwall, but according to others, of the whole of Britain, and known to all as the husband of the Fair Isoult, and the uncle of Sir Tristrem. But as a deformed deity of the underworld he can be found in Gaelic as well as in British myth. He cannot be considered as originally different from Morc, a king of the Fomors at the time when from their Glass Castle they so fatally oppressed the Children of Nemed. The Fomors were distinguished by their animal features, and March had the same peculiarity. When Sir Thomas Malory relates how, to please Arthur and Sir Launcelot, Sir Dinadan made a song about Mark, 'which was the worst lay that ever harper sang with harp or any other instruments', he does not tell us wherein the sting of the lampoon lay. It no doubt reminded King Mark of the unpleasant fact that he had – not like his Phrygian counterpart, ass's but – horse's ears. He was, in fact, a Celtic Midas, a distinction which he shared with one of the mythical kings of early Ireland.

Neither can we pass over Urien, a deity of the underworld akin to, or perhaps the same as, Brân. Like that son of Llyr, he was at once a god of battle and of minstrelsy; he was adored by the bards as their patron; his badge was the raven (*bran*, in Welsh); while, to make his identification complete, there is an extant poem which tells how Urien, wounded, ordered his own head to be cut off by his attendants. His wife was Modron, known as the mother of Mabon, the sun-god to whom inscriptions exist as *Maponos*. Another of the children of Urien and Modron is Owain, which was perhaps only another name for Mabon. Taliesin calls him 'chief of the glittering west', and he is as certainly a sun-god as his father Urien, 'lord of the evening', was a ruler of the dark underworld.

It is by reason of the pre-eminence of Arthur that we find gathered round him so many gods, all probably various tribal personifications of the same few mythological ideas. The Celts, both of the Gaelic and the British branches, were split up into numerous petty tribes, each with its own local deities embodying the same essential conceptions under different names. There was the god of the underworld, gigantic in figure, patron alike of warrior and minstrel, teacher of the arts of eloquence and literature, and owner of boundless wealth, whom some of the British tribes worshipped as Brân, others as Urien, others as Pwyll, or March, or Mâth, or Arawn, or Ogyrvran. There was the lord of an elysium – Hades in its aspect of a paradise of the departed rather than of the primeval subterranean realm where all things originated – whom the Britons of Wales called Gwyn, or Gwynwas; the Britons of Cornwall, Melwas; and the Britons of Somerset, Avallon, or Avallach. Under this last title, his realm is called *Ynys Avallon*, 'Avallon's Island', or, as we know the word, Avilion. It was said to be in the 'Land of Summer', which, in the earliest myth, signified Hades; and it was only in later days that the mystic Isle of Avilion became fixed to earth as Glastonbury, and the Elysian 'Land of Summer' as Somerset. There was a mighty ruler of heaven, a 'god of battles', worshipped on high places, in whose hands was 'the stern arbitrament of war'; some knew him as Lludd, others as

Myrddin, or as Emrys. There was a gentler deity, friendly to man, to help whom he fought or cajoled the powers of the underworld; Gwydion he was called, and Arthur. Last, perhaps, to be imagined in concrete shape, there was a long-armed, sharp-speared sun-god who aided the culture-god in his work, and was known as Lleu, or Gwalchmei, or Mabon, or Owain, or Peredur, and no doubt by many another name; and with him is usually found a brother representing not light, but darkness. This expression of a single idea by different names may be also observed in Gaelic myth, though not quite so clearly. In the hurtling of clan against clan, many such divinities perished altogether out of memory, or survived only as names, to make up, in Ireland, the vast, shadowy population claiming to be Tuatha Dé Danann, and, in Britain, the long list of Arthur's followers. Others – gods of stronger communities – would increase their fame as their worshippers increased their territory, until, as happened in Greece, the chief deities of many tribes came together to form a national Pantheon.

We have already tried to explain the 'Coming of Arthur' historically. Mythologically, he came, as, according to Celtic ideas, all things came originally, from the underworld. His father is called Uther Pendragon. But Uther Pendragon is (for the word 'dragon' is not part of the name, but a title signifying 'war-leader') *Uther Ben*, that is, Brân, under his name of the 'Wonderful Head', so that, in spite of the legend which describes Arthur as having disinterred Brân's head on Tower Hill, where it watched against invasion, because he thought it beneath his dignity to keep Britain in any other way than by valour, we must recognize the King of Hades as his father. This being so, it would only be natural that he should take a wife from the same eternal country, and we need not be surprised to find in Gwynhwyvar's father, Ogyrvran, a personage corresponding in all respects to the Celtic conception of the ruler of the underworld. He was of gigantic size; he was the owner of a cauldron out of which three Muses had been born; and he was the patron of the bards, who deemed him to have been the originator of their art. More than this, his very name, analysed into its original *ocur vran*, means the evil *bran*, or raven, the bird of death.

But Welsh tradition credits Arthur with three wives, each of them called Gwynhwyvar. This peculiar arrangement is probably due to the Celtic love of triads; and one may compare them with the three Etains who pass through the mythico-heroic story of Eochaid Airem, Etain, and Mider. Of these three Gwynhwyvars, besides the Gwynhwyvar, daughter of Ogyrvran, one was the daughter of Gwyrd Gwent, of whom we know nothing but the name, and the other of Gwyrthur ap Greidawl, the same 'Victor son of Scorcher' with whom Gwyn son of Nudd, fought, in earlier myth, perpetual battle for the possession of Creudylad, daughter of the sky-god Lludd. This same eternal strife between the powers of light and darkness for the possession of a symbolical damsel is waged again in the Arthurian cycle; but it is no longer for Creudylad that Gwyn contends, but for Gwynhwyvar, and no longer with Gwyrthur, but with Arthur. It would seem to have been a Cornish form of the myth; for the dark god is called 'Melwas', and not 'Gwynwas', or 'Gwyn', his name in Welsh. Melwas lay in ambush for a whole year, and finally succeeded in carrying off Gwynhwyvar to his palace in Avilion. But Arthur pursued, and besieged that stronghold, just as Eochaid Airem had, in the Gaelic version of the universal story, mined and sapped at Mider's *sídh* of Bri Leith. Mythology, as well as history, repeats itself; and Melwas was obliged to restore Gwynhwyvar to her rightful lord.

It is not Melwas, however, that in the best-known versions of the story contends with Arthur for the love of Gwynhwyvar. The most widespread early tradition makes Arthur's rival his nephew Medrawt. Here Professor Rhys traces a striking parallel between the British legend of Arthur, Gwynhwyvar, and Medrawt, and the Gaelic story of Airem, Etain, and Mider. The two myths are practically counterparts; for the names of all the three pairs agree in their essential meaning. 'Airem', like 'Arthur', signifies the 'Ploughman', the divine institutor of agriculture; 'Etain', the 'Shining One', is a fit parallel to 'Gwynhwyvar', the 'White Apparition'; while 'Mider' and 'Medrawt' both come from the same root, a word meaning 'to hit', either literally, or else metaphorically, with the mind, in the sense of coming to a decision. To attempt to explain this myth is to raise the vexed question of the meaning of mythology. Is it day and dark that strive for dawn, or summer and winter for the lovely spring, or does it shadow forth the rescue of the grain that makes man's life from the devouring underworld by the farmer's wit? When this can be finally resolved, a multitude of Celtic myths will be explained. Everywhere arise the same combatants for the stolen bride; one has the attributes of light, the other is a champion of darkness.

Even in Sir Thomas Malory's version of the Arthurian story, taken by him from French romances far removed from the original tradition, we find the myth subsisting. Medrawt's original place as the lover of Arthur's queen had been taken in the romances by Sir Launcelot, who, if he was not some now undiscoverable Celtic god, must have been an invention of the Norman adapters. But the story which makes Medrawt Arthur's rival has been preserved in the account of how Sir Mordred would have wedded Guinevere by force, as part of the rebellion which he made against his king and uncle. This strife was Celtic myth long before it became part of the pseudo-history of early Britain. The triads tell us how Arthur and Medrawt raided each other's courts during the owner's absence. Medrawt went to Kelli Wic, in Cornwall, ate and drank everything he could find there, and insulted Queen Gwynhwyvar, in revenge for which Arthur went to Medrawt's court and killed man and beast. Their struggle only ended with the Battle of Camlan; and that mythical combat, which chroniclers have striven to make historical, is full of legendary detail. Tradition tells how Arthur and his antagonist shared their forces three times during the fight, which caused it to be known as one of the 'Three Frivolous Battles of Britain', the idea of doing so being one of 'Britain's Three Criminal Resolutions'. Four alone survived the fray: one, because he was so ugly that all shrank from him, believing him to be a devil; another, whom no one touched because he was so beautiful that they took him for an angel; a third, whose great strength no one could resist; and Arthur himself, who, after revenging the death of Gwalchmei upon Medrawt, went to the island of Avilion to heal him of his grievous wounds.

And thence – from the Elysium of the Celts popular belief has always been that he will some day return. But just as the gods of the Gaels are said to dwell sometimes in the 'Land of the Living', beyond the western wave, and sometimes in the palace of a hollow hill, so Arthur is sometimes thought to be in Avilion, and sometimes to be sitting with his champions in a charmed sleep in some secret place, waiting for the trumpet to be blown that shall call him forth to reconquer Britain. The legend is found in the Eildon Hills; in the Snowdon district; at Cadbury, in Somerset, the best authenticated Camelot; in the Vale of Neath, in South Wales; as well as in other places. He slumbers, but he has not died. The ancient Welsh poem called 'The Verses of the Graves of the Warriors' enumerates the last resting-places of most of the British gods and demi-gods. 'The grave of Gwydion is in the marsh of Dinlleu', the grave of Lieu Llaw Gyffes is 'under the protection of the sea with which he was familiar', and 'where the wave makes a sullen sound is the grave of Dylan'; we know the graves of Pryderi, of Gwalchmei, of March, of Mabon, even of the great Beli, but

'Not wise the thought – a grave for Arthur'.

XVIII

THE TREASURES OF BRITAIN

It is in keeping with the mythological character of Arthur that the early Welsh tales recorded of him are of a different nature from those which swell the pseudo-histories of Nennius and of Geoffrey of Monmouth. We hear nothing of that subjugation of the countries of Western Europe which fills so large a part in the two books of the *Historia Britonum* which Geoffrey has devoted to him. Conqueror he is, but his conquests are not in any land known to geographers. It is against Hades, and not against Rome, that he achieves his highest triumphs. This is the true history of King Arthur, and we may read more fragments and snatches of it in two prose-tales preserved in the Red Book of Hergest. Both these tales date, in the actual form in which they have come down to us, from the twelfth century. But, in each of them, the writer seems to be stretching out his hands to gather in the dying traditions of a very remote past.

When a Welsh man-at-arms named Rhonabwy lay down, one night, to sleep upon a yellow calf-skin, the only furniture in a noisome hut, in which he had taken shelter, that was comparatively free from vermin, he had the vision which is related in the tale called 'The Dream of Rhonabwy'. He thought that he was travelling with his companions towards the Severn, when they heard a rushing noise behind them, and, looking back, saw a gigantic rider upon a monstrous horse. So terrible was the horseman's appearance that they all started to run from him. But their running was of no avail, for every time the horse drew in its breath, it sucked them back to its very chest, only, however, to fling them forward as it breathed out again. In despair they fell down and besought their pursuer's mercy. He granted it, asked their names, and told them, in return, his own. He was known as Iddawc the Agitator of Britain; for it was he who, in his love of war, had purposely precipitated the Battle of Camlan. Arthur had sent him to reason with Medrawt; but though Arthur had charged him with the fairest sayings he could think of, Iddawc translated them into the harshest he could devise. But he had done seven years' penance, and had been forgiven, and was now riding to Arthur's camp. Thither he insisted upon taking Rhonabwy and his companions.

Arthur's army was encamped for a mile around the ford of Rhyd y Groes, upon both sides of the road; and on a small flat island in the middle of the river was the Emperor himself, in converse with Bedwini the Bishop and Gwarthegyd, the son of Kaw. Like Ossian, when he came back to Ireland after his three hundred years' sojourn in the 'Land of Promise', Arthur marvelled at the puny size of the people whom Iddawc had brought for him to look at. 'And where, Iddawc, didst thou find these little men?' 'I found them, Lord, up yonder on the road.' Then the Emperor smiled. 'Lord,' said Iddawc, 'wherefore dost thou laugh?' 'Iddawc,' replied Arthur, 'I laugh not; but it pitieth me that men of such stature as these should have this island in their keeping, after the men that guarded it of yore.' Then he turned away, and Iddawc told Rhonabwy and his companions to keep silent, and they would see what they would see.

The scope of such a book as this allows no space to describe the persons and equipments of the warriors who came riding down with their companies to join Arthur, as he made his great march to fight the Battle of Badon, thought by some to be historical, and located at Bath. The reader who turns to the tale itself will see what Rhonabwy saw. Many of Arthur's warriors he will know by name: Caradawc the Strong-armed, who is here called a son, not of Brân, but of Llyr; March son of Meirchion, the underworld king; Kai, described as 'the fairest horseman in all Arthur's court'; Gwalchmei, the son of Gwyar and of Arthur himself; Mabon, the son of Modron; Trystan son of Tallwch, the lover of 'The Fair Isoult'; Goreu, Arthur's cousin and his rescuer from Manawyddan's bone-prison; these, and many more, will pass before him, as they passed before Rhonabwy during the three days and three nights that he slept and dreamed upon the calf-skin.

This story of the 'Dream of Rhonabwy', elaborate as it is in all its details, is yet, in substance, little more than a catalogue. The intention of its unknown author seems to have been to draw a series of pictures of what he considered to be the principal among Arthur's followers. The other story – that of 'Kulhwch and Olwen' – also takes this catalogue form, but the matters enumerated are of a different kind. It is not so much a record of men as of things. Not the heroes of Britain, but the treasures of Britain are its subject. One might compare it with the Gaelic story of the adventures of the three sons of Tuirenn.

The 'Thirteen Treasures of Britain' were famous in early legend. They belonged to gods and heroes, and were current in our island till the end of the divine age, when Merlin, fading out of the world, took them with him into his airy tomb, never to be seen by mortal eyes again. According to tradition, they consisted of a sword, a basket, a drinking-horn, a chariot, a halter, a knife, a cauldron, a whetstone, a garment, a pan, a platter, a chess-board, and a mantle, all possessed of not less marvellous qualities than the apples, the pig-skin, the spear, the horses and chariot, the pigs, the hound-whelp, and the cooking-spit which the sons of Tuirenn obtained for Lugh. It is these same legendary treasures that reappear, no doubt, in the story of 'Kulhwch and Olwen'. The number tallies, for there are thirteen of them. Some are certainly, and others probably, identical with those of the other tradition. That there should be discrepancies need cause no surprise, for it is not unlikely that there were several different versions of their legend. Everyone had heard of the Thirteen Treasures of Britain. Many, no doubt, disputed as to what they were. Others might ask whence they came. The story of 'Kulhwch and Olwen' was composed to tell them. They were won by Arthur and his mighty men.

Kulhwch is the hero of the story and Olwen is its heroine, but only, as it were, by courtesy. The pair provide a love-interest which, as in the tales of all primitive people, is kept in the background. The woman, in such romances, takes the place of the gold and gems in a modern 'treasure-hunt' story; she is won by overcoming external obstacles, and not by any difficulty in obtaining her own consent. In this romance, Kulhwch was the son of a king who afterwards married a widow with a grown-up daughter, whom his stepmother urged Kulhwch to marry. On his modestly replying that he was not yet of an age to wed, she laid the destiny on him that he should never have a wife at all, unless he could win Olwen, the daughter of a terrible father called 'Hawthorn, Chief of Giants'.

The 'Chief of Giants' was as hostile to suitors as he was monstrous in shape; and no wonder! for he knew that on his daughter's marriage his own life would come to an end. Both in this peculiarity and in the description of his ponderous eyebrows, which fell so heavily over his eyes that he could not see until they had been lifted up with forks, he reminds one of the Fomor, Balor. Of his daughter, on the other hand, the Welsh tale gives a description as beautiful as Olwen was, herself. 'More yellow was her head than the flower of the broom, and her skin was whiter than the foam of the wave, and fairer were her hands and her fingers than the blossoms of the wood anemone amidst the spray of the meadow-fountain. The eye of the trained hawk, the glance of the three-mewed falcon was not brighter than hers. Her bosom was more snowy than the breast of the white swan, her cheek was redder than the reddest roses. Whoso beheld her was filled with her love. Four white trefoils sprung up wherever she trod. And therefore was she called Olwen.'

Kulhwch had no need to see her to fall in love with her. He blushed at her very name, and asked his father how he could obtain her in marriage. His father reminded him that he was Arthur's cousin, and advised him to claim Olwen from him as a boon.

So Kulhwch 'pricked forth upon a steed with head dappled grey, of four winters old, firm of limb, with shell-formed hoofs, having a bridle of linked gold on his head, and upon him a saddle of costly gold. And in the youth's hand were two spears of silver, sharp, well-tempered, headed with steel, three ells in length, of an edge to wound the wind, and cause blood to flow, and swifter than the fall of the dewdrop from the blade of reed-grass upon the earth when the dew of June is at the heaviest. A gold-hiked sword was upon his thigh, the blade of which was of gold, bearing a cross of inlaid gold of the hue of the lightning of heaven; his war-horn was of ivory. Before him were two brindled white-breasted greyhounds, having strong collars of rubies about their necks, reaching from the shoulder to the ear. And the one that was on the left side bounded across to the right side, and the one on the right to the left, and like two sea-swallows sported around him. And his courser cast up four sods with his four hoofs, like four swallows in the air, about his head, now above, now below. About him was a four-cornered cloth of purple, and an apple of gold was at each corner, and every one of the apples was of the value of an hundred kine. And there was precious gold of the value of three hundred kine upon his shoes, and upon his stirrups, from his knee to the tip of his toe. And the blade of grass bent not beneath him, so light was his courser's tread as he journeyed towards the gate of Arthur's palace.'

Nor did this bold suitor stand greatly upon ceremony. He arrived after the portal of the palace had been closed for the night, and, contrary to all precedent, sent to Arthur demanding instant entry. Although, too, it was the custom for visitors to dismount at the horse-block at the gate, he did not do so, but rode his charger into the hall. After greetings had passed between him and Arthur, and he had announced his name, he demanded Olwen for his bride at the hands of the Emperor and his warriors.

Neither Arthur nor any of his court had ever heard of Olwen. However, he promised his cousin either to find her for him, or to prove that there was no such person. He ordered his most skilful warriors to accompany Kulhwch; Kai, with his companion Bedwyr, the swiftest of men; Kynddelig, who was as good a guide in a strange country as in his own; Gwrhyr, who knew all the languages of men, as well as of all other creatures; Gwalchmei, who never left an adventure unachieved; and Menw, who could render himself and his companions invisible at will.

They travelled until they came to a castle on an open plain. Feeding on the plain was a countless herd of sheep, and, on a mound close by, a monstrous shepherd with a monstrous dog. Menw cast a spell over the dog, and they approached the shepherd. He was called Custennin, a brother of Hawthorn, while his wife was a sister of Kulhwch's own mother. The evil chief of giants had reduced his brother to servitude, and murdered all his twenty-four sons save one, who was kept hidden in a stone chest. Therefore he welcomed Kulhwch and the embassy from Arthur, and promised to help them secretly, the more readily since Kai offered to take the one surviving son under his protection. Custennin's wife procured Kulhwch a secret meeting with Olwen, and the damsel did not altogether discourage her wooer's suit.

The party started for Hawthorn's castle. Without raising any alarm, they slew the nine porters and the nine watch-dogs, and came unhindered into the hall. They greeted the ponderous giant, and announced the reason of their coming. 'Where are my pages and my servants?' he said. 'Raise up the forks beneath my two eyebrows which have fallen over my eyes, so that I may see the fashion of my son-in-law.' He glared at them, and told them to come again upon the next day.

They turned to go, and, as they did so, Hawthorn seized a poisoned dart, and threw it after them. But Bedwyr caught it, and cast it back, wounding the giant's knee. They left him grumbling, slept at the house of Custennin, and returned, the next morning.

Again they demanded Olwen from her father, threatening him with death if he refused. 'Her four great-grandmothers, and her four great-grandsires are yet alive,' replied Hawthorn; 'it is needful that I take counsel of them.' So they turned away, and, as they went, he flung a second dart, which Menw caught, and hurled back, piercing the giant's body.

The next time they came, Hawthorn warned them not to shoot at him again, unless they desired death. Then he ordered his eyebrows to be lifted up, and, as soon as he could see, he flung a poisoned dart straight at Kulhwch. But the suitor himself caught it, and flung it back, so that it pierced Hawthorn's eyeball and came out through the back of his head. Here again we are reminded of the myth of Lugh and Balor. Hawthorn, however, was not killed, though he was very much discomforted. 'A cursed ungentle son-in-law, truly!' he complained. 'As long as I remain alive, my eyesight will be the worse. Whenever I go against the wind, my eyes will water; and peradventure my head will burn, and I shall have a giddiness every new moon. Cursed be the fire in which it was forged! Like the bite of a mad dog is the stroke of this poisoned iron.'

It was now the turn of Kulhwch and his party to warn the giant that there must be no more dart-throwing. He appeared, indeed, more amenable to reason, and allowed himself to be placed opposite to Kulhwch, in a chair, to discuss the amount of his daughter's bride-price.

Its terms, as he gradually unfolded them, were terrific. The blood-fine paid for Cian to Lugh seems, indeed, a trifle beside it. To obtain grain, for food and liquor at his daughter's wedding, a vast hill which he showed to Kulhwch must be rooted up, levelled, ploughed, sown, and harvested in one day. No one could do this except Amaethon son of Dôn, the divine husbandman, and Govannan son of Dôn, the divine smith, and they must have the service of three pairs of magic oxen. He must also have returned to him the same nine bushels of flax which he had sown in his youth, and which had never come up; for only out of this very flax should be made the white wimple for Olwen's head. For mead, too, he must have honey 'nine times sweeter than the honey of the virgin swarm'.

Then followed the enumeration of the thirteen treasures to be paid to him as dowry. Such a list of wedding presents was surely never known! No pot could hold such honey as he demanded but the magic vessel of Llwyr, the son of Llwyryon. There would not be enough food for all the wedding-guests, unless he had the basket of Gwyddneu Garanhir, from which all the men in the world could be fed, thrice nine at a time. No cauldron could cook the meat, except that of Diwrnach the Gael. The mystic drinking-horn of Gwlgawd Gododin must be there, to give them drink. The harp of Teirtu, which, like the Dagda's, played of itself, must make music for them. The giant father-in-law's hair could only be shorn with one instrument – the tusk of White-tooth, King of the Boars, and not even by that unless it was plucked alive out of its owner's mouth. Also, before the hair could be cut, it must be spread out, and this could not be done until it had been first softened with the blood of the perfectly black sorceress, daughter of the perfectly white sorceress, from the Source of the Stream of Sorrow, on the borders of hell. Nor could the sorceress's blood be kept warm enough unless it was placed in the bottles of Gwyddolwyn Gorr, which preserved the heat of any liquor put into them, though it was carried from the east of the world to the west. Another set of bottles he must also have to keep milk for his guests in – those bottles of Rhinnon Rhin Barnawd in which no drink ever turned sour. For himself, he required the sword of Gwrnach the Giant, which that personage would never allow out of his own keeping, because it was destined that he himself should fall by it. Last of all, he must be given the comb, the razor, and the scissors which lay between the ears of Twrch Trwyth, a king changed into the most terrible of wild boars.

It is the chase of this boar which gives the story of 'Kulhwch and Olwen' its alternative title – 'The Twrch Trwyth'. The task was one worthy of gods and demi-gods. Its contemplation might well have appalled Kulhwch, who, however, was not so easily frightened. To every fresh demand, every new obstacle put in his way, he gave the same answer:

'It will be easy for me to compass this, although thou mayest think that it will not be easy'.

Whether it was easy or not will be seen from the conditions under which alone the hunt could be brought to a successful end. No ordinary hounds or huntsmen would avail. The chief of the pack must be Drudwyn, the whelp of Greid the son of Eri, led in the one leash that would hold him, fastened, by the one chain strong enough, to the one collar that would contain his neck. No huntsman could hunt with this dog except Mabon son of Modron; and he had, ages before, been taken from between his mother and the wall when he was three nights old, and it was not known where he was, or even whether he were living or dead. There was only one steed that could carry Mabon, namely Gwynn Mygdwn, the horse of Gweddw. Two other marvellous hounds, the cubs of Gast Rhymhi, must also be obtained; they must be held in the only leash they would not break, for it would be made out of the beard of the giant Dissull, plucked from him while he was still alive. Even with this, no huntsman could lead them except Kynedyr Wyllt, who was himself nine times more wild than the wildest beast upon the mountains. All Arthur's mighty men must come to help, even Gwyn son of Nudd, upon his black horse; and how could he be spared from his terrible duty of restraining the devils in hell from breaking loose and destroying the world?

Here is material for romance indeed! But, unhappily, we shall never know the full story of how all these magic treasures were obtained, all these magic hounds captured and compelled to hunt, all these magic huntsmen brought to help. The story – which Mr. Nutt considers to be, 'saving the finest tales of the 'Arabian Nights', the greatest romantic fairy tale the world has ever known' – is not, as we have it now, complete. It reads fully enough; but, on casting backwards and forwards, between the list of feats to be performed and the body of the tale which is supposed to relate them all, we find many of them wanting. 'The host of Arthur', we are told, 'dispersed themselves into parties of one and two', each party intent upon some separate quest. The adventures of some of them have come down, but those of others have not. We are told how Kai slew Gwrnach the Giant with his own sword; how Gwyrthur son of Greidawl, Gwyn's rival for the love of Creudylad, saved an anthill from fire, and how the grateful ants searched for and found the very flax-seeds sown by Hawthorn in his youth; how Arthur's host surrounded and took Gast Rhymhi's cubs, and how Kai and Bedwyr overcame Dissull, and plucked out his beard with wooden tweezers, to make a leash for them. We learn how Arthur went to Ireland, and brought back the cauldron of Diwrnach the Gael, full of Irish money; how White-tusk the Boar-king was chased and killed; and how Arthur condescended to slay the perfectly black sorceress with his own hand. That others of the treasures were acquired is hinted rather than said. Most important of all (for so much depended on him), we find out where the stolen Mabon was, and learn how he was rescued.

So many ages had elapsed since Mabon had disappeared that there seemed little hope of ever finding news of him. Nevertheless Gwrhyr, who spoke the languages of all creatures, went to enquire of that ancient bird, the Ousel of Cilgwri. But the Ousel, though in her time she had pecked a smith's anvil down to the size of a nut, was yet too young to have heard of Mabon. She sent Gwrhyr to a creature formed before her, the Stag of Redynvre. But though the Stag had lived to see an oak-sapling slowly grow to be a tree with a thousand branches, and as slowly decay again till it was a withered stump, he had never heard of Mabon.

Therefore he sent him on to a creature still older than himself – the Owl of Cwm Cawlwyd. The wood she lived in had been thrice rooted up, and had thrice resown itself, and yet, in all that immense time, she had never heard of Mabon. There was but one who might have, she told Gwrhyr, and he was the Eagle of Gwern Abwy.

Here, at last, they struck Mabon's trail. 'The Eagle said: "I have been here for a great space of time, and when I first came hither there was a rock here, from the top of which I pecked at the stars every evening; and now it is not so much as a span high. From that day to this I have been here, and I have never heard of the man for whom you inquire, except once when I went in search of food as far as Llyn Llyw. And when I came there, I struck my talons into a salmon, thinking he would serve me as food for a long time. But he drew me into the deep, and I was scarcely able to escape from him. After that I went with my whole kindred to attack him, and to try to destroy him, but he sent messengers, and made peace with me; and came and besought me to take fifty fish spears out of his back. Unless he know something of him whom you seek, I cannot tell who may. However, I will guide you to the place where he is."'

It happened that the Salmon did know. With every tide he went up the Severn as far as the walls of Gloucester, and there, he said, he had found such wrong as he had never found anywhere else. So he took Kai and Gwrhyr upon his shoulders and carried them to the wall of the prison where a captive was heard lamenting. This was Mabon son of Modron, who was suffering such imprisonment as not even Lludd of the Silver Hand or Greid, the son of Eri, the other two of the 'Three Paramount Prisoners of Britain', had endured before him. But it came to an end now; for Kai sent to Arthur, and he and his warriors stormed Gloucester, and brought Mabon away.

All was at last ready for the final achievement – the hunting of Twrch Trwyth, who was now, with his seven young pigs, in Ireland. Before he was roused, it was thought wise to send the wizard Menw to find out by ocular inspection whether the comb, the scissors, and the razor were still between his ears. Menw took the form of a bird, and settled upon the Boar's head. He saw the coveted treasures, and tried to take one of them, but Twrch Trwyth shook himself so violently that some of the venom from his bristles spurted over Menw, who was never quite well again from that day.

Then the hunt was up, the men surrounded him, and the dogs were loosed at him from every side. On the first day, the Irish attacked him. On the second day, Arthur's household encountered him and were worsted. Then Arthur himself fought with him for nine days and nine nights without even killing one of the little pigs.

A truce was now called, so that Gwrhyr, who spoke all languages, might go and parley with him. Gwrhyr begged him to give up in peace the comb, the scissors, and the razor, which were all that Arthur wanted. But the Boar Trwyth, indignant of having been so annoyed, would not. On the contrary, he promised to go on the morrow into Arthur's country, and do all the harm he could there.

So Twrch Trwyth with his seven pigs crossed the sea into Wales, and Arthur followed with his warriors in the ship 'Prydwen'. Here the story becomes wonderfully realistic and circumstantial. We are told of every place they passed through on the long chase through South Wales, and can trace the course of the hunt over the map. We know of every check the huntsmen had, and what happened every time the boars turned to bay. The 'casualty-list' of Arthur's men is completely given; and we can also follow the shrinking of Twrch Trwyth's herd, as his little pigs fell one by one. None were left but Trwyth himself by the time the Severn estuary was reached, at the mouth of the Wye.

Here the hunt came up with him, and drove him into the water, and in this unfamiliar element he was outmatched. Osla Big-Knife, Manawyddan son of Llyr, Kacmwri, the servant of Arthur, and Gwyngelli caught him by his four feet and plunged his head under water, while the two chief huntsmen, Mabon son of Modron, and Kyledyr Willt, came, one on each side of him, and took the scissors and the razor. Before they could get the comb, however, he shook himself free, and struck out for Cornwall, leaving Osla and Kacmwri half-drowned in the Severn.

And all this trouble, we are told, was mere play compared with the trouble they had with him in Cornwall before they could get the comb. But, at last, they secured it, and drove the boar out over the deep sea. He passed out of sight, with two of the magic hounds in pursuit of him, and none of them have ever been heard of since.

The sight of these treasures, paraded before Hawthorn, chief of giants, was, of course, his death-warrant. All who wished him ill came to gloat over his downfall. But they should have been put to shame by the giant, whose end had, at least, a certain dignity. 'My daughter', he said to Kulhwch, 'is yours, but you need not thank me for it, but Arthur, who has accomplished all this. By my free will you should never have had her, for with her I lose my life.'

Thereupon they cut off his head, and put it upon a pole; and that night the undutiful Olwen became Kulhwch's bride.

XIX

THE GODS AS KING ARTHUR'S KNIGHTS

It is not, however, by such fragments of legend that Arthur is best known to English readers. Not Arthur the god, but Arthur the 'blameless king', who founded the Table Round, from which he sent forth his knights 'to ride abroad redressing human wrongs', is the figure which the name conjures up. Nor is it even from Sir Thomas Malory's Morte Darthur that this conception comes to most of us, but from Tennyson's *Idylls of the King*. But Tennyson has so modernized the ancient tradition that it retains little of the old Arthur but the name. He tells us himself that his poem had but very slight relation to –

> 'that gray king, whose name, a ghost,
> Streams like a cloud, man-shaped, from mountain-peak,
> And cleaves to cairn and cromlech still; or him
> Of Geoffrey's book, or him of Malleor's ... ';

but that he merely used the legend to give a substantial form to his ideal figure of the perfect English gentleman – a title to which the original Arthur could scarcely have laid claim. Still less does there remain in it the least trace of anything that could suggest mythology.

As much as this, however, might be said of Malory's book. We may be fairly certain that the good Sir Thomas had no idea that the personages of whom he wrote had ever been anything different from the Christian knights which they had become in the late French romances from which he compiled his own fifteenth-century work. The old gods had been, from time to time, very completely euhemerized. The characters of the 'Four Branches of the Mabinogi' are still recognizable as divine beings. In the later Welsh stories, however, their divinity merely hangs about them in shreds and tatters, and the first Norman adapters of these stories made them still more definitely human. By the time Malory came to build up his Morte Darthur from the foreign romances, they had altered so much that the shapes and deeds of gods could only be recognized under their mediæval knightly disguises by those who had known them in their ancient forms.

We have chosen Malory's Morte Darthur, as almost the sole representative of Arthurian literature later than the Welsh poems and prose stories, for three reasons. Firstly, because it is the English Arthurian romance *par excellence* from which all later English authors, including Tennyson, have drawn their material. Secondly, because the mass of foreign literature dealing with the subject of Arthur is in itself a life-study, and could not by any possibility be compressed within the limits of a chapter. Thirdly, because Malory's fine judgment caused him to choose the best and most typical foreign tales to weave into his own romance; and hence it is that we find most of our old British gods – both those of the earlier cycle and those of the system connected with Arthur – striding disguised through his pages.

Curiously enough, Sir Edward Strachey, in his preface to the 'Globe' edition of Caxton's Morte Darthur, uses almost the same image to describe Malory's prose-poem that Matthew Arnold handled with such effect, in his *Study of Celtic Literature*, to point out the real nature of the Mabinogion. 'Malory', he says, 'has built a great, rambling, mediæval castle, the walls of which enclose rude and even ruinous work of earlier times.' How rude and how ruinous these relics were Malory doubtless had not the least idea, for he has completely jumbled the ancient mythology. Not only do the gods of the older and newer order appear together, but the same deities, under very often only slightly varying names, come up again and again as totally different characters.

Take, for example, the ancient deity of death and Hades. As King Brandegore, or Brandegoris (Brân of Gower), he brings five thousand mounted men to oppose King Arthur; but, as Sir Brandel, or Brandiles (Brân of Gwales), he is a valiant Knight of the Round Table, who dies fighting in Arthur's service. Again, under the name of Uther Pendragon (Uther Ben), he is Arthur's father; though as King Ban of Benwyk (the 'Square Enclosure', doubtless the same as Taliesin's *Caer Pedryvan* and Malory's *Carbonek*), he is a foreign monarch, who is Arthur's ally. Yet again, as the father of Guinevere, Ogyrvran has become Leodegrance. As King Uriens, or Urience, of Gore (Gower), he marries one of Arthur's sisters, fights against him, but finally tenders his submission, and is enrolled among his knights. Urien may also be identified in the Morte Darthur as King Rience, or Ryons, of North Wales, and as King Nentres of Garloth; while, to crown the varied disguises of this Proteus of British gods, he appears in an isolated episode as Balan, who fights with his brother Balin until they kill one another.

One may generally tell the divinities of the underworld in these romances by their connection, not with the settled and civilized parts of England, but with the wild and remote north and west, and the still wilder and remoter islands. Just as Brân and Urien are kings of Gower, so Arawn, under the corruptions of his name into 'Anguish' and 'Anguissance', is made King of Scotland or Ireland, both countries having been probably confounded, as the same land of the Scotti, or Gaels. Pwyll, Head of Annwn, we likewise discover under two disguises. As Pelles, 'King of the Foreign Country' and Keeper of the Holy Grail, he is a personage of great mythological significance, albeit the real nature of him and his surroundings has been overlaid with a Christian veneer as foreign to the original of Pelles as his own kingdom was to Arthur's knights. The Chief of Hades figures as a 'cousin nigh unto Joseph of Arimathie', who, 'while he might ride supported much Christendom, and holy church'. He is represented as the father of Elayne (Elen), whom he gives in marriage to Sir Launcelot, bestowing upon the couple a residence called 'Castle Bliant', the name of which, there is good evidence to show, is connected with that of Pwyll's vassal called Teirnyon Twryf Vliant in the first of the Mabinogi. Under his other name of 'Sir Pelleas' – the hero of Tennyson's *Idyll of Pelleas and Ettarre* – the primitive myth of Pwyll is touched at a different point. After his unfortunate love-passage with *Ettarre* (or Ettard, as Malory calls her), Pelleas is represented as marrying Nimue, whose original name, which was Rhiannon, reached this form, as well as that of 'Vivien', through a series of miscopyings of successive scribes.

With Pelles, or Pelleas, is associated a King Pellean, or Pellam, his son, and, equally with him, the Keeper of the Grail, who can be no other than Pryderi. Like that deity in the Mabinogi of Mâth, he is defeated by one of the gods of light. The dealer of the blow, however, is not Arthur, as successor to Gwydion, but Balin, the Gallo-British sun-god Belinus.

Another dark deity, Gwyn son of Nudd, we discover under all of his three titles. Called variously 'Sir Gwinas', 'Sir Guynas', and 'Sir Gwenbaus' by Malory, the Welsh Gwynwas (or Gwyn) is altogether on Arthur's side. The Cornish Melwas, split into two different knights, divides his allegiance. As Sir Melias, or Meleaus, de Lile ('of the Isle'), he is a Knight of the Round Table, though, on the quarrel between Arthur and Launcelot, he sides with the knight against the king. But as Sir Meliagraunce, or Meliagaunce, it is he who, as in the older myth, captures Queen Guinevere and carries her off to his castle. Under his Somerset name of Avallon, or Avallach, he is connected with the episode of the Grail. King Evelake is a Saracen ruler who was converted by Joseph of Arimathea, and brought by him to Britain. In his convert's enthusiasm, he attempted the quest of the holy vessel, but was not allowed to succeed. As a consolation, however, it was divinely promised him that he should not die until he had seen a knight of his blood in the ninth degree who should achieve it. This was done by Sir Percivale, King Evelake being then three hundred years old.

Turning from deities of darkness to deities of light, we find the sky-god figuring largely in the Morte Darthur. The Lludd of the earlier mythology is Malory's King Loth, or Lot, of Orkney, through an intrigue with whose wife Arthur becomes the father of Sir Mordred. Lot's wife was the mother also of Sir Gawain, whose birth Malory does not, however, attribute to Arthur, though such must have been the original form of the myth. Sir Gawain, of the Arthurian legend, is the Gwalchmei of the Welsh stories, the successor of the still earlier Lieu Llaw Gyffes, just as Sir Mordred – the Welsh Medrawt – corresponds to Lieu's brother Dylan. As Sir Mordred retains the dark character of Medrawt, so Sir Gawain, even in Malory, shows the attributes of a solar deity. We are told that his strength increased gradually from dawn till high noon, and then as gradually decreased again – a piece of pagan symbolism which forms a good example of the appositeness of Sir Edward Strachey's figure; for it stands out of the mediæval narrative like an ancient brick in some more modern building.

The Zeus of the later cycle, Emrys or Myrddin, appears in the Morte Darthur under both his names. The word 'Emrys' becomes 'Bors', and King Bors of Gaul is made a brother of King Ban of Benwyck – that is, Brân of the Square Enclosure, the ubiquitous underworld god. Myrddin we meet under no such disguise. The ever-popular Merlin still retains intact the attributes of the sky-god. He remains above, and apart from all the knights, higher even in some respects than King Arthur, to whom he stands in much the same position as Mâth does to Gwydion in the Mabinogi. Like Mâth, he is an enchanter, and, like Mâth, too, who could hear everything said in the world, in however low a tone, if only the wind met it, he is practically omniscient. The account of his final disappearance, as told in the Morte Darthur, is only a re-embellishment of the original story, the nature-myth giving place to what novelists call 'a feminine interest'. Everyone knows how the great magician fell into a dotage upon the 'lady of the lake' whom Malory calls 'Nimue', and Tennyson 'Vivien' – both names being that of 'Rhiannon' in disguise. 'Merlin would let her have no rest, but always he would be with her . . . and she was ever passing weary of him, and fain would have been delivered of him, for she was afeard of him because he was a devil's son, and she could not put him away by no means. And so on a time it happed that Merlin showed to her in a rock whereas was a great wonder, and wrought by enchantment, that went under a great stone. So, by her subtle working, she made Merlin to go under that stone to let her wit of the marvels there, but she wrought so there for him that he never came out for all the craft that he could do. And so she departed and left Merlin.'

Merlin's living grave is still to be seen at the end of the *Val des Fées*, in the forest of Brécilien, in Brittany. The tomb of stone is certainly but a prosaic equivalent for the tower of woven air in which the heaven-god went to his rest. Still, it is not quite so unpoetic as the leather sack in which Rhiannon, the original of Nimue, caught and imprisoned Gwawl, the earlier Merlin, like a badger in a bag.

Elen, Myrddin's consort, appears in Malory as five different 'Elaines'. Two of them are wives of the dark god, under his names of 'King Ban' and 'King Nentres'. A third is called the daughter of King Pellinore, a character of uncertain origin. But the two most famous are the ladies who loved Sir Launcelot – 'Elaine the Fair, Elaine the lovable, Elaine the lily maid of Astolat', and the luckier and less scrupulous Elaine, daughter of King Pelles, and mother of Sir Launcelot's son, Galahad.

But it is time, now that the most important figures of British mythology have been shown under their knightly disguises, and their place in Arthurian legend indicated, to pass on to some account of the real subject-matter of Sir Thomas Malory's romance. Externally, it is the history of an Arthur, King of Britain, whom most people of Malory's time considered as eminently a historical character. Around this central narrative of Arthur's reign and deeds are grouped, in the form of episodes, the personal exploits of the knights believed to have supported him by forming a kind of household guard. But, with the exception of a little magnified and distorted legendary history, the whole cycle of romance may be ultimately resolved into a few myths, not only retold, but recombined in several forms by their various tellers. The Norman adapters of the *Matière de Bretagne* found the British mythology already in process of transformation, some of the gods having dwindled into human warriors, and others into hardly less human druids and magicians. Under their hands the British warriors became Norman knights, who did their deeds of prowess in the tilt-yard, and found their inspiration in the fantastic chivalry popularized by the Trouveres, while the druids put off their still somewhat barbaric druidism for the more conventional magic of the Latin races. More than this, as soon as the real sequence and *raison d'être* of the tales had been lost sight of, their adapters used a free hand in reweaving them. Most of the romancers had their favourite characters whom they made the central figure in their stories. Sir Gawain, Sir Percival, Sir Tristrem, and Sir Owain (all of them probably once local British sun-gods) appear as the most important personages of the romances called after their names, stories of the doughty deeds of christened knights who had little left about them either of Briton or of pagan.

It is only the labours of the modern scholar that can bring back to us, at this late date, things long forgotten when Malory's book was issued from Caxton's press. But oblivion is not annihilation, and Professor Rhys points out to us the old myths lying embedded in their later setting with almost the same certainty with which the geologist can show us the fossils in the rock. Thus treated, they resolve themselves into three principal *motifs*, prominent everywhere in Celtic mythology: the birth of the sun-god; the struggle between light and darkness; and the raiding of the underworld by friendly gods for the good of man.

The first has been already dealt with. It is the retelling of the story of the origin of the sun-god in the Mabinogi of Mâth, son of Mâthonwy. For Gwydion we now have Arthur; instead of

Arianrod, the wife of the superannuated sky-god Nwyvre, we find the wife of King Lot, the superannuated sky-god Lludd; Lleu Llaw Gyffes rises again as Sir Gawain (Gwalchmei), and Dylan as Sir Mordred (Medrawt); while the wise Merlin, the Jupiter of the new system, takes the place of his wise prototype, Mâth. Connected with this first myth is the second – the struggle between light and darkness, of which there are several versions in the Morte Darthur. The leading one is the rebellion of the evilly-disposed Sir Mordred against Arthur and Sir Gawain; while, on other stages, Balan – the dark god Brân – fights with Balin – the sun-god Belinus; and the same Balin, or Belinus, gives an almost mortal stroke to Pellam, the Pryderi of the older mythology.

The same myth has also a wider form, in which the battle is waged for possession of a maiden. Thus (to seek no other instances) Gwynhwyvar was contended for by Arthur and Medrawt, or, in an earlier form of the myth, by Arthur and Gwyn. In the Morte Darthur, Gwyn, under the corruption of his Cornish name Melwas into 'Sir Meliagraunce', still captures Guinevere, but it is no longer Arthur who rescues her. That task, or privilege, has fallen to a new champion. It is Sir Launcelot who follows Sir Meliagraunce, defeats and slays him, and rescues the fair captive. But Sir Launcelot, it must be stated – probably to the surprise of those to whom the Arthurian story without Launcelot and Queen Guinevere must seem almost like the play of 'Hamlet with Hamlet left out', – is unknown to the original tradition. Welsh song and story are silent with regard to him, and he is not improbably a creation of some Norman romancer who calmly appropriated to his hero's credit deeds earlier told of other 'knights'.

But the romantic treatment of these two myths by the adapters of the *Matière de Bretagne* are of smaller interest to us at the present day than that of the third. The attraction of the Arthurian story lies less in the battles of Arthur or the loves of Guinevere than in the legend that has given it its lasting popularity – the Christian romance of the Quest of the Holy Grail. So great and various has been the inspiration of this legend to noble works both of art and literature that it seems almost a kind of sacrilege to trace it back, like all the rest of Arthur's story, to a paganism which could not have even understood, much less created, its mystical beauty. None the less is the whole story directly evolved from primitive pagan myths concerning a miraculous cauldron of fertility and inspiration.

In the later romances, the Holy Grail is a Christian relic of marvellous potency. It had held the Paschal lamb eaten at the Last Supper; and, after the death of Christ, Joseph of Arimathea had filled it with the Saviour's blood. But before it received this colouring, it had been the magic cauldron of all the Celtic mythologies – the Dagda's 'Undry' which fed all who came to it, and from which none went away unsatisfied; Brân's cauldron of Renovation, which brought the dead back to life; the cauldron of Ogyrvran the Giant, from which the Muses ascended; the cauldrons captured by Cuchulainn from the King of the Shadowy City, and by Arthur from the chief of Hades; as well as several other mythic vessels of less note.

In its transition from pagan to Christian form, hardly one of the features of the ancient myth has been really obscured. We may recount the chief attributes, as Taliesin tells them in his 'Spoiling of Annwn', of the cauldron captured by Arthur. It was the property of Pwyll, and of his son Pryderi, who lived in a kingdom of the other world called, among other titles, the 'Revolving Castle', the 'Four-cornered Castle', the 'Castle of Revelry', the 'Kingly Castle', the 'Glass Castle', and the 'Castle of Riches'. This place was surrounded by the sea, and in other ways made difficult of access; there was no lack of wine there, and its happy inhabitants spent with music and feasting an existence which neither disease nor old age could assail. As for the cauldron, it had a rim of pearls around its edge; the fire beneath it was kept fanned by the breaths of nine maidens; it spoke, doubtless in words of prophetic wisdom; and it would not cook the food of a perjurer or coward. Here we have considerable data on which to base a parallel between the pagan cauldron and the Christian Grail.

Nor have we far to go in search of correspondences, for they are nearly all preserved in Malory's romance. The mystic vessel was kept by King Pelles, who is Pwyll, in a castle called 'Carbonek', a name which resolves itself, in the hands of the philologist, into *Caer bannawg*, the 'square' or 'four-cornered castle' – in other words, the *Caer Pedryvan* of Taliesin's poem. Of the character of the place as a 'Castle of Riches' and a 'Castle of Revelry', where 'bright wine was the drink of the host', we have more than a hint in the account, twice given, of how, upon the appearance of the Grail – borne, it should be noticed, by a maiden or angel – the hall was filled with good odours, and every knight found on the table all the kinds of meat and drink he could imagine as most desirable. It could not be seen by sinners, a Christian refinement of the savage idea of a pot that would not cook a coward's food; but the sight of it alone would cure of wounds and sickness those who approached it faithfully and humbly, and in its presence neither old age nor sickness could oppress them. And, though in Malory we find no reference either to the spot having been surrounded by water, or to the castle as a 'revolving' one, we have only to turn from the Morte Darthur to the romance entitled the *Seint Greal* to discover both. Gwalchmei, going to the castle of King Peleur (Pryderi), finds it encircled by a great water, while Peredur, approaching the same place, sees it turning with greater speed than the swiftest wind. Moreover, archers on the walls shoot so vigorously that no armour can resist their shafts, which explains how it happened that, of those that went with Arthur, 'except seven, none returned from Caer Sidi'.

It is noticeable that Arthur himself never attempts the quest of the Grail, though it was he who had achieved its pagan original. We find in Malory four competitors for the mantle of Arthur – Sir Pelleas, Sir Bors, Sir Percivale, and Sir Galahad. The first of these may be put out of court at once, Sir Pelleas, who, being himself Pelles, or Pwyll, the keeper of it, could have had no reason for such exertions. At the second we may look doubtfully; for Sir Bors is no other than Emrys, or Myrddin, and, casting back to the earlier British mythology, we do not find the sky-god personally active in securing boons by force or craft from the underworld. The other two have better claims – Sir Percivale and Sir Galahad. 'Sir Percivale' is the Norman-French name for Peredur, the hero of a story in the Red Book of Hergest which gives the oldest form of a Grail quest we have. It is anterior to the Norman romances, and forms almost a connecting-link between tales of mythology and of chivalry. Peredur, or Sir Percivale, therefore, is the oldest, most primitive, of Grail seekers. On the other hand, Sir Galahad is the latest and youngest. But there is reason to believe that Galahad, in Welsh 'Gwalchaved', the 'Falcon of Summer', is the same solar hero as Gawain, in Welsh 'Gwalchmei', the 'Falcon of May'. Both are made, in the story of 'Kulhwch and Olwen', sons of the same mother, Gwyar. Sir Gawain himself is, in one Arthurian romance, the achiever of the Grail. It is needless to attempt to choose between these two. Both have the attributes of sun-gods. Gwalchmei, the successor of Lleu Llaw Gyffes, and Peredur Paladrhir, that is to say, the 'Spearman with the Long Shaft', may be allowed to claim equal honours. What is important is that the quest of the Grail, once the chief treasure of Hades, is still accomplished by one who takes in later legend the place of Lleu Llaw Gyffes and Lugh Lamhfada in the earlier British and Gaelic myths as a long-armed solar deity victorious in his strife against the Powers of Darkness.

XX

THE DECLINE AND FALL OF THE GODS

If there be love of fame in celestial minds, those gods might count themselves fortunate who shared in the transformation of Arthur. Their divinity had fallen from them, but in their new rôles, as heroes of romance, they entered upon vivid reincarnations. The names of Arthur's Knights might almost be described as 'household words', while the gods who had no portion in the Table Round are known only to those who busy themselves with antiquarian lore. It is true that a few folk-tales still survive in the remoter parts of Wales, in which the names of such ancient British deities as Gwydion, Gwyn, Arianrod, and Dylan appear, but it is in such a chaos of jumbled and distorted legend that one finds it hard to pick out even the slenderest thread of story. They have none of the definite coherence of the contemporary Gaelic folk-tales quoted in a previous chapter as still preserving the myths about Goibniu, Lugh, Cian, Manannán, Ethniu, and Balor. Indeed, they have reached such a stage of disintegration that they can hardly now survive another generation.

There have been, however, other paths by which the fame of a god might descend to a posterity which would no longer credit his divinity. The rolls of early British history were open to welcome any number of mythical personages, provided that their legends were attractive. Geoffrey of Monmouth's famous *Historia Britonum* is, under its grave pretence of exact history, as mythological as the Morte Darthur, or even the Mabinogion. The annals of early British saintship were not less accommodating. A god whose tradition was too potent to be ignored or extinguished was canonized, as a matter of course, by clerics who held as an axiom that 'the toleration of the cromlech facilitated the reception of the Gospel.' Only the most irreconcilable escaped them – such a one as Gwyn son of Nudd, who, found almost useless by Geoffrey and intractable by the monkish writers, remains the last survivor of the old gods – dwindled to the proportions of a fairy, but unsubdued.

This part of resistance is perhaps the most dignified; for deities can be sadly changed by the caprices of their euhemerizers. Dôn, whom we knew as the mother of the heaven gods, seems strangely described as a *king* of Lochlin and Dublin, who led the Irish into north Wales in AD 267. More recognizable is *his* son Gwydion, who introduced the knowledge of letters into the country of his adoption. The dynasty of 'King' Dôn, according to a manuscript in the collection of Mr. Edward Williams – better known under his bardic name of Iolo Morganwg – held north Wales for a hundred and twenty-nine years, when the North British king, Cunedda, invaded the country, defeated the Irish in a great battle, and drove them across sea to the Isle of Man. This battle is historical, and, putting Dôn and Gwydion out of the question, probably represented the last stand of the Gael, in the extreme west of Britain, against the second and stronger wave of Celtic invasion. In the same collection of *Iolo Manuscripts* is found a curious, and even comic, euhemeristic version of the strange myth of the Bone Prison of Oeth and Anoeth which Manawyddan son of Llyr, built in Gower. The new reading makes that ghastly abode a real building, constructed out of the bones of the 'Caesarians' (Romans) killed in battle with the Cymri. It consisted of numerous chambers, some of large bones and some of small, some above ground and some under. Prisoners of war were placed in the more comfortable cells, the underground dungeons being kept for traitors to their country. Several times the 'Caesarians' demolished the prison, but, each time, the Cymri rebuilt it stronger than before. At last, however, the bones decayed, and, being spread upon the ground, made an excellent manure! 'From that time forth' the people of the neighbourhood 'had astonishing crops of wheat and barley and of every other grain for many years'.

It is not, however, in these, so to speak, unauthorized narratives that we can best refind our British deities, but in the compact, coherent, and at times almost convincing *Historia Britonum* of Geoffrey of Monmouth, published in the first half of the twelfth century, and for hundreds of years gravely quoted as the leading authority on the early history of our islands. The modern critical spirit has, of course, relegated it to the region of fable. We can no longer accept the pleasant tradition of the descent of the Britons from the survivors of Troy, led westward in search of a new home by Brutus, the great-grandson of the pious Æneas. Nor indeed does any portion of the *History*, from Æneas to Athelstan, quite persuade the latter-day reader. Its kings succeed one another in plausible sequence, but they themselves are too obviously the heroes of popular legend.

A large part of Geoffrey's chronicle – two books out of twelve – is, of course, devoted to Arthur. In it he tells the story of that paladin's conquests, not only in his own country, against the Saxons, the Irish, the Scots, and the Picts, but over all western Europe. We see the British champion, after annexing Ireland,

Iceland, Gothland, and the Orkneys, following up these minor victories by subduing Norway, Dacia (by which Denmark seems to have been meant), Aquitaine, and Gaul. After such triumphs there was clearly nothing left for him but the overthrow of the Roman empire; and this he had practically achieved when the rebellion of Mordred brought him home to his death, or rather (for even Geoffrey does not quite lose hold of the belief in the undying Arthur) to be carried to the island of Avallon to be healed of his wounds, the crown of Britain falling to 'his kinsman Constantine, the son of Cador, Duke of Cornwall, in the five hundred and forty-second year of our Lord's incarnation'. Upon the more personal incidents connected with Arthur, Geoffrey openly professes to keep silence, possibly regarding them as not falling within the province of his history, but we are told shortly how Mordred took advantage of Arthur's absence on the Continent to seize the throne, marry Guanhamara (Guinevere), and ally himself with the Saxons, only to be defeated at that fatal battle called by Geoffrey 'Cambula', in which Mordred, Arthur, and Walgan – the 'Sir Gawain' of Malory and the Gwalchmei of the earlier legends – all met their dooms.

We find the gods of the older generation standing in the same position with regard to Arthur in Geoffrey's 'History' as they do in the later Welsh triads and tales. Though rulers, they are yet his vassals. In 'three brothers of royal blood', called Lot, Urian, and Augusel, who are represented as having been chiefs in the north, we may discern Lludd, Urien, and Arawn. To these three Arthur restored 'the rights of their ancestors', handing over the semi-sovereignty of Scotland to Augusel, giving Urian the government of Murief (Moray), and re-establishing Lot 'in the consulship of Loudonesia (Lothian), and the other provinces belonging to him'.

Two other rulers subject to him are Gunvasius, King of the Orkneys, and Malvasius, King of Iceland, in whom we recognize Gwyn, under Latinized forms of his Welsh name Gwynwas and his Cornish name Melwas. But it is characteristic of Geoffrey of Monmouth's loose hold upon his materials that, not content with having connected several of these gods with Arthur's period, he further endows them with reigns of their own. 'Urien' was Arthur's vassal, but 'Urianus' was himself King of Britain centuries before Arthur was born. Lud (that is, Lludd) succeeded his father Beli. We hear nothing of his silver hand, but we learn that he was 'famous for the building of cities, and for rebuilding the walls of Trinovantum, which he also surrounded with innumerable towers . . . and though he had many other cities, yet he loved this above them all, and resided in it the greater part of the year; for which reason it was afterwards called Kaerlud, and by the corruption of the word, Caerlondon; and again by change of languages, in process of time, London; as also by foreigners who arrived here, and reduced this country under their subjection, it was called Londres. At last, when he was dead, his body was buried by the gate which to this time is called in the British tongue after his name Parthlud, and in the Saxon, Ludesgata.' He was succeeded by his brother, Cassibellawn (Cassivelaunus), during whose reign Julius Caesar first invaded Britain.

Lludd, however, is not entirely dependent upon Geoffrey of Monmouth for his reputation as a king of Britain. One of the old Welsh romances, translated by Lady Charlotte Guest in her Mabinogion, relates the rebuilding of London by Lludd in almost the same words as Geoffrey. The story which these pseudo-historical details introduce is, however, an obviously mythological one. It tells us how, in the days of Lludd, Britain was oppressed

THE DECLINE AND FALL OF THE GODS

by three plagues. The first was the arrival of a strange race of sorcerers called the 'Coranians', who had three qualities which made them unpopular; they paid their way in 'fairy money', which, though apparently real, returned afterwards – like the shields, horses, and hounds made by Gwydion son of Dôn, to deceive Pryderi – into the fungus out of which it had been charmed by magic; they could hear everything that was said over the whole of Britain, in however low a tone, provided only that the wind met it; and they could not be injured by any weapon. The second was 'a shriek that came on every May eve, over every hearth in the Island of Britain, and went through people's hearts and so scared them that the men lost their hue and their strength, and the women their children, and the young men and the maidens their senses, and all the animals and trees and the earth and the waters were left barren'. The third was a disappearance of the food hoarded in the king's palace, which was so complete that a year's provisions vanished in a single night, and so mysterious that no one could ever find out its cause.

By the advice of his nobles, Lludd went to France to obtain the help of its king, his brother Llevelys, who was 'a man great of counsel and wisdom'. In order to be able to consult with his brother without being overheard by the Coranians, Llevelys caused a long tube of brass to be made, through which they talked to one another. The sorcerer tribe, however, got to know of it, and, though they could not hear what was being said inside the speaking-tube, they sent a demon into it, who whispered insulting messages up and down it, as though from one brother to the other. But Lludd and Llevelys knew one another too well to be deceived by this, and they drove the demon out of the tube by flooding it with wine. Then Llevelys told Lludd to take certain insects, which he would give him, and pound them in water. When the water was sufficiently permeated with their essence, he was to call both his own people and the Coranians together, as though for a conference, and, in the midst of the meeting, to cast it over all of them alike. The water, though harmless to his own people, would nevertheless prove a deadly poison to the Coranians.

As for the shriek, Llevelys explained it to be raised by a dragon. This monster was the Red Dragon of Britain, and it raised the shriek because it was being attacked by the White Dragon of the Saxons, which was trying to overcome and destroy it. The French king told his brother to measure the length and breadth of Britain, and, when he had found the exact centre of the island, to cause a pit to be dug there. In this pit was to be placed a vessel containing the best mead that could be made, with a covering of satin over it to hide it. Lludd was then to watch from some safe place. The dragons would appear and fight in the air until they were exhausted, then they would fall together on to the top of the satin cloth, and so draw it down with them into the vessel full of mead. Naturally they would drink the mead, and, equally naturally, they would then sleep. As soon as Lludd was sure that they were helpless, he was to go to the pit, wrap the satin cloth round both of them, and bury them together in a stone coffin in the strongest place in Britain. If this were safely done, there would be no more heard of the shriek.

And the disappearance of the food was caused by 'a mighty man of magic', who put everyone to sleep by charms before he removed the king's provisions. Lludd was to watch for him, sitting by the side of a cauldron full of cold water. As often as he felt the approach of drowsiness, he was to plunge into the cauldron. Thus he would be able to keep awake and frustrate the thief.

So Lludd came back to Britain. He pounded the insects in the water, and then summoned both the men of Britain and the Coranians to a meeting. In the midst of it, he sprinkled the water over everyone alike. The natives took no harm from this mythological 'beetle powder', but the Coranians died.

Lludd was then ready to deal with the dragons. His careful measurements proved that the centre of the island of Britain was at Oxford, and there he caused the pit to be dug, with the vessel of mead in it, hidden by the satin covering. Having made everything ready, he watched, and soon saw the dragons appear. For a long time they fought desperately in the air; then they fell down together on to the satin cloth, and, drawing it after them, subsided into the mead. Lludd waited till they were quite silent, and then pulled them out, folded them carefully in the wrapping, and took them to the district of Snowdon, where he buried them in the strong fortress whose remains, near Beddgelert, are still called 'Dinas Emrys'. After this the terrible shriek was not heard again until Merlin had them dug up, five hundred years later, when they recommenced fighting, and the red dragon drove the white one out of Britain.

Last of all, Lludd prepared a great banquet in his hall, and watched over it, armed, with the cauldron of water near him. In the middle of the night, he heard soft, drowsy music, such as nearly put him to sleep; but he kept awake by repeatedly dipping himself in the cold water. Just before dawn a huge man, clad in armour, came into the hall, carrying a basket, which he began to load with the viands on the table. Like the bag in which Pwyll captured Gwawl, its holding capacity seemed endless. However, the man filled it at last, and was carrying it out, when Lludd stopped him. They fought, and Lludd conquered the man of magic, and made him his vassal. Thus the 'Three Plagues of Britain' came to an end.

Lludd, in changing from god to king, seems to have lost most of his old mythological attributes. Even his daughter Creudylad is taken from him and given to another of the ancient British deities. Why Lludd, the sky-god, should have been confounded with Llyr, the sea-god, is not very apparent, but it is certain that 'Creudylad' of the early Welsh legends and poems is the same as Geoffrey's 'Cordeilla' and Shakespeare's 'Cordelia'. The great dramatist was ultimately indebted to the Celtic mythology for the groundwork of the legend which he wove into the tragic story of *King Lear*. 'Leir', as Geoffrey calls him, was the son of Bladud, who built Caer Badus (Bath), and perished, like Icarus, as the result of an accident with a flying-machine of his own invention. Having no sons, but three daughters, Gonorilla, Regan, and Cordeilla, he thought in his old age of dividing his kingdom among them. But, first of all, he decided to make trial of their affection for him, with the idea of giving the best portions of his realm to the most worthy. Gonorilla, the eldest, replied to his question of how much she loved him, 'that she called heaven to witness, she loved him more than her own soul'. Regan answered 'with an oath, "that she could not otherwise express her thoughts, but that she loved him above all creatures"'. But when it came to Cordeilla's turn, the youngest daughter, disgusted with her sisters' hypocrisy, spoke after a quite different fashion. '"My father," said she, "is there any daughter that can love her father more than duty requires? In my opinion, whoever pretends to it, must disguise her real sentiments under the veil of flattery. I have always loved you as a father, nor do I yet depart from my purposed duty; and if you insist to have something more extorted from me, hear now the greatness of my affection, which I always bear you, and take this for a short answer to all your questions; look how much you have, so much is your value, and so much do I love you.'" Her enraged father immediately bestowed his kingdom upon his two other daughters, marrying them to the two highest of his nobility, Gonorilla to Maglaunus, Duke of Albania, and Regan to Henuinus, Duke of Cornwall. To Cordeilla he not only refused a share in his realm, but even a dowry. Aganippus, King of the Franks, married her, however, for her beauty alone.

Once in possession, Leir's two sons-in-law rebelled against him, and deprived him of all regal authority. The sole recompense for his lost power was an agreement by Maglaunus to allow him maintenance, with a body-guard of sixty soldiers. But, after two years, the Duke of Albania, at his wife Gonorilla's instigation, reduced them to thirty. Resenting this, Leir left Maglaunus, and went to Henuinus, the husband of Regan. The Duke of Cornwall at first received him honourably, but, before a year was out, compelled him to discharge all his attendants except five. This sent him back in a rage to his eldest daughter, who, this time, swore that he should not stay with her, unless he would be satisfied with one serving-man only. In despair, Leir resolved to throw himself upon the mercy of Cordeilla, and, full of contrition for the way he had treated her, and of misgivings as to how he might be received, took ship for Gaul.

Arriving at Karitia, he sent a messenger to his daughter, telling her of his plight and asking for her help. Cordeilla sent him money, robes, and a retinue of forty men, and, as soon as he was fully equipped with the state suitable to a king, he was received in pomp by Aganippus and his ministers, who gave the government of Gaul into his hands until his own kingdom could be restored to him.

This the king of the Franks did by raising an army and invading Britain. Maglaunus and Henuinus were routed, and Leir replaced on the throne, after which he lived three years. Cordeilla, succeeding to the government of Britain, 'buried her father in a certain vault, which she ordered to be made for him under the River Sore, in Leicester ("Llyr-cestre"), and which had been built originally under the ground to the honour of the god Janus. And here all the workmen of the city, upon the anniversary solemnity of that festival, used to begin their yearly labours.'

Exactly what myth is retold in this history of Leir and his three daughters we are hardly likely ever to discover. But its mythological nature is clear enough in the light of the description of the underground temple dedicated to Llyr, at once the god of the subaqueous, and therefore subterranean, world and a British Dis Pater, connected with the origin of things, like the Roman god Janus, with whom he was apparently identified.

Ten kings or so after this (for any more exact way of measuring the flight of time is absent from Geoffrey's *History*) we recognize two other British gods upon the scene. Brennius (that is, Brân) disputes the kingdom with his brother Belinus. Clearly this is a version of the ancient myth of the twin brothers, Darkness and Light, which we have seen expressed in so many ways in Celtic mythology. Brân, the god of death and the underworld, is opposed to Belinus, god of the sun and health. In the original, lost myth, probably they alternately conquered and were conquered – a symbol of the alternation of night and day and of winter and summer. In Geoffrey's *History*, they divided Britain, Belinus taking 'the crown of the island with the dominions of Loegria, Kambria, and Cornwall, because, according to the Trojan constitution, the right of inheritance would come to him as the elder', while

Brennius, as the younger, had 'Northumberland, which extended from the River Humber to Caithness'. But flatterers persuaded Brennius to ally himself with the King of the Norwegians, and attack Belinus. A battle was fought, in which Belinus was conqueror, and Brennius escaped to Gaul, where he married the daughter of the Duke of the Allobroges, and on that ruler's death was declared successor to the throne. Thus firmly established with an army, he invaded Britain again. Belinus marched with the whole strength of the kingdom to meet him, and the armies were already drawn out opposite to one another in battle array when Conwenna, the mother of the two kings, succeeded in reconciling them. Not having one another to fight with, the brothers now agreed upon a joint expedition with their armies into Gaul. The Britons and the Allobroges conquered all the other kings of the Franks, and then entered Italy, destroying villages and cities as they marched to Rome. Gabius and Porsena, the Roman consuls, bought them off with large presents of gold and silver and the promise of a yearly tribute, whereupon Brennius and Belinus withdrew their army into Germany and began to devastate it. But the Romans, now no longer taken by surprise and unprepared, came to the help of the Germans. This brought Brennius and Belinus back to Rome, which, after a long siege, they succeeded in taking. Brennius remained in Italy, 'where he exercised unheard-of tyranny over the people'; and one may take the whole of this veracious history to be due to a patriotic desire to make out the Brennus of 'Vae Victis' fame – who actually did sack Rome, in BC 390 – a Briton. Belinus, the other brother, returned to England. 'He made a gate of wonderful structure in Trinovantum, upon the bank of the Thames, which the citizens call after his name Billingsgate to this day. Over it he built a prodigiously large tower, and under it a haven or quay for ships.

... At last, when he had finished his days, his body was burned, and the ashes put up in a golden urn, which they placed at Trinovantum, with wonderful art, on the top of the tower above mentioned.' He was succeeded by Gurgiunt Brabtruc, who, as he was returning by way of the Orkneys from a raid on the Danes, met the ships of Partholon and his people as they came from Spain to settle in Ireland.

Llyr and his children, large as they bulk in mythical history, were hardly less illustrious as saints. The family of Llyr Llediath is always described by the early Welsh hagiologists as the first of the 'Three chief Holy Families of the Isle of Britain'. The glory of Llyr himself, however, is but a reflected one; for it was his son Brân 'the Blesséd' who actually introduced Christianity into Britain. Legend tells us that he was taken captive to Rome with his son Caradawc (who was identified for the purpose with the historical Caratacus), and the rest of his family, and remained there seven years, during which time he became converted to the Gospel, and spread it enthusiastically on his return. Neither his son Caradawc nor his half-brother Manawyddan exactly followed in his footsteps, but their descendants did. Caradawc's sons were all saintly, while his daughter Eigen, who married a chief called Sarrlog, lord of Caer Sarrlog (Old Sarum), was the first female saint in Britain. Manawyddan's side of the family was less adaptable. His son and his grandson were both pagans, but his great-grandson obtained Christian fame as St. Dyfan, who was sent as a bishop to Wales by Pope Eleutherius, and was martyred at Merthyr Dyvan. After this, the saintly line of Llyr increases and flourishes.

Singularly inappropriate persons are found in it – Mabon, the Gallo-British Apollo, as well as Geraint and others of King Arthur's court.

THE DECLINE AND FALL OF THE GODS

It is so quaint a conceit that Christianity should have been, like all other things, the gift of the Celtic Hades, that it seems almost a pity to cast doubt on it. The witness of the classical historians sums up, however, dead in its disfavour. Tacitus carefully enumerates the family of Caratacus, and describes how he and his wife, daughter, and brother were separately interviewed by the Emperor Claudius, but makes no mention at all of the chieftain's supposed father Brân. Moreover, Dio Cassius gives the name of Caratacus's father as Cunobelinus – Shakespeare's 'Cymbeline' – who, he adds, had died before the Romans first invaded Britain. The evidence is wholly against Brân as a Christian pioneer. He remains the grim old god of war and death, 'blesséd' only to his pagan votaries, and especially to the bards, who probably first called him *Bendigeid Vran*, and whose stubborn adherence must have been the cause of the not less stubborn efforts of their enemies, the Christian clerics, to bring him over to their own side by canonization.

They had an easier task with Brân's sister, Branwen of the 'Fair Bosom'. Goddesses, indeed, seem to have stood the process better than gods – witness 'Saint' Brigit, the 'Mary of the Gael'. The British Aphrodité became, under the name of Brynwyn, or Dwynwen, a patron saint of lovers. As late as the fourteenth century, her shrine at Llandwynwyn, in Anglesey, was the favourite resort of the disappointed of both sexes, who came to pray to her image for either success or forgetfulness. To make the result the more certain, the monks of the church sold Lethean draughts from her sacred well. The legend told of her is that, having vowed herself to perpetual celibacy, she fell in love with a young chief called Maelon. One night, as she was praying for guidance in her difficulty, she had a vision in which she was offered a goblet of delicious liquor as a draught of oblivion, and she also saw the same sweet medicine given to Maelon, whom it at once froze into a block of ice. She was then, for her faith, offered the granting of three boons. The first she chose was that Maelon might be allowed to resume his natural form and temperature; the second, that she should no longer desire to be married; and the third, that her intercessions might be granted for all true-hearted lovers, so that they should either wed the objects of their affection or be cured of their passion. From this cause came the virtues of her shrine and fountain. But the modern generation no longer flocks there, and the efficacious well is choked with sand. None the less, she whom the Welsh bards called the 'Saint of Love' still has her occasional votaries. Country girls of the neighbourhood seek her help when all else fails. The water nearest to the church is thought to be the best substitute for the now dry and ruined original well.

A striking contrast to this easy victory over paganism is the stubborn resistance to Christian adoption of Gwyn son of Nudd. It is true that he was once enrolled by some monk in the train of the 'Blesséd Brân', but it was done in so half-hearted a way that, even now, one can discern that the writer felt almost ashamed of himself. His fame as at least a powerful fairy was too vital to be thus tampered with. Even Spenser, though, in his *Faerie Queene*, he calls him 'the good Sir Guyon . . . in whom great rule of Temp'raunce goodly doth appeare', does not attempt to conceal his real nature. It is no man, but

'an Elfin born, of noble state
And mickle worship in his native land',

who sets forth the beauties of that virtue for which the original Celtic paradise, with its unfailing ale and rivers of mead and wine, would hardly seem to have been the best possible school. Save for Spenser, all authorities agree in making Gwyn the determined opponent of things Christian. A curious and picturesque legend is told of him in connection with St. Collen, who was himself the great-grandson of Brân's son, Caradawc. The saint, desirous of still further retirement from the world, had made himself a cell beneath a rock near Glastonbury Tor, in Gwyn's own 'island of Avilion'. It was close to a road, and one day he heard two men pass by talking about Gwyn son of Nudd, and declaring him to be King of Annwn and the fairies. St. Collen put his head out of the cell, and told them to hold their tongues, and that Gwyn and his fairies were only demons. The two men retorted by warning the saint that he would soon have to meet the dark ruler face to face. They passed on, and not long afterwards St. Collen heard someone knocking at his door. On asking who was there, he got the answer: 'I am here, the messenger of Gwyn ap Nudd, King of Hades, to bid thee come by the middle of the day to speak with him on the top of the hill.' The saint did not go; and the messenger came a second time with the same message. On the third visit, he added a threat that, if St. Collen did not come now, it would be the worse for him. So, a little disquieted, he went, but not unarmed. He consecrated some water, and took it with him.

On other days the top of Glastonbury Tor had always been bare, but on this occasion the saint found it crowned by a splendid castle. Men and maidens, beautifully dressed, were going in and out. A page received him and told him that the king was waiting for him to be his guest at dinner. St. Collen found Gwyn sitting on a golden chair in front of a table covered with the rarest dainties and wines. He invited him to share them, adding that if there was anything he especially liked, it should be brought to him with all honour. 'I do not eat the leaves of trees,' replied the saint, who knew what fairy meats and drinks were made of. Not taken aback by this discourteous answer, the King of Annwn genially asked the saint if he did not admire his servants' livery, which was a motley costume, red on one side and blue on the other. 'Their dress is good enough for its kind,' said St. Collen. 'What kind is that?' asked Gwyn. 'The red shows which side is being scorched, and the blue shows which side is being frozen,' replied the saint, and, splashing his holy water all round him, he saw castle, serving-men, and king vanish, leaving him alone on the bare, windy hill-top.

Gwyn, last of the gods of Annwn, has evidently by this time taken over the functions of all the others. He has the hounds which Arawn once had – the *Cwn Annwn*, 'dogs of hell', with the white bodies and the red ears. We hear more of them in folklore than we do of their master, though even their tradition is dying out with the spread of newspapers and railways. We are not likely to find another Reverend Edmund Jones to insist upon belief in them, lest, by closing our minds to such manifest witnesses of the supernatural world, we should become infidels. Still, we may even now find peasants ready to swear that they have heard them sweeping along the hill-sides upon stormy nights, as they pursued the flying souls of unshriven men or unbaptized babes. The tales told of them agree curiously. Their cry is like that of a pack of fox-hounds, but softer in tone. The nearer they are to a man, the less loud their voices seem, and the farther off they are, the louder. But they are less often seen than heard, and it has been suggested that the sounds were the cries of migrating bean-geese, which are not unlike those of hounds in chase. The superstition is widely spread. The *Cwn Annwn* of Wales are called in North Devon the

'Yeth' (Heath or Heathen), or 'Yell' Hounds, and on Dartmoor, the 'Wish' Hounds. In Durham and Yorkshire they are called 'Gabriel' Hounds, and they are known by various names in Norfolk, Gloucestershire, and Cornwall. In Scotland it is Arthur who leads the Wild Hunt, and the tradition is found over almost the whole of western Europe.

Not many folk-tales have been preserved in which Gwyn is mentioned by name. His memory has lingered longest and latest in the fairy-haunted Vale of Neath, so close to his 'ridge, the Tawë abode . . . not the nearest Tawë . . . but that Tawë which is the farthest'. But it may be understood whenever the king of the fairies is mentioned. As the last of the greater gods of the old mythology, he has been endowed by popular fancy with the rule of all the varied fairy population of Britain, so far, at least, as it is of Celtic or pre-Celtic origin. For some of the fairies most famous in English literature are Teutonic. King Oberon derives his name, through the French *fabliaux*, from Elberich, the dwarf king of the *Niebelungenlied*, though his queen, Titania, was probably named out of Ovid's *Metamorphoses*. Puck, another of Shakespeare's fays, is merely the personification of his race, the 'pwccas' of Wales, 'pookas' of Ireland, 'poakes' of Worcestershire, and 'pixies' of the West of England. It is Wales that at the present time preserves the most numerous and diverse collection of fairies. Some of them are beautiful, some hideous; some kindly, some malevolent. There are the gentle damsels of the lakes and streams called Gwragedd Annwn, and the fierce and cruel mountain fairies known as the Gwyllion. There are the household sprites called Bwbachod, like the Scotch and English 'brownies'; the Coblynau, or gnomes of the mines (called 'knockers' in Cornwall); and the Ellyllon, or elves, of whom the pwccas are a branch. In the North of England the spirits belong more wholly to the lower type. The bogies, brownies, killmoulis, redcaps, and their like seem little akin to the higher, Aryan-seeming fairies. The Welsh bwbach, too, is described as brown and hairy, and the coblynau as black or copper-faced. We shall hardly do wrong in regarding such spectres as the degraded gods of a pre-Aryan race, like the Irish leprechauns and pookas, who have nothing in common with the still beautiful, still noble figures of the Tuatha Dé Danann.

Of these numberless and nameless subjects of Gwyn, some dwell beneath the earth or under the surface of lakes – which seem to take, in Wales, the place of the Gaelic 'fairy hills' – and others in Avilion, a mysterious western isle of all delights lying on or just beneath the sea. Pembrokeshire – the ancient Dyfed – has kept the tradition most completely. The story goes that there is a certain square yard in the hundred of Cemmes in that county which holds the secret of the fairy realm. If a man happens to set his feet on it by chance, his eyes are opened, and he can see that which is hidden from other men – the fairy country and commonwealth, – but, the moment he moves from the enchanted spot, he loses the vision, and he can never find the same place again. That country is upon the sea, and not far from shore; like the Irish paradise of which it is the counterpart, it may sometimes be sighted by sailors. The 'Green Meadows of Enchantment' are still an article of faith among Pembrokeshire and Caermarthenshire sailors, and evidently not without some reason. In 1896 a correspondent of the *Pembroke County Guardian* sent in a report made to him by a certain Captain John Evans to the effect that, one summer morning, while trending up the Channel, and passing Gresholm Island (the scene of the entertaining of Brân's head), in what he had always known as deep water, he was surprised to see to windward of him a large tract of land covered with a beautiful green meadow. It was not, however, above water, but two or three feet below it, so that the grass waved or swam about as the ripple floated over it, in a way that made one who watched it feel drowsy. Captain Evans had often heard of the tradition of the fairy island from old people, but admitted that he had never hoped to see it with his own eyes. As with the 'Hounds of Annwn' one may suspect a quite natural explanation. Mirage is at once common enough and rare enough on our coasts to give rise to such a legend, and it must have been some such phenomenon as the 'Fata Morgana' of Sicily which has made sober men swear so confidently to ocular evidence of the Celtic Paradise, whether seen from the farthest western coasts of Gaelic Ireland or Scotland, or of British Wales.